MW01121168

Global Development and Colonial Power

Kilombo: International Relations and Colonial Questions

This is the first series to mark out a dedicated space for advanced critical inquiry into colonial questions across International Relations. The ethos of this book series is reflected by the bricolage constituency of Kilombos – settlements of African slaves, rebels and indigenous peoples in South America who became self-determining political communities that retrieved and renovated the social practices of its diverse constituencies while being confronted by colonial forces. The series embraces a multitude of methods and approaches, theoretical and empirical scholarship, alongside historical and contemporary concerns. Publishing innovative and top-quality peer-reviewed scholarship, Kilombo enquires into the shifting principles of colonial rule that inform global governance and investigates the contestation of these principles by diverse peoples across the globe. It critically re-interprets popular concepts, narratives and approaches in the field of IR by reference to the 'colonial question' and, in doing so, the book series opens up new vistas from which to address the key political questions of our time.

Series Editors:

Mustapha K. Pasha, Aberystwyth University

Meera Sabaratnam, SOAS University of London

Robbie Shilliam, Queen Mary University of London

Titles in the Series

Global Development and Colonial Power

German Development Policy at Home and Abroad

Daniel Bendix

ROWMAN &
LITTLEFIELD
————INTERNATIONAL
London • New York

Published by Rowman & Littlefield International Ltd
Unit A, Whitacre Mews, 26–34 Stannary Street, London SE11 4AB
www.rowmaninternational.com

Rowman & Littlefield International Ltd. is an affiliate of Rowman & Littlefield
4501 Forbes Boulevard, Suite 200, Lanham, Maryland 20706, USA
With additional offices in Boulder, New York, Toronto (Canada), and Plymouth (UK)
www.rowman.com

British Library Cataloguing in Publication Data
A catalogue record for this book is available from the British Library

ISBN: HB 978-1-78660-349-4

Library of Congress Cataloging-in-Publication Data
Names: Bendix, Daniel, 1980– author.
Title: Global development and colonial power : German development
    policy at home and abroad / Daniel Bendix.
Description: London ; New York : Rowman & Littlefield International, Ltd,
    [2018] | Series: Kilombo : international relations and colonial questions |
    Includes bibliographical references and index.
Identifiers: LCCN 2017048660 (print) | LCCN 2018001865 (ebook) |
    ISBN 9781786603517 (electronic) | ISBN 9781786603494
    (cloth : alk. paper)
Subjects: LCSH: Postcolonialism—Germany. | Postcolonialism—
    Africa, East. | Germany—Relations—Africa, East. |
    Africa, East—Relations—Germany.
Classification: LCC JV2027 (ebook) | LCC JV2027 .B46 2018 (print) |
    DDC 338.91/430676—dc23
LC record available at https://lccn.loc.gov/2017048660

Printed in the United States of America

Contents

List of Figures

Acronyms

BMZ:	Bundesministerium für wirtschaftliche Zusammenarbeit und Entwicklung (German Federal Ministry for Economic Cooperation and Development)
BUKO:	Bundeskoordination Internationalismus (Federal Coordination of Internationalism)
CBD:	Community-based distributor
CDU:	Christlich Demokratische Union (Christian Democratic Union)
CF:	Curriculum framework
CIA:	Central Intelligence Agency
CIM:	Centrum für internationale Migration und Entwicklung (Centre for International Migration and Development)
CONCORD:	European NGO Confederation for Relief and Development
CSI:	Contraceptive Security Initiative
DE:	Development education
DED:	Deutscher Entwicklungsdienst (German Development Service)
DHS:	Demographic and Health Survey
DSW:	Deutsche Stiftung Weltbevölkerung (German Foundation for World Population)
DZI:	Deutsches Zentralinstitut für soziale Fragen (German Central Institute for Social Issues)
FDP:	Freie Demokratische Partei (Free Democratic Party)
FRG:	Federal Republic of Germany
G20:	Group of Twenty
GDR:	German Democratic Republic
GIZ:	Deutsche Gesellschaft für Internationale Zusammenarbeit (German Agency for International Cooperation)

GNI:	Gross national income
GTZ:	Deutsche Gesellschaft für Technische Zusammenarbeit (German Agency for Technical Cooperation)
ICF Macro:	Inner City Fund Macro
InWEnt:	Internationale Weiterbildung und Entwicklung (Capacity Building International)
ISD:	Initiative Schwarze Menschen in Deutschland (Initiative Black People in Germany)
JSI:	John Snow, Inc.
KfW:	Kreditanstalt für Wiederaufbau (German Development Bank)
KMK:	Kultusministerkonferenz (Standing Conference of the Ministers of Education and Cultural Affairs of the *Länder* in the Federal Republic of Germany)
MDG:	Millennium Development Goal
MSD:	Medical Stores Department
NGO:	Non-governmental organisation
ODA:	Official development assistance
OECD:	Organisation for Economic Co-operation and Development
PR:	Public relations
PSI:	Population Services International
SAIH:	The Norwegian Students and Academics International Assistance Fund
SAP:	Structural Adjustment Programme
SPD:	Sozialdemokratische Partei Deutschlands (Social Democratic Party)
SRHR:	Sexual and reproductive health and rights
SWP:	Stiftung Wissenschaft und Politik (German Institute for International and Security Affairs)
TBA:	Traditional birth attendant
TGPSH:	Tanzanian German Programme to Support Health
UK:	United Kingdom
UN:	United Nations
UNDP:	United Nations Development Programme
UNFPA:	United Nations Population Fund
US:	United States
USAID:	United States Agency for International Development
VENRO:	Verband Entwicklungspolitik deutscher Nichtregierungsorganisationen (Confederation Development Policy of German NGOs)
WWI:	World War I
WWII:	World War II

Acknowledgements

This book would not have been possible without the help and support of the wonderful people around me. My utmost gratitude goes to Uma Kothari and Encarnación Gutiérrez Rodríguez, the exceptional supervisors of my PhD thesis at the University of Manchester. Chapters 5 and 6 draw on my PhD research and are derived, in part, from articles published in *Progress in Development Studies* (Bendix 2016a) and in *Postcolonial Studies* (Bendix 2016b). Uma and Encarna were always there to guide me through the mysterious world of academic research and writing. In Germany, Aram Ziai took over their role and has never failed to support me. Chapters 3 and 4 are, in many ways, the outcome of collective thinking at the Berlin NGO glokal during the past ten years, challenging the way global inequality and colonial legacies have been addressed in Germany. Here, I am particularly indebted to Chandra-Milena Danielzik, Tahir Della, Jana Döll, Juliane Juergensohn, Timo Kiesel, Kristina Kontzi and Carolin Philipp. Papers on which chapters 3 and 4 build have been published in *PERIPHERIE – Zeitschrift für Ökonomie und Politik in der Dritten Welt* (Kiesel and Bendix 2010), *Critical Literacy: Theories and Practices* (Bendix 2013b; Bendix, Danielzik, and Kiesel 2015), and *Darkmatter. In the Ruins of Imperial Culture* (Bendix et al. 2016). Throughout the writing of this book, I relied on the unequivocal support of Helene Decke-Cornill and Chandra, and also of Paul Bendix and Timo. I will forever be grateful for their commitment. And I owe sincere gratitude to all those in Germany and Tanzania who were willing to support my research; spend their time with me; share their knowledge, experience, opinions and food; and be interviewed by me.

It is a pleasure to thank the many teachers, activists, colleagues and friends who helped make this book possible, especially various adbusters, Rob Ahearne, Afrique-Europe-Interact, Joshua Kwesi Aikins, Vanessa Andreotti, Lotte Arndt, Susan Arndt, Chambi Chachage, decolonize orientierungsrahmen!

(decolonize curriculum framework!), Maria Eriksson Baaz, Minu Hashemi Yekani, Susanne Hofmann, Brigitte Kerchner, Clare Land, Cheryl McEwan, Mpaki Molapo, Franziska Müller, Markus-Michael Müller, Tanja Müller, Kum'a Ndumbe III, Bernd Overwien, *PERIPHERIE*, Lisa Ann Richey, Musa Sadock, Julia Schäfer, Susanne Schultz, Robbie Shilliam, Natasha Shivji, Ruth Stanley and Elizabeth Wardle. Many other friends provided their generous support throughout the process. In particular, I would like to thank Christoph Bendix, David Berdonces Labairu, Renate Decke-Cornill, Felix Dahmen, Teboho Edkins, Tillmann Fiehn, Maria Geier, Ann Greenberg, Mark Griffiths, Wilfried Grauert, Jan Hanson, Paula Herm, Rosa Hoppe, Jonas Huber, Barak Kayanor, Vinzenz Kremer, Hama Mamoudou, Richardi Milanzi, Kathrin Ohlmann, Sophie Perry, Martha Areli Ramirez, Ole Schwabe, Leon Thompson, James Vybiral and Ricardo Zürn.

I am most grateful to those who funded the research for and the writing of this book: the UK Economic and Social Research Council; the School of Environment and Development and the Institute for Development Policy and Management of the University of Manchester, UK; the Section Development and Postcolonial Studies and the Institute of Political Science at the University of Kassel, Germany; and the research group 'Landnahme, Acceleration, Activation. Dynamic(s) and (De-)Stabilisation of Modern Growth Societies' at the University of Jena, Germany. I thank the Tanzania Commission for Science and Technology for allowing me to conduct research in Tanzania. Last but not least, I thank the editors of *Kilombo: International Relations and Colonial Questions* and the staff of Rowman & Littlefield International for their patience and open-mindedness.

Chapter 1

Introduction

'German-Tanzanian Cooperation in Health can be followed back to the 19th century' (Tanzanian German Programme to Support Health 2008). When I began my research on colonial power in German development policy in 2008, I was surprised to find this allusion to the colonial period on the website of the Tanzanian German Programme to Support Health (TGPSH), the most significant German development programme on health in Africa. I was surprised because there is a general agreement in Germany – and in formerly colonising nations more generally – that development policy constitutes a break with the colonial past. As it turned out, the reference to the period of German colonial rule was the product of a short research project initiated by a former senior manager of the German health programme in Tanzania. In my interview with him, he recounted his fascination with the German activities in health care during the colonial period. At the same time, he pointed out that Germany's colonial past was a delicate topic for the German government:

> Well, it was new to me how systematically the German colonial medical personnel or the German Colonial Office had already acted in the establishment of a health system back then. That was really exciting. . . . The German government, well, I know that BMZ [the German Federal Ministry for Economic Cooperation and Development] was, of course, never interested and very reluctant when it came to dealing with German colonial times, research-wise or other. That was politically taboo . . . but one would have to, I think, ask again from time to time, whether the times are not changing; that it has just become more of a historical thing, and not political.[1] (Interview 10, 21 October 2010)

German development staff may have made similar political considerations – to declare colonialism a thing of the past – and, when relaunching its website, TGPSH avoided all references to the colonial history that connects Germany

1

and Tanzania. It appears that non-recognition of the colonial past and denial of colonial legacies is characteristic of global development in general (e.g., Biccum 2002; Kapoor 2008; Kothari 2011). This book addresses this denial and reconstructs traces of colonial power in contemporary development. It does so by investigating the presence of colonial modes of thought and practice in the specific case of Germany's transnational development policy.

Unlike the previously mentioned research by the German health programme manager, who would have liked to consign the topic of German colonialism to the past, this research pursues an understanding of history as put forward by Michel Foucault (1977, 1979) and described by the German postcolonial scholar Kien Nghi Ha as follows:

> As long as the overlapping of sediments of time and society is not acknowledged and academic reappraisal remains purely historical, the influences of colonial effects on the racist imprints of present German society cannot be focused on. To not comprehend history as an open and dynamic field means to disallow the question of the topicality of colonial presences. (2005, 106)

A critical approach understands history as a realm that is still active and refrains from treating colonialism as historical in the sense of being over and done with. It acknowledges that the past affects our present.

THE RELEVANCE OF THIS BOOK

Challenging the notion of a clear and thorough break between colonial-era interventions and post-World War II (WWII) development, postcolonial approaches have urged us 'to unnaturalize stories of development' (Power 2006, 28). While the impact of British colonialism on contemporary global development policy has been subject to revision and critique, this book turns the spotlight on the neglected case of Germany. It applies the postcolonial development studies' assumption that colonialism affects contemporary development to various fields of German policy and undertakes an empirical investigation of specific German interventions. Investigating German development in a transnational sense as interrelated interventions 'at home' and 'abroad', this book shows how colonial power – conceived as discourses which emerged during colonisation, interconnected with practices, institutions and political-economic conditions – functions in global development to stabilise relations of inequality to the advantage of the global North.[2]

The book builds on and complements important work in postcolonial development studies (Eriksson Baaz 2005; Heron 2007; Kapoor 2008; Wainwright 2008; McEwan 2009; Wilson 2012). It takes up their theoretical insights to specific contexts (policy fields as well as country context) in order to empirically test the hypothesis that development policy and colonialism are interrelated. The book explores colonial power in German development policy both empirically and as a transnational phenomenon. It understands the colonialism-development nexus as productive in the interrelationship between policies directed at informing and educating the German public, on the one hand, and development activities aimed at the global South, on the other. Scholars of postcolonial development studies have mainly focused on one side of the coin only: some have investigated the coloniality of development in interventions in the South (Wainwright 2008), while others have focused on the production of colonial development mentalities in the North (Kontzi 2015). Moving beyond the common strategy of understanding racism, colonialism and development through the lens of the British (post-)colonial context, and bringing forward the under-researched case of Germany, this book suggests more generally that the colonial power of international development can best be understood in the complex transnational interrelationship between interventions at home and abroad. Postcolonial development studies have to date not undertaken a comprehensive analysis of a single donor country's development endeavours in such a transnational manner. By linking interventions abroad with activities in the name of global development inside Germany, this book highlights the concerted – and at times contradictory – efforts of national policies towards international development.

The overall argument here is that contemporary transnational German development endeavours are fundamentally shaped by the colonial past. By disavowing that legacy, development policy risks creating or perpetuating the very inequalities and injustices it claims to battle against. More specifically, the book highlights the fact that international development activities inside Germany in its current orientation contribute to stabilising colonial and racialised relations of inequality at the national and global levels by disregarding the development-colonialism nexus. The examples taken as evidence are development education (DE), on the one hand, and advertising by non-governmental organisations (NGOs) and government, on the other. Furthermore, the book demonstrates that contemporary German development interventions in the global South display striking similarities to colonial-era policy and practice with regard to discourse and its interrelation with practices and political-economic interests. The two examples taken here are obstetric care policy in Tanzania and population control in the global South.

WHY GERMANY? WHY TANZANIA AND 'GERMAN EAST AFRICA'?

Germany as a country is a worthy case for investigating questions around the development/colonial issue. It displays the singular characteristics of a country 'in-between': Acknowledgement of historical facts and critical

assessment of today's development policy run concurrently with the denial
of Germany's part in European colonialism and its lasting effects (see
chapter 2). Despite the facts that 'Germans are a colonizing people with
centuries of experience' (Friedrichsmeyer, Lennox, and Zantop 1998, 9)
and that Germany, as part of the European Union, profits immensely from
the ongoing pan-European colonial project (cf. Hansen and Jonsson 2014),
its involvement in colonialism is often denied or – if acknowledged –
downplayed with reference to the colonising endeavours of other European
nations. Germany's image as not lumbered with a colonial burden regularly
serves to justify its particular suitability as an unfettered authority in questions of development in the South. Studies on the colonial legacy of development policy have focused on activities by British (Wilson 2012; Kothari
2006b; Wainwright 2008; Slater and Bell 2002; Biccum 2005; Noxolo 2006;
Hodge 2007) and, to a lesser degree, Canadian (Heron 2007), Scandinavian
(Eriksson Baaz 2005), Portuguese (Power 2006) and Slovak (Profant 2015)
agencies, institutions and professionals. Despite the fact that Germany is the
European Union's largest and the world's second largest 'aid donor' (OECD
2017a) and once was one of the principal colonising nations in Africa (and
the Pacific), colonial power in German development policy has remained
comfortably ignored or denied.

While both Germanys shared the legacy of a colonial past, they practised
different approaches in their relations to the global South. Thus, the German Democratic Republic (GDR) distanced itself from Western 'foreign
aid' semantically and 'preferred to use terms such as "economic socialist
assistance" rather than "aid" which it associated with the neo-imperialism
of the Federal Republic of Germany' (Howell 1994, 305). According to
Jude Howell, the GDR's 'assistance' 'provided the possibility of pursuing a
strategy of development that was founded on radically different economic,
ideological, and political premises' to the 'neo-liberal paradigm' (1994,
328). This possibility for alternative South-North relations, which was in
fact welcomed by some recipient countries, came to a halt with the 'unification' of the two Germanys (Büschel 2010). Germany's 'unification' has
been described as 'annexation' or even 'colonisation' by some observers
(Vilmar and Dumcke 1996), because GDR's economic, political, cultural
and social life was destroyed or devaluated in its process (Behrend 1995).
This also applies to GDR's thought and practice on 'socialist international
solidarity' (Weiter 2000). While I am aware of the danger of reproducing
the effacement of the GDR's history and legacy, this research does not
cover the colonial legacy of the GDR's development policy or its repercussions after 'annexation'. In the following, 'Germany', when used for the
period of the existence of the GDR, thus only refers to the Federal Republic
of Germany (FRG).

The chapters that examine development policy abroad concentrate on German-Tanzanian development 'cooperation'. Present-day Tanzania seems a particularly fitting case for investigating colonial power in global development. It previously formed part of Germany's largest colony 'German East Africa', and the significance of 'German East Africa' for German colonialism is reflected in the centrality of German-Tanzanian relations to this day. What is more, German development policy and practice have in fact emerged during German colonial occupation and were particularly evident in 'German East Africa'. Even though the GDR also had extensive relations with Tanzania, the focus of this book, as mentioned earlier, is on development engagement by the FRG. It has been argued that among all of Germany's development partners, Tanzania is the country with which Germany has the broadest and deepest relations (Köhler 2000). Health, and more specifically population and reproductive health, is one of German development 'cooperation's' priority areas in Tanzania (BMZ 2011b; TGPSH 2009c).

DEVELOPMENT POLICY

Despite ample criticism, there appears to be much faith by governments, NGOs and the general public in development 'cooperation' as a philanthropic, altruistic endeavour by the rich nations of the North to support the 'development' of poor countries in the South. Multi- and bilateral donor agencies and NGOs in the North present their objectives as selfless improvements of the economic, social, ecological and political conditions in so-called developing countries. However, such an understanding of development is also contested (Sachs 1992; Escobar 1994). Some scholars suggest that development perpetuates asymmetrical power constellations that serve the economic interests of the North (Duffield 2006; Kapoor 2008). Others have highlighted the fact that societies in the South are evaluated, and development policies are implemented, on the basis of a racialised and gendered modernity-tradition dichotomy (Crush 1995b; Noxolo 2006). This book adds to existing studies by exploring the ways in which racialisation, developmentalism, trusteeship and political-economic interests interconnect in the particular case of German development policy. To date, postcolonial development research has largely refrained from analysing specific policy fields and interventions and primarily focused on general policy orientations (Biccum 2005; Noxolo 2006; Slater and Bell 2002). By undertaking a concrete scrutiny of particular policy fields (see later) and by rereading present interventions through the lens of the colonial past, this book offers an empirical, 'real-world' assessment of the colonial power in present-day development. It investigates that power empirically, in the interaction between the intranational (political education, development advertisement) and the international (interventions into obstetric care and population development in the global South) and traces influences of colonial modes of thought and practice in contemporary development.

Development studies focus on practical interventions and are largely future oriented (Kothari 2011). Recently, however, scholars have shown increasing interest in the history of development (Bayly et al. 2011; Woolcock, Szreter, and Rao 2011). Michael Woolcock, Simon Szreter and Vijayendra Rao (2011) regard history as a resource for self-reflection: Why are certain issues focused on and not others, and why have interventions come to take their particular form in the present? While existing historical approaches in development studies tend to focus on the evolution of institutions and economic development (van de Walle 2009; Bayly et al. 2011), this book provides evidence that rereading discourses and practices of contemporary development through the theoretical lens of colonial power (chapters 3 and 4) or through an actual comparison with colonial times (chapters 5 and 6) gives substance and sophistication to the postcolonial claim that particular 'racial formations constructed through colonial processes are re-presented and re-articulated' in international development (Kothari 1996, 3). Such an in-depth understanding of the influence of colonialism on contemporary issues of development provides the necessary ground for imagining 'de-colonized, de-whitened, post-colonial' international cooperation (Crush 1994, 334).

Benita Parry and others (e.g., Lambert and Lester 2006) have argued that colonial rule was never 'monolithic' but rather characterised by a 'dispersed space of power . . . effecting multiple situations and relations' (2004, 14). Thus, differences between colonialisms and their legacies must also be taken into account. Even though colonialism was a distinctly trans-European project, one cannot assume that Germans held the same convictions, followed the same policies and carried out the same practices as other European colonisers in other territories. This also means that contemporary development policy by different countries of the global North draws on different cultural experiences and backgrounds. This book elaborates on the specificity of one individual national case of colonial power in international development. It highlights, for example, the simultaneity of German development professionals' philanthropic arguments to legitimise interventions, on the one hand, and their ignorance regarding considerable German economic stakes in reproductive health in the South, on the other hand (chapter 6). It also ascertains how obstetric practices were introduced by Germans during colonial rule and are now presented as evidence of African backwardness (chapter 5). German professionals are situated within the legacy of not only a general but also a specific colonial past. Because colonialism was both a European and a multifaceted endeavour, postcolonial development studies must take account of similarities and divergences in colonial power in contemporary development.

SELECTED AREAS OF INTERVENTION

Alongside its transnational perspective, the focus of this book lies on two areas of intervention *within* Germany that are key to conveying or negotiating ideas of development and North-South relations intranationally: DE (chapter 3) and billboard advertising strategies by NGOs and government (chapter 4). DE 'is the only strand of education that organises itself around North-South relations and therefore is located right in the middle of local-global processes and debates' (Andreotti 2006, 2). While it is supposed to raise awareness of power relations and interdependence, it may also, inadvertently, restrict its perspective to notions of the global South based on Western superiority or charity. Germany's financial investment in DE is higher than that of any other OECD (Organisation for Economic Co-operation and Development) country. In addition to schools and universities, about 16,000 German NGOs are involved in DE activities. Billboard advertising is equally crucial in educating the German public on issues of global development and in conveying measures to counteract poverty and inequality – albeit in a more implicit way. Growing up in Germany means to be exposed from day to day to public images that locate destitution in the South and solution in the North. It is common to not 'take these billboards seriously and [think] they [are] just about donations. . . . However, these images in and of themselves inform notions of the Global South and of Black people' (Kahlon et al. 2016, 19). Charity advertisements by humanitarian and 'aid' NGOs in the form of large billboards are omnipresent in public places and train stations all over Germany. Some campaigns comprise up to 100,000 posters along the streets and train stations of the country. DE and billboard advertising provide the necessary ideological legitimation for development policy abroad as well as the background for the socialisation of those Germans active in global development.

In terms of development policy abroad, the book focuses on two areas (maternal health and family planning) within a policy field that is generally understood as altruistically motivated, common sense and non-negotiable – sexual and reproductive health and rights (SRHR) – and analyses their colonial legacy. While population policy had occasionally been subject to criticism for its neocolonial, patriarchal and authoritarian orientation, the institutionalisation of the concept of SRHR at the United Nations International Conference on Population and Development in Cairo in 1994 allegedly rid the field of reasons for such critique. An examination of the policy field of reproductive health and population is instructive because it is one of Germany's main concerns today and was a focus, too, during German colonisation in Africa and the Pacific. Questions of reproduction in the colonised territories in Africa and the Pacific were also discussed by German politicians, administrators, missionaries and physicians from around 1905 to the end of German colonisation around 1920. This book zooms in on two distinct strands in development policy on sexual and reproductive health and rights. 'Maternal health' or 'pregnancy and delivery' (chapter 5) is one of the focal areas of the German Federal Ministry for Economic Cooperation and Development's (BMZ) endeavours in the field of 'reproductive health' (BMZ 2011b). Childbirth-related issues lend themselves to an analysis of colonial power in development because they were a prime target of colonial policies for transforming the colonised people in the name of civilisation and modernity (Ram and Jolly 1998; Vaughan 1991). Furthermore, this book takes a closer look at 'family planning' and 'population dynamics' (chapter 6). Contemporary German development policy closely links the subject of SRHR to warnings about population growth. During German colonialism, colonial stakeholders cautioned against a population decline and perceived the colonies' inhabitants as a resource in need of protection and enhancement. However, Germany's colonial past is seldom viewed as significant in German development 'aid' and, on the rare occasion that a connection between the period of colonial occupation and contemporary development 'cooperation' is suggested, it typically appears in a positive light, as evident in the initial quote taken from the opening paragraph of the web page of TGPSH on the history of the 'German technical cooperation in the health sector' in Tanzania.

BIOGRAPHICAL CONNECTION TO COLONIAL POWER IN DEVELOPMENT

Postcolonial approaches in the social sciences, and particularly in anthropology, have urged us to account for the positionality of the researcher in relation to the field and people under scrutiny. It is necessary to bring to the forefront the ways in which researchers are 'historically and socially ... linked with the areas we study' (Gupta and Ferguson 1997, 38). The choice of the field – German development policy – and how I encountered it was influenced by my socialisation in development 'aid' circles; my social position as a white, bourgeois, male German; and my family's entanglements with German colonialism and National Socialism – as perpetrators and beneficiaries in the case of the former, as victims, survivors and perpetrators or beneficiaries of the latter.

My father worked as a development professional for German governmental and non-governmental organisations (NGOs) in Germany, Lesotho and South Africa. I was active as volunteer and intern in development organisations in various African countries as well as in Switzerland and Germany and continue to work as seminar facilitator and consultant for German development agencies and NGOs. From an early age, I learned how to talk the development talk and walk the development walk. I thus partly consider this book 'insider ethnography' (Gupta and Ferguson 1997, 30), influenced by my experience of growing up and moving around in the framework and 'culture' of German development policy.

My desire for a critical inquiry into the colonial legacy of development has its roots in my experience of consciously living whiteness in Lesotho and South Africa during my teens. Having had the uneasy feeling that something was fundamentally wrong in the encounters and relationships between over-seas development professionals (or people from the West more generally) and the inhabitants of Lesotho, my subsequent engagement with Afrocentric, anti-colonial, postcolonial and race-critical perspectives provided me with the tools to investigate my uneasiness by digging into the politics of development and its connection to colonialism and racism. My desire to 'decolonise' my own and others' minds and actions as well as global structures has inspired me to investigate 'my culture' and pursue the question of colonial imprints on German development. I am aware that focusing on the (former) colonisers and their agency poses ethico-political problems, given that one of the key aims of postcolonial studies is, in fact, to decentre the global North and its people. Postcolonial studies have at times been accused of exaggerating the influence of colonialism (Ahmad 1995) and, instead of decentring history, recentring everything around colonialism (McClintock 1992). They have thus been criticised for reinforcing colonialism's universalising tendencies and for overlooking indigenous agency (Loomba 2005). I would, however, maintain that a critical perspective on the (former) colonisers and a focus on the (formerly) colonised people are not mutually exclusive. Both moves are necessary for destabilising colonial power and are essentially part of the same decolonising strategy (McEwan 2009). For this research, I follow Ilan Kapoor's assertion that the critique of the (former) colonisers is not a 'navel-gazing exercise that reinforces Western ethnocentrism', if it is explicitly 'car-ried out *in order to* clear the way *for* an ethical relationship with the Other' (2008, 57). And, I would like to add, an ethical relationship does not only have to be built vis-à-vis 'the Other' but also vis-à-vis 'the Self'. As Robbie Shilliam points out with regard to (re-)building decolonial relations, 'Even the children of Arcadian Hermes might have a part to play – or a relation to redeem – in this enterprise' (2015, 30).

Coming to terms with my relation to the project of international develop-ment has motivated large parts of my studies and inspired my PhD thesis on German development interventions in Tanzania. It also intrigued me to join glokal, a Berlin-based collective for postcolonial development and anti-racist education and consulting, on whose work chapters 3 and 4 draw. I have recently been digging deeper into my family connections to colo-nialism. I had known its Shoah experience for a while: My Jewish-born,

Christian-converted great-grandfather had been wise enough to pass away one year before the National Socialist German Workers' Party rose to power in Germany; his three sons – half-Jewish according to the Nazi Nuremburg laws – survived the Shoah when they were able to escape from a labour camp in Kassel (where I now work at university) only days before their planned deportation to the gas chambers. A couple of years after the liberation of Germany, my grandfather decided to leave for either Brazil or South Africa with his wife, my grandmother, and young son, my father, to try his luck. He opted for South Africa in 1952, four years after the official beginning of Apartheid – having just survived a racist, colonial, fascist regime on the 'losing' side, he now joined the 'winning' one.

While this family history explains my father's decision to return to Southern Africa after the end of Apartheid to work as a development professional, another colonial connection came to my knowledge only recently. In 2015, I received an e-mail from my father with the subject 'Bendix in Namibia'. But it had nothing to do with my aunt who had married a Boer farmer and co-owns farms in southern Namibia. At least not in a straightforward way. The e-mail entailed a short article on the discovery of a war memorial in the hometown of my father's family, Dülmen in North Rhine-Westphalia, on which was engraved the name Joseph Bendix, the year of his death given as 1904 and the place as Owikokorero. My great-grandfather's cousin Joseph had taken up a job as railway engineer to 'develop' what was then called 'German Southwest Africa' (see chapter 3 on how infrastructure, the railway in particular, is today presented as a positive effect of colonialism in German DE) and was then ordered to take part in the genocidal war against the Ovaherero. In hindsight, he took part in conquering the land that now serves the wealth of my aunt's family. Had he survived his colonial experience, he would have died in the gas chambers of Nazi Germany, just like his siblings did. During the work on this book, I thus learnt how intimately my personal family history is imbued with the colonialism-development nexus. I suspect I am one of many similarly involved in one way or another.

SOURCES, WRITING PROCESS AND CHAPTER OUTLINE

In order to investigate the influences of colonial modes of thought and practice on contemporary development, this book draws on original research in both Germany and Tanzania. It brings together a broad and deep range of materials in order to address the question of colonial power in global development. Sources include archives, documents, statistics, billboard advertising and observation, as well as interviews conducted with about sixty professionals in Germany and Tanzania between 2009 and 2011 (see appendix). For chapter 3 on DE and chapter 4 on billboard advertising, I also draw on my experiences as freelance educator, facilitator and consultant for various international volunteer organisations and NGOs – as well as on many exchanges with peers in this field and in the context of glokal's work. My interest in the connections between development at home and abroad was particularly stimulated by seminars and workshops with young Germans going abroad for – or returning from – a volunteer year through a programme by the BMZ. Not only the connection between their socialisation into the ideology of global development and their experiences in development abroad became apparent but also the possibility of transformation through the confrontation with anti-colonial thought and histories of struggle against colonialism and Western development.

As I have been connected to colonialism and the field of development policy for a considerable time, I am unable to tell a clear-cut story of my entry into the field. This is a typical requirement expected from scholars in order to 'authenticate and authorize the material that follows' (Gupta and Ferguson 1997, 12–13). Furthermore, postcolonial anthropological perspectives on fieldwork have urged scholars to question the boundaries between 'home' and 'abroad' (Gupta and Ferguson 1997). During the research process, I moved between various different spaces and contexts: my desks in Manchester, Dar es Salaam, Berlin, Kassel and Jena; the German Federal Archives and the State Library in Berlin; the BMZ, development agencies, NGOs and companies in Bonn, Frankfurt, Berlin and Heidelberg; people's private homes and offices in Germany and Tanzania; TGPSH headquarters in Dar es Salaam; hospitals in the Tanzanian countryside; bars and restaurants in Tanzania in which I met German development professionals; seminars with young volunteers and workshops with facilitators of DE; and the streets and train stations of Germany decorated with billboard advertisings.

My positionality and socialisation significantly shaped the way I accessed and encountered the field. While my reading of DE materials and billboard advertising departs from particular analytical positions, it is also informed by whiteness, Westernness or Germanness. Charity adverts that expose Black and People of Color's bodies to the stares of passers-by are not a direct attack on my Self – as is the case for artist Rajkamal Kahlon, quoted in chapter 4. Instead, people like me are the implicit target audience, those expected to feel compelled to act as the provider of 'aid' and to identify with 'the helping hero' (Kahlon et al. 2016, 18–19). Moreover, in Tanzania, it was striking how easily I was able to make contacts and forge relationships with German (and other white, non-German) development professionals.[3] This resonates with the experiences of other white researchers who have carried out fieldwork on their country's development 'aid' in Africa (Eriksson Baaz 2005). While German professionals only occasionally invited me to their homes in Germany, the openness increased considerably in Tanzania: We met up on weekends at the beach, they took me along on tourist activities, invited me to their homes, let me stay overnight, had me look after their children and so on. Being on a first-name basis, which is a lot less common in Germany than in the Anglo-American world, was almost a given – and when Germany beat Argentina in the 2010 Football World Cup, I found myself receiving 'high fives' from German interviewees who were twice my age and with whom I personally had little in common. I experienced what Barbara Heron observed in her study with Canadian women working in development 'aid' in East Africa: 'dissimilarities that might have loomed large in Canada vanish in the face of the real difference, that of the culture of the African Other' (2007, 79). My positionality also facilitated my attendance at staff meetings and access to Tanzanian hospital wards alongside my interviewees. This experience of power cannot only be attributed to my status as researcher but also has to do with whiteness. For example, entering hospital settings as a white person had the effect that I was regularly mistaken for a doctor.

Chapter 2 lays out the framework for the subsequent empirical studies. It provides an introduction to the history of German colonialism as well as to discussions on Germany's postcolonial condition in the present. Furthermore, it sketches the emergence of development ideology during German colonialism and outlines post-WWII and contemporary German development policy. Last but not least, it presents the theoretical perspective of colonial power in development as well as this book's methodological approach.

Chapter 3 explores the ways in which Germans are socialised into development discourse, and in particular, how far DE in Germany has broached or neglected postcolonial power relations. It analyses key policy papers on DE as well as educational materials. It takes into account recent debates between advocates of postcolonial critique and those accusing this perspective of being normative and authoritarian. The chapter argues that, despite some significant postcolonial sensitivity, German DE in general continues to refrain from fundamentally questioning historically developed relations of power and domination.

Another dimension of German development policy at home is scrutinised in chapter 4, namely, the public relations strategies of the German government as well as secular and faith-based NGOs. The focus is on billboard advertising. Billboard advertising is one of the central means of educating the general public about 'development' and global inequality. The chapter analyses dominant narratives in NGO billboard advertising with an in-depth study of a specific campaign by the BMZ. Subsequently, new directions in advertising as well as the potential for critique through adbusting are explored. They show that development billboards in Germany tend to de-historicise and de-politicise global inequality and manifest colonial legacies. On the other hand, some campaigns and adbusting activities oppose such tendencies.

Chapter 5 turns to development abroad and investigates German interventions in childbirth-related practices in East Africa during colonial occupation and the present. Drawing on archives as well as interviews, it finds that colonial power continues to shape German policy on and practice in obstetric care in Tanzania: They can be considered colonial in that they are marked by a combination of racialisation, developmentalism and trusteeship. However, these interventions are also challenged by German professionals in this field. The chapter thus shows that colonial power today is fractured: Development professionals' accounts of their work display a considerable degree of hesitancy and admissions of failure to induce change.

Chapter 6 presents the last of the four empirical studies. It continues the exploration of German interventions abroad and zooms in on German policy aimed at population control in East Africa. While German policy during colonial rule was concerned about 'underpopulation', contemporary German policy is concerned about 'population growth'. An analysis of archives and interviews as well as regarding the dissemination of contraceptives by German industry demonstrates the persistence of discourses and material interest. The chapter's findings are that racialised, gendered discourses continue to be interconnected with the political economy of population control and the interests of capital in German policy today.

The conclusion wraps up the insights into the four discussed policy realms and highlights the book's contribution to the general debate on colonialism and development. It emphasises the interconnectedness of policies at home and abroad that allow for the stability of the colonialism-development nexus. This final chapter also stresses the instructiveness of the German case for discussions in postcolonial development studies. After some reflections on research into colonial power in development, the book ends with thoughts on how to challenge and transform colonial power.

NOTES

1. All translations are my own.
2. 'Global North' and 'global South' refer to those countries and world regions commonly called developed/industrialised and developing/underdeveloped, respectively, while trying to avoid the hierarchy inherent in such terminology. Countries of the global South share a common history of having been subjected to colonial imposition. The 'West' is used interchangeably with global North in this book. 'Western' and 'European' as adjectives are used in this book to denote thinking and acting characteristic of the global North and marked by 'enlightenment', 'modernity' and

colonialism. For a discussion of the problems with, and pitfalls of, these terminologies, see Chandra Talpade Mohanty (2002).

3. Coincidentally, to prepare for my volunteer service almost two decades ago, I had taken the same course at the German development training organisation InWEnt as many of my interviewees had taken.

Chapter 2

German Colonialism, Development Policy and Colonial Power

This chapter provides the framework for the following empirical analyses. It proceeds in two steps. In the first four sections – 'German Colonialism', '(Dis-)Remembering Colonialism', 'The Emergence of German Development Policy during Colonialism', 'Post-WWII German Development Policy' – the historical and contemporary context of German colonialism and development policy is laid out, while the later sections outline the book's theoretical and methodological basis.

Given that German colonialism is not widely known – at the University of Manchester I was often asked whether Germany actually even had a colonial past – I first introduce the histories of German colonialism. In the second section of the chapter, '(Dis-)Remembering Colonialism', I describe the particularities of how colonialism is remembered, or rather disremembered, in Germany in general and in the particular context of German development. While development ideas and practice are often considered to have emerged after World War II (WWII), the chapter's third section, 'The Emergence of German Development Policy during Colonialism' shows how German development ideology already surfaced during the period of colonisation at the beginning of the twentieth century. This insight is particularly crucial for the analyses in chapters 5 and 6 of German interventions in East Africa. To contextualise more recent and contemporary German development at home and abroad, the fourth section, 'Post-WWII German Development Policy', provides an overview of development endeavours by German actors in the middle of twentieth century.

Based on this introduction to the field and through dialogue with literature on colonialism and development, the second part of this chapter outlines the specific theoretical perspective of colonial power and the methodological approach of dispositif analysis that form the analytical angle of the book's empirical chapters.

GERMAN COLONIALISM

German colonialism is commonly equated with the formal colonisation or 'state-sponsored colonialism' (cf. Friedrichsmeyer, Lennox, and Zantop 1998, 9) which effectively lasted from the mid-1880s through approximately 1920 (Colwell 2001). However, it 'dates back at least to the 15th and 16th centuries, when thousands of Germans took part in the conquest and colonisation of the "New World" – as adventurers, mercenaries, merchants, scientists, explorers, interpreters' (Friedrichsmeyer, Lennox, and Zantop 1998, 8). For example, as early as 1499, the trading families Fugger and Welser financed expeditions and brought miners from Germany as well as enslaved Africans to South America (Friedrichsmeyer, Lennox, and Zantop 1998, 9). The Americas played an important role for early German colonialist aspirations (Zantop 1997). Later on, particularly in the nineteenth century, millions of Germans emigrated to participate in settler colonialism in the USA. The first independent German occupation, however, took place in 1683 in Africa, on the territory of what is today Ghana. The Brandenburgisch-Africanische Compagnie established the trading colony 'Groß-Friedrichsburg' and trafficked enslaved Africans across the Atlantic (Stelzer 1984). This was followed by conquests in what are now Benin, Mauritania, the US Virgin Islands, Puerto Rico and the British Virgin Islands.

The zenith of German colonialism lasted from the mid-1880s through 1920. During large-scale 'state-sponsored' formal colonisation, a total of 2,953,000 square kilometres in Africa and Asia was occupied by Germany, a geographical area five times that of its national surface area (van Laak 2005). In these territories, approximately 25,000 Germans ruled over 12 million colonised people (Kößler and Melber 2004). The focus of German colonial endeavours was Africa. There, the German Empire conquered and occupied 'German East Africa' (present-day Tanzania as well as Rwanda, Burundi and parts of Kenya and Mozambique); 'German South-West Africa' (present-day Namibia and parts of Botswana); 'Kamerun' (today's Cameroon); and 'Togoland' (present-day Togo and parts of Ghana). The centrality of Africa to German colonisation led to Africa and colonialism becoming synonymous (Eckert and Wirz 2002). However, between the mid-1880s and approximately 1920, Germany also occupied territories and exploited people in the South Pacific ('German New Guinea' and 'German Samoa') and in China ('German Kiautschou' and Chefoo). Compared to that of other colonising nations, German 'state-sponsored colonialism' was short-lived but nonetheless not dramatically different from that of other colonising nations, such as France and Great Britain (Smith 2011).

There were diverging opinions within Germany on the legitimacy and form of German colonial rule (Speitkamp 2005). Criticism was voiced across a number of social milieus and political groups but was most emphatically pronounced among the Social Democratic Party (SPD). In an 1889 parliamentary debate, Germany's leading Social Democrat, August Bebel (1889), criticised government's support for colonisation because he believed that the 'entrepreneurial class' would, due to their racism, exploit colonised people even more than they exploited workers in Germany. The SPD tended to 'reject the colonial civilizing mission as part of its larger refusal of paternalist state socialism' (Kontzi 2015, 198). While some Social Democrats (including Bebel) at a later stage promoted a socialist colonialism consisting of a supposedly more humane civilising mission (Conrad 2008), this position was rejected by others as no better than the reformist colonialism proposed by the state secretary of the Imperial Colonial Office Bernhard Dernburg and others. The Social Democrat Karl Kautsky went furthest in his critique; he viewed socialist colonial policy as a 'logical contradiction' and criticised the view that 'there exist[ed] childish peoples unable to rule themselves' (cited in Kontzi 2015, 197). Within generally pro-colonial circles, positions varied. For example, German colonialism was marked by the conflict over modes of colonisation ('settlement' versus 'plantations' versus 'trade'). 'Settlers' and colonial reformists also disagreed over how to economically exploit and treat the colonised people.

According to Sara Friedrichsmeyer, Sara Lennox and Susanne Zantop, Germany's colonial policy was 'almost exclusively economic' when compared to 'Britain, which wished to convert the rest of the globe to the English way of life, and France, committed to its mission civilisatrice' (1998, 11). In general, economic reasoning was the common and predominant ground of all stakeholders, but the motive of bringing 'civilisation' was also apparent (Pogge von Strandmann 2009). In purely economic terms, the colonies were a 'national losing deal' for the German Empire (van Laak 2004, 3). That did not mean that German enterprises and individuals at the time, or contemporary German society as a whole, did not profit immensely from the pan-European 500-year project of colonialism. As will be discussed in detail in chapters 5 and 6, self-interest as well as philanthropic considerations marked colonial-era German interventions in health, population and reproduction.

'German East Africa' constituted the largest German colony and served as a 'plantation colony', facilitating economic exploitation via agricultural enterprises. Colonial historiography suggests that, by the turn of the twentieth century, colonial administrations had begun to initiate discussions regarding population decline (see chapter 6) in the context of colonial reforms towards 'rationality' and 'efficiency' (Widmer 2008; Grosse 2000). Accordingly, German missionaries, physicians and administrators showed great concern for practices of birth control as well as for obstetric care and child-rearing in the colonised territories (see chapter 5). This concern was part of a larger European project of discussing and intervening into the reproductive sphere of colonised people (Ram and Jolly 1998; Hunt 1999).

In the light of German colonial activities since the fifteenth century, Friedrichsmeyer, Lennox and Zantop conclude that 'Germans are a colonizing people with centuries of experience' (1998, 9). German colonial aspirations and endeavours did not end with the loss of the occupied territories to other colonising nations after World War I (WWI). The Weimar Republic was replete with revisionists who demanded a return of the lost colonies (Campt, Grosse, and Lemke-Muniz de Faria 2001). In 1927, the German politician Konrad Adenauer, who later became the first chancellor of West Germany, stated the following: 'The German Empire needs to pursue the acquisition of colonies. There is too little space for the large population within the Empire' (cited in Gründer 1999, 327). Such aspirations were matched in practice by state-sponsored efforts to secure new land for settlement in Namibia or by the promotion of colonial products from German-owned plantations in former colonies (Kößler 2015, 62). The colonial quest was kept in the public mind by civil society organisations such as the Deutsche Kolonialgesellschaft ('German Colonial Society'). It maintained a growing membership throughout the 1920s and into the 1930s, when it was 'absorbed into *Gleichschaltung*, the enforced conformity imposed on civil society organisations under Nazi rule' (Kößler 2015, 63).

The Nazi regime had detailed plans to colonise large sections of Africa (Ndumbe 1993). During this time, former agents, institutions and enterprises involved in colonialism were implicated in the occupation of Eastern European countries and the Soviet Union (Zimmerer 2010, chap. 10). Scholars such as Jürgen Zimmerer equate the Nazi rule of these territories to colonialism with reference to practices of occupation and statements by Adolf Hitler that 'the Russian space is our India' and that it was 'our colonial space' (Zimmerer 2012, 16). According to Reinhart Kößler, 'The colonial discourse remained largely unbroken in Germany right up to the cataclysmic end of any dreams about territorial expansion, be it in Africa, in Eastern Europe or elsewhere, with the complete defeat of Nazi Germany in 1945' (2015, 63). Even after the end of German fascist rule and until the great wave of decolonisation in Africa in the 1960s, Germans continued to envisage a role for Germany as a colonising power alongside England, France, Portugal, Spain and Holland (van Laak 2005). In the following, we will see how this past has been dealt with in German society.

(DIS-)REMEMBERING COLONIALISM

Although the word 'postcolonial' is useful in indicating a general process with some shared features across the globe, if uprooted from specific

> locations, 'postcoloniality' cannot be meaningfully investigated, and, instead, the term begins to obscure the very relations of domination that it seeks to uncover. (Loomba 2005, 22)

Postcolonialism characterises the conditions, processes and struggles of coming to terms with a presence that is imbued with the colonial past (Schilling 2015). This section outlines the particularities of German postcolonialism: In the contemporary German public, the colonial past is rarely mentioned or is played down and whitewashed (Eckert and Wirz 2002; Kößler 2015, chap. 2). Involvement in colonialism is disremembered or – if acknowledged – considered as having had no lasting effects or, sometimes, as having had positive effects. In 2004, Chancellor Gerhard Schröder erased Germany's colonial past altogether when he said that one of the reasons why Germany should promote security policy in several African countries was that this should not be left to the former colonising powers (Kößler and Melber 2004).

Responding to my question whether the colonial past played a role for the German non-governmental organisations (NGOs) working on reproductive health in Tanzania, one of my interviewees acknowledged that she did not know much about colonialism and added: 'The German colonial history . . . that it was so short and also over so quickly, that it was over fairly early. It's not really contained in the structures in Tanzania' (Interview 01, November 11, 2009). This is exemplary for the way German colonialism is characterised if brought up or remembered: It is generally reduced to the period of state-sponsored colonialism, considered to have been short-lived, and characterised as having had little effect on colonising as well as colonised societies. This was also epitomised by a similar official statement uttered by the left-leaning Green Bundestag deputy Hans-Christian Ströbele, in 2001, in his capacity as his party's leader in the Bundestag Committee for Development Cooperation: 'Germany has been driven out of colonialisation early on. . . . Germany can now act in an unencumbered way and assume the role of avant-garde' in Africa (cited in Kößler and Melber 2004, 37).

While the impact of colonialism on the colonised societies is sometimes deemed insignificant, as evident in the previous quote by one of my interviewees, at times its allegedly positive sides are highlighted. In 1980, the writer Uwe Timm summarised the relation of the majority of Germans to their colonial past as follows:

> In the public consciousness, the German colonial past is, if at all, still present today in the same way as before 1945: as the legend of the hard-working Germans who built roads and railroads in Africa and taught the blacks their ABCs. That this legend survives so stubbornly can probably also be explained by the fact that – after the horrors of German fascism – Germans thought that in this area at least they had an edge on other peoples. (Cited in Friedrichsmeyer, Lennox, and Zantop 1998, 24)

While overtly pro-colonial circles remain in existence – for instance, the *Traditionsverband ehemaliger Schutz- und Überseetruppen – Freunde der früheren deutschen Schutzgebiete* ('Association for the Tradition of Former Protection and Overseas Troops – Friends of the Former German Protectorates') – positive sides of German colonialism are also implicitly put forward in academic texts that are otherwise critical of colonialism: 'The African work force was subsequently treated better. Around 1913, about 150,000 Africans had been baptised, and 120,000 learnt at German schools. Moreover, 3,754 kilometres of railway had been built in the German colonies by 1914' (van Laak 2005, 8–9). Even though the eminent historian Dirk van Laak refrains from explicitly qualifying Christianisation, schooling and infrastructure development as positive, at least the associations attached to formal education and mobility as well as the listing of these supposed achievements right after stating that the colonised had been treated better in that episode of colonisation allow such a reading.

A similar perspective is also reflected in statements from German development policy circles. While German occupation of the territory of present-day Tanzania lasted over thirty years, that is, more than twice as long as the Nazi regime, and cost hundreds of thousands of East African lives, the Ministry for Economic Cooperation and Development (BMZ), for example, states that 'Tanzania and Germany are bound to one another by a *brief* and, *in some ways*, painful colonial history' (BMZ 2012; my emphasis). The German Foreign Office (2012) suggests that this colonial past was largely amicable and unproblematic in terms of relations between Germany and Tanzania, often referring solely to Germany's engineering interventions during colonial times:

> Germany is highly esteemed in Tanzania, where there is a greater public awareness than here of the country's colonial past, thanks to the substantial architectural and infrastructure heritage from the German colonial era. The good bilateral relations are reflected in Germany's intensive engagement, particularly in development cooperation.

Most interviewees quoted in chapters 5 and 6 also played down Germany's colonial past in Tanzania and did not see any negative repercussions for present-day German-Tanzanian relations. Highlighting the allegedly positive aspects of colonisation is also mirrored internally in the case of development education (DE) (see chapter 3).

According to Britta Schilling, public discourse on German colonialism was laid to rest after the 1968 movement (2014, 10), but since the turn to the twenty-first century that silence has started to crumble due to lobbying by social movements and civil society organisations in Germany as well as in former German colonies. Commemorations of milestones in German colonial history have been used to push the issue of German colonialism and postcolonialism into the limelight: 100 years of the genocide against the Ova-herero and Nama in 2004, 100 years of the Maji Maji War in 'German East Africa' in 2005 and 125 years of the Berlin Conference in 2009. Over the past years, initiatives of the groups affected by the genocide as well as German civil society have led to further publicity and acknowledgement of this past (No Amnesty on Genocide! 2017). Ovaherero and Nama initiatives demand 'to be directly involved in negotiating a comprehensive solution, including recognition of the genocide, a sincere and appropriate apology, as well as just reparations to the Ovaherero and Nama communities who continue to suffer the adverse effects of the genocide' (Delegates to the I. Transnational Congress on the Ovaherero and Nama Genocides 2016). In 2017, Ovaherero and Nama representatives filed a lawsuit for damages against Germany. The Tanzanian government has also announced its inclination to seek compensa-tion for the victims of German military campaigns between 1905 and 1907 (Ayeko-Kümmeth 2017).

This, albeit small, surge in public attention to German occupation of African territories in particular is accompanied by a growing academic inter-est in the impact of German colonialism on the colonies and on German society. Prior to that, the history of imperialism and colonialism was only really of interest to Marxist approaches in German historiography. Accord-ing to Andreas Eckert and Albert Wirz (2002), this was due to its fixation on national history, on everyday history and on German fascism and the Holo-caust. In addition, the lack of a postcolonial presence in Germany that could have lobbied for a change of perspective (as was the case for France and Britain) must not be underestimated. As Schilling puts it, 'Germany never had the experience of the "empire striking back"', and in the cultural-literary sense, for instance, '[p]ostcolonial . . . refers to the postwar immigration of Turkish "guest workers"' (2014, 5).

While the acknowledgement of state-sponsored colonialism remains mar-ginal, the disavowal of German involvement in colonialism predating 1884 is almost comprehensive: Slavery is readily associated with Great Britain, France, Holland, Portugal and Spain but not with Germany. A couple of years ago, an attempt to erect a statue for Heinrich Karl Schimmelmann (1724–1782) – business man, politician and one of the richest and most influential men of his times – at the Wandsbeker Market in Hamburg was only just prevented by anti-racist activists. The supporters of the monument remembered him as responsible for the industrialisation of Wandsbek, while the adversaries pointed out that he had made his money through kidnapping and trafficking African men, women and children.

Kößler's understanding of colonial amnesia as 'a public attitude of not addressing a past that in principle is known, but for various reasons is not a topic of attention and discussion' (2015, 64–65) – what I prefer to call 'dis-remembering' in order to highlight it as an active social and cultural process (Raghuram, Madge, and Noxolo 2009, 10) – seems to be useful for a description of the state of contemporary Germany and, in particular, the field of development policy. The German development scene is aware of Germany's colonial past but deals with it in a peculiar way. Among other strategies, it takes care to dissociate ideas and practices of development and the colonial past (see in particular chapter 3 and its investigation of DE).

THE EMERGENCE OF GERMAN DEVELOPMENT POLICY DURING COLONIALISM

Development studies commonly date the emergence of development policy and practice back to the post-WWII era and in particular to the period after the former colonies gained independence. However, some scholars of colonialism and development challenge the notion of a clear break between colonial-era interventions and development and note that the idea and practice of 'developing' the global South arose during colonisation (Hodge 2007; Cooke 2001; Kothari 2006b). In line with this latter position, this section addresses the emergence of German development policy and practice in the first decade of the twentieth century. Its main concern is in childbirth-related policy and population policy in 'German East Africa', which are the empirical focus of chapters 5 and 6.

The year 1906 is repeatedly mentioned as a turning point in German policy and practice towards its African colonies (Iliffe 1969). Immediately after the turn of the century, German colonialism in Africa experienced a crisis. This was in part due to major wars that the Germans fought in 'German South-West Africa' from 1904 to 1907 and in 'German East Africa' from 1905 to 1907. The latter, the Maji Maji War, 'was a resistance against plantation owners, cash crops' communal production under supervision of colonial agents, and harsh German colonial rule in general' (Chachage 2006). The German chancellor at the time utilised the critiques of malfeasance, corruption and brutality uttered by the SPD and the Centre Party against the wars and the colonial administration to disband parliament. The outcome of the subsequent elections changed the balance of political power and paved the way for a renewal of the colonial administration with regard to both structure and personnel: The Kolonialabteilung des Auswärtigen Amtes (Colonial Department of the Foreign Office) was transformed into an independent Reichskolonial-amt (Imperial Colonial Office), and Dernburg became the first state secretary of the Imperial Colonial Office in May 1907.

In Dernburg's reformist agenda, the 'natives' were '[t]he most important resource in Africa' (1907, 7). With the introduction of wage labour and measures to force people to take up such labour, Africans were supposed to become 'economic persons' who would enable the exploitation of the colony and who would also be able to purchase German products (Gann 1987). Despite opposition from settlers, 'the goals for export crops and commercial development' were revised towards a 'social policy' (Beck 1977, 22). This turn in policy is summarised by Dernburg's vision of an 'enlightened colonialism' (Beck 1977, 47): 'While one used to colonise by means of destruction, one can now colonise by means of preservation, which encompasses the missionary as well as the doctor, the railway and the machine, i.e. the progressive theoretical and practical science in all fields' (Dernburg 1907, 60).

Such a centrality of science and technology has been identified as characteristic of the emergence of development ideology during the period of colonial occupations (Hodge 2007). German colonial reformist agendas were not specific to the German Empire but were embedded in wider European debates which had commenced prior to the major colonial wars and Dernburg's appointment. Pascal Grosse (2000) argues that the new administration was not the vanguard of European colonial 'reforms' but merely responded to international debate over colonial reform and reflected internal debates in Germany on social reform as a third path – between uninhibited capitalism and socialist reform. According to John Iliffe, it is reasonable to understand the changes in German colonial policy as 'stimulated by fears engendered by the Maji Maji rebellion of 1905–07' and thus as a reaction to an African initiative rather than a decision controlled by the Germans (1969, 7). Reforms were regularly opposed by European settlers who feared for their economic interests and security (Iliffe 1969). While some scholars – as mentioned earlier – hold that 'the African work force was subsequently treated better' and schooling and health care were expanded (van Laak 2005, 9), the reforms did not 'necessarily imply liberalisation, in the sense of developments more acceptable to the African peoples' (Iliffe 1969, 8). Whether intervention actually led to 'development', in the sense of improvement of the lives of East Africans, is a matter of debate in the literature (e.g., Colwell 2001). As far as this research is concerned, it is crucial to note that ideas and practices to 'develop' colonised people had emerged.

POST-WWII GERMAN DEVELOPMENT POLICY

Former colonialists continued to influence post-WWII Germany. They upheld a positive image of German colonialism and established a continuity from colonial paternalism to post-war development (van Laak 2004, 366–72). The Federal Republic of Germany (FRG) officially initiated development 'aid' in the early 1950s (Ziai 2007, 95). The tendency to perceive development policy as part of economic foreign policy was expressed in the creation of a Federal Ministry for Economic Cooperation in 1961. This ministry's name received the addendum 'and Development' only three decades later. From the outset, and for a considerable time, one of the primary foreign policy functions of 'aid' by the FRG was to prevent decolonising nations from recognising the German Democratic Republic as a sovereign state. From the 1980s, German development policy has pushed for an economic reorientation in line with neoliberal principles and has asserted such a policy via conditionality, that is, providing 'official development assistance' (ODA) on the condition that certain policies and practices are implemented. From 1998 to 2009, BMZ leadership was held by Heidemarie Wieczorek-Zeul from the SPD. During her leadership, German development policy shifted increasingly from an approach focused on projects and programmes to 'global structural policy', which aimed to promote a development-friendly international policy environment (Ziai 2007).

When Minister Dirk Niebel of the Free Democratic Party took office in 2009, the BMZ began to emphasise cooperation with the private sector (Kuhn 2011). Gerd Müller of the Christian Social Union followed Niebel to head the BMZ in 2013. At the beginning of 2017 – and in the context of Germany's G20 presidency – the BMZ unveiled its new Africa policy framework entitled 'Africa and Europe – A New Partnership for Development, Peace, and a Better Future. Cornerstones of a Marshall Plan with Africa' (BMZ 2017a). It claims that 'the days of "aid" and of "donors and recipients" [must be] put behind us' and that the focus is now on 'fair trade, more private investment, more bottom-up economic development, more entrepreneurial spirit and, above all, more jobs and employment' (BMZ 2017a, 4). The fact that Germany has become more explicit in linking national (and sometimes European) interests to its development policy is evident in the 'Marshall Plan with Africa': 'As the world's last untapped market . . . Africa holds great opportunities, not least for the German private sector' (BMZ 2017a, 16). The other, more hidden agenda of the paper is the prevention of migration to Europe (Bauer 2017; Bernau 2017). Aram Ziai and Josephine Brämer (2015) have differentiated recent BMZ policy according to the logics of geopolitics, economics and 'genuine' development and find that economic policy – in contrast to the other two – remains constant despite changes in office. As a specific form of foreign policy, development policy follows the primacy of national interest in a peculiar way: It 'ensures the accumulation of national capital' by 'stabilising the international system through improvements of living conditions of people in "less developed" countries' (Ziai and Brämer 2015, 415). Here, and exemplified in the 'Marshall Plan with Africa', one of the central 'discursive tricks of development policy' (Ziai and Brämer 2015, 403) becomes clear, that is, to present the interests of investors from the North as compatible with the interests of the poor in the South. How this is conveyed to the German public will be discussed in chapter 3 with regard to a government billboard advertising campaign, while chapter 6 will demonstrate how German economic interests are implicated in reproductive health-related development policy abroad. Germany has a 'complex and decentralized aid governance structure' (CONCORD 2012, 48). The BMZ as 'the hub in an organisational network' (Nuscheler 2006, 196) is responsible for the majority of Germany's ODA. The second-largest portion of 'aid' funds goes towards the budget of the European Union's development 'cooperation'. Other important actors in the 'aid' network are various ministries, government-owned organisations responsible for implementation and secular as well as faith-based NGOs (Nuscheler 2006). From 1974 until recently, most bilateral development 'aid' of the BMZ and the other ministries was implemented by the Deutsche Gesellschaft für Technische Zusammenarbeit (German Agency for Technical Cooperation, GTZ) (responsible for technical cooperation) and Kreditanstalt für Wiederaufbau (German Development Bank, KfW) (responsible for financial cooperation). At the beginning of 2011, shortly after I had completed my fieldwork in Tanzania, the Deutsche Gesellschaft für Internationale Zusammenarbeit (German Agency for International Cooperation, GIZ) was formed by merging GTZ; Deutscher Entwicklungsdienst (German Development Service, DED), which deployed development workers on behalf of BMZ; and InWEnt (Capacity Building International), which was active in 'human resource' development and training. The motivation behind this merger was for German development 'assistance' to have a centralised, uniform appearance; to eliminate triple structures; and to make it easier for the BMZ to control the implementing agencies (Stockmann et al. 2010). Today, most German 'aid' – in 2015, 78 per cent of ODA went into bilateral cooperation (CONCORD 2016, 13) – is managed by the three implementing agencies KfW, GIZ and Engagement Global. As with most donor countries, German 'aid' policy is an integral part of the international 'aid' system. Not only is a large share of ODA distributed via multilateral donor agencies, but German 'aid' is also geared towards fulfilling the 2015 United Nations' (UN) Sustainable Development Goals (that build on the Millennium Development Goals) and the Paris Declaration on Aid Effectiveness of 2005.

In 2011, Germany had a net disbursement of about €10.5 billion (CONCORD 2012, 48). However, as it contributed only 0.4 per cent of its gross national income (GNI) (or, according to the European NGO Confederation for Relief and Development's [CONCORD] calculation of genuine 'aid',[1] a mere €8.9 billion, or 0.34%), it was among the OECD (Organisation for Economic Co-operation and Development) member countries which were furthest from reaching the UN goal of contributing 0.7 per cent of GNI as ODA. In 2015, Germany had increased its net 'aid' disbursement to €15.7 billion or 0.52 per cent and its genuine 'aid' to €11.8 billion or 0.39 per cent (CONCORD 2016, 13). The increase in net 'aid' disbursement in 2015 was mainly due to a new way of calculating ODA whereby the German government included refugee costs. According to the OECD (2017b), Germany met the UN target to keep ODA at or above 0.7 per cent of GNI for the first time in 2016 and became the world's second-largest 'aid donor'. This was 'due to the scaling up of its overall "aid" programme as well the doubling of in-donor refugee costs compared to 2015' (OECD 2017a). Partner countries were reduced from sixty-eight countries in 2000 to fifty-five in 2008, and the number today stand at fifty (Faust and Ziaja 2012; BMZ 2017b). All Germany's former colonies are partner countries, although 'cooperation' with Togo had temporarily been suspended and resumed only in 2011. Africa is the focal region of German 'aid': In 2010, about one-third of German ODA went to African countries (German Federal Foreign Office 2011). And German NGOs also direct about half their funds to the African continent (BMZ 2016). As will become evident in the empirical analyses, the focus on Africa is also evident in DE and billboard advertising. For the chapters on development policy abroad, I have thus chosen to investigate German interventions on the African continent.

Kapoor (2008, chap. 5) argues that donors often cover up problematic conditionalities in order to appear benevolent and generous. According to CONCORD, 'Donors still informally tie aid by biasing supposedly competitive procurement processes in favour of their own companies, who win an estimated 60% of formally untied aid contracts' (2012, 21). Even though Germany promotes its 'aid' as almost wholly untied, in 2011 less than 50 per cent of its 'free-standing technical cooperation' was 'channeled through local procurement procedures', and the ministry expressed the desire to 'strengthen cooperation with the private sector' and 'open business opportunities' to German companies (CONCORD 2012, 21). Bilateral 'aid' has a significant, positive influence on German exports to partner countries (Larch et al. 2007) – and the proportion of bilateral 'aid' of total ODA has increased considerably in the past years. Chapter 6 will address the stakes of German companies in the market for family planning and how they are intertwined with German development 'aid'.

With regard to the issues of population, family planning and maternal health, which are the focus of this book's analysis of development abroad, the FRG significantly expanded its activities in the 1980s and has since been particularly active in Africa (Schlebusch 1994). Germany's current official development 'assistance' on issues of population and reproductive health is outlined in the policy papers 'Sexual and Reproductive Health and Rights, and Population Dynamics' (BMZ 2008) and 'Population Dynamics

in German Development Cooperation' (BMZ 2014a). 'Sexual and reproductive health' is understood as 'encompassing issues of physical, mental
and social well-being in matters related to sexuality and the reproductive
system' (BMZ 2008, 4). While this shows a very broad understanding of
sexual and reproductive health and rights, issues raised as facts to highlight
a problematic situation in the global South are narrower and rather pertain to
questions of maternal mortality (see chapter 5), population growth and family
planning (see chapter 6). This narrowing of the concept is also discernible in
other publications by government agencies as well as NGOs. In 2011, BMZ
launched a specific 'Initiative on Rights-based Family Planning and Maternal Health'. It places emphasis on 'improv[ing] knowledge and acceptance
of modern family planning methods', 'expand[ing] access to modern family
planning methods and services' (see chapter 6) and 'increas[ing] the number
of births attended by health professionals' (see chapter 5) (BMZ 2011a). In
the past years, a renewed emphasis on economic demographic concepts such
as 'demographic dividend' and 'population dynamics' is discernible. In 2014,
the German government declared itself 'a pioneering force in Europe on the
cross-sector issue of population dynamics' (BMZ 2014a, 3), and the 2017
'Marshall Plan with Africa' is strongly influenced by these concepts.

German development policy abroad, it has to be noted, does not only take
place via the government or state institutions. German NGOs transfer more
than €1 billion annually – mainly from membership contributions and donations – to 'developing countries' (BMZ 2016). As the BMZ states, '[a]nybody
can get involved: by donating cash, by getting involved in development-
policy initiatives and organisations, by supporting fair trade or working on
the ground in a partner country' (BMZ 2017d). The BMZ regards '[d]evel-
opment policy . . . the duty of society as a whole' and in order to ensure the
'involvement of German civil society . . . supports development information
and education work' (BMZ 2017d). The aim is 'to communicate the vision
of sustainable development', to 'arouse interest in developing countries [and]
explain global contexts', to 'motivate people to become actively involved'
and to 'support development activities inside Germany' (BMZ 2017d). About
16,000 NGOs are active in development awareness and educational work
in Germany (VENRO 2009, 21). While the BMZ 'supports campaigns and
effective PR events, issues audio-visual media, lends films, [and] produces
publications on the entire spectrum of development cooperation issues',
Engagement Global is the institution 'that implements state development
education programmes' (BMZ 2017d). In 2015, the German government
spent €24 million on DE and about €30 million on development exchange
and volunteer services, which can also be considered part of DE (Asbrand and
Scheunpflug 2014). The budget for 2017 was increased by about €10 million
for each field (Federal Ministry of Finance 2017, 23–24).

COLONIAL POWER IN DEVELOPMENT

This and the following sections put forward the specific theoretical perspective of the book. As the aim of this book is to examine the connections between contemporary development and the colonial past, it is part of
postcolonial studies with their interest in 'the persistence of colonial forms
of power and knowledge into the present' (Kothari 2011, 69). Postcolonial
approaches are distinct in their theoretical and epistemological perspectives
as they provide 'critiques of the process of production of knowledge about the
other' (Williams and Chrisman 1994, 8). Refuting the differentiation between
colonisation 'as a system of rule, of power and exploitation, and colonisation
as a system of knowledge and representation' (Hall 1996, 254), postcolonial
approaches to development examine the colonial imprint on knowledge,
subjectivities, practices, institutions and political economy (Kapoor 2008;
McEwan 2009).

I employ colonial power as an analytic concept to characterise the kinds
of power that emerged during European colonialism and are still operative in
the present (Mbembe 2001; Gutiérrez Rodríguez 2010). By not reserving the
notion of colonial power to refer to the period of actual territorial occupation,
the difference between the period of formal colonial rule and the postcolonial
era can be examined 'as the reconfiguration of a field, rather than as movement of linear transcendence between two mutually exclusive states' (Hall
1996, 254). In Latin America, the persistence of colonial modes of thinking
and colonial economic, political and social relations has been discussed with
reference to the notion of 'coloniality' (Moraña, Dussel, and Jauregui 2008).
While this book is inspired by this debate, it acknowledges that the concept
of 'coloniality' is closely related to the particular context of Latin America.
I have chosen to use the term *colonial power* for my analysis of Germany's
colonial present, so as to underline the specificity of that context, and to
understand, for example, 'how the specifics of the German colonial and postcolonial experience facilitated the survival of thought structures that are still
discernible today' (Friedrichsmeyer, Lennox, and Zantop 1998, 29).

Colonial Difference and Racism

Postcolonial perspectives on development are, first of all, concerned with the
manner in which development policy is based on and establishes differences
and hierarchies between the global North and South (McEwan 2009). Colonialism was enabled and legitimised through the establishment of difference
between the colonising Self and the colonised Other (Said 1978; Mudimbe
1994), and thus, the colonised were discursively and materially positioned
as fundamentally different from and inferior to the colonisers (Fanon 2008).

Scholars have argued that principles of development policy such as partnership, which suggests equality between donors and recipients, are called into question by the self-conception of Western nations as superior (Noxolo 2006; Eriksson Baaz 2005). Patricia Noxolo (2006), for instance, suggests that the impossibility of 'partnership' between the UK and its former colonies has its roots in colonial-era racialised, gendered hierarchies that continue to operate in the present. Referring to colonial-era representations of Africans as idle and irrational, Maria Eriksson Baaz (2005) highlights the manner in which the self-conception of development professionals, as different from and superior to their counterparts in the global South, leads them to interpret the resistance of these partners to their proposals as passivity rather than as a sign of autonomy.

Scholars from Latin America in particular have argued that 'colonial difference' has been the essence of colonial power ever since the conquest of the Americas (Quijano 2000). For the purpose of this book, the concept of colonial difference is meant to highlight the 'consequence of coloniality of power', not 'an epistemic location' (Mignolo 2002, 90). Allowing for differentiation, classification and hierarchisation of the colonised vis-à-vis the colonisers, 'colonial difference' assumed different forms under 'different global designs' (Christianisation, 'civilising mission', post-WWII development, neoliberalism and so on). However, '[b]arbarians, primitives, underdeveloped people, and people of colour are all categories that established epistemic dependencies' (Mignolo 2002, 84–85). Whether difference was established on the basis of religion, biology, civilisation, modernity, culture or development, these concepts shared an underlying construct of race. Racism is an ideology according to which people are categorised into 'racial' groups based on arbitrary physical markers (Arndt and Ofuatey-Alazard 2011). It 'is about the ability to be able to manage human populations by dividing them and ordering them in some kind of way' (Lentin and Karakayali 2016, 147). Since the beginning of colonialism (and before within Europe), Europeans have used race to justify conquest, exploitation, annihilation and subordination of people constructed as racially inferior. Commonly, agents from the global North have made reference to oppressive gender relations in the global South to establish racial superiority and justify intervention (Spivak 2003; Mohanty 1991).

According to Achille Mbembe, 'In relation to Africa the notion of "absolute otherness" has been taken farthest' and 'the simplistic and narrow prejudice persists that African social formations belong to a specific category, that of simple societies or of traditional societies' (2001, 2–3). In this manner, Africa is typically associated with resistance to change, ' "absence", "lack", and "non-being"' (Mbembe 2001, 3–4). Here, 'to differ from something or somebody is not simply not to be [similar, DB]; it is not to be at all (non-being). What is more, it is being nothing (nothingness)' (Mbembe 2001, 4).

Building on the insight that 'the silence on race is a determining silence that both masks and marks its centrality to the development project' (White 2002, 408) and that 'racial hierarchies remain as master frameworks within contemporary development thought and practice' (Shilliam 2014, 41), this book explores the establishment of colonial difference in German development endeavours both at home and abroad.

The concept of racism within Germany continues to be reserved for the period of German fascism, anti-Semitism and the Shoah, and, related to that, for contemporary right-wing extremism (Lentin and Karakayali 2016). As to the former, it means that other 'necropolitical' projects (Mbembe 2003), such as the Porajmos – the attempt to exterminate all Roma and Sinti – or the persecution and killing of Slavs and Blacks, and racism as part of German colonialism has not been given much attention (Goldberg 2006). Regarding the latter, the UN's 'Report of the Special Rapporteur on Contemporary Forms of Racism, Racial Discrimination, Xenophobia and Related Intolerance' has ascertained that 'one of the central problems in furthering the fight against racism in Germany is the narrow understanding of racism in practice that for many years prevailed within society at large. Due to Germany's historical experience, racism has traditionally been equated with extremist right-wing ideology and violence' (2010, 16). Contemporary Germany is marked by a 'postcolonial, postnationalsocialist, postsocialist situation as well as by several consecutive regimes of migration, emigration and genocide' (Steyerl 2003, 39). While some postcolonial scholars argue that 'Germany's recent history is not significantly characterised by its own relatively short and brutal phase of colonial rule' (Steyerl 2003, 41), German colonialism has – as noted earlier – a much longer trajectory (before and after the period of formal colonisation). What is more, for the purpose of scrutinising development policy, Germany's history of colonial occupations in and exploitations of the global South is of central relevance.

It is for lack of historical consciousness regarding colonial racism that, for instance, Blackface imagery in the German media, racial profiling by the German police or depictions of Black children as symbols of misery (see chapter 4) are not widely regarded as problematic. Here, the United Nations' Working Group of Experts on People of African Descent (2017) found that 'Germany's colonial past, the genocide of the Ovaherero and Nama peoples, and the sterilization, incarceration, and murder of Black people during Nazi Germany, is not adequately addressed in the national narrative'. The tendency to disregard non-white participants in DE (chapter 4) can be related to the fact that citizenship and belonging in German have for long time – and particularly since state-sponsored colonialism – been related to an ethnicised understanding of Germanness as a subform of whiteness, in which the reference point is not a common state but a common *Volkstum* (a concept mixing nation and folklore) (Walgenbach 2005, 169–71; Grosse 2000; El-Tayeb 2016).

Linearity of Development and Trusteeship

In addition to the workings of colonial difference, the global North and global South are commonly seen as being at different stages of a single universal time in development policy (Eriksson Baaz 2005; Kothari 2011). There is a tendency to perceive all phenomena in the global South in terms of the history of the global North (Robinson 2006). This is epitomised in modernisation theory, which has dominated post-WWII development thinking and practice. The idea that people, societies and world regions inhabit different yet continuous temporal spaces dates back to the period of colonial rule. Colonial thinking entailed an assumption of history, social change and development taking place in a linear manner (Dussel 1995). Western Europe was seen as the culmination of history and development; other regions allegedly lagged behind (Kebede 2004). Africa in particular was perceived by Europeans as a place of stagnation. This assumption was first and foremost formulated and propagated during the European 'Enlightenment' by philosophers such as G. W. F. Hegel (1822). Europe and white people were construed as the human norm and associated with 'progress', 'development', and mandated to subdue other regions of the world and peoples (Farr 2005). This book addresses the question of whether notions of linear, teleological societal development are invoked in German development policy. For example, it discusses whether such assumptions are evident in policy papers and materials for DE in Germany (see chapter 3).

The idea of linear, teleological development is connected to the practice of trusteeship (Cowen and Shenton 1996) – legitimising Western tutelage and imposing Western epistemology and 'modes of organization on the non-West' (Slater 2005, 227). Scholars have criticised development policy and practice for postulating Western positivist, scientific rationality as the only legitimate means of knowledge production (Escobar 1994; Goldman 2005). According to John Briggs and Joanne Sharp, the prevailing conviction in international development is 'that either Western science and rationality are more advanced or refined than other positions or, more simply, that they are the norm – "knowledge" in the singular form – from which others deviate in their fallibility' (2004, 662). These authors highlight that donors tend to incorporate indigenous knowledge in the name of 'ownership' as a mere complement to scientific and expert solutions, thereby reducing it to technical knowledge without taking underlying social norms and world views into account. Scholars have also shown that, by employing force to subjugate the rest of the world, Western societies have attempted to shape the non-Western world according to their desires (Hauck 2003). Local European knowledge and modes of organisation have thereby been projected across the globe. Such universalisation entailed the destruction of other knowledge systems through annihilation and transformation of societies and institutions and the parallel installation of Western institutional and epistemological apparatuses (for instance, Western education and schooling, or hospitals and health care). In this manner, colonial power operates not only through the conviction that non-Western societies should follow the European model but also through putting this into practice on a material level. This is, for instance, particularly relevant for understanding German interventions in childbirth-related practices in East Africa (see chapter 5) or for understanding German endeavours to influence population numbers abroad (see chapter 6).

Capitalism and the Continuity of Colonial Inequality and Exploitation

It is hence crucial to acknowledge that colonial discourses interact with 'material events and circumstance, the forms through which discourse is, as it were, entangled in the material world' (Young 2001, 387). Or, as Thomas Lemke (1997, 48–50) has argued, an understanding of discourse as self-regulating and not connected to non-discursive dimensions leads into an analytical cul-de-sac. Discourses take effect in the material world, are expressed in actions, located in institutions and brought to life by people. However, in some approaches to development, a tendency of regarding the social sphere in terms of self-contained discourse is evident. Eriksson Baaz, for instance, conceptualises speech, action and economic relations as solely discursive (2005, 10–13). While I concur with her argument that discourses define how phenomena may be understood and circumscribe a certain type of practice, I believe that taking for granted the primacy of discourses is theoretically flawed and politically problematic. This is evident in Eriksson Baaz's conclusion; she suggests that 'the possibility of change is located primarily in the issue of representation, in providing alternative meanings' (2005, 173–74). In my view, trying to understand all phenomena in development as discursive reduces the usefulness of discourse as an analytical tool (Crewe and Harrison 1998, 17). It also runs the danger of diverting attention away from pivotal issues in development such as actual practices, institutions and the global political economy. Rather than being autonomous, self-referential producers of knowledge, discourses are conceived in this book as materially embedded and yielding effects: 'Development discourse is constituted and reproduced within a set of material relationships, activities and powers – social, cultural and geopolitical. To comprehend the real power of development, we cannot ignore either the immediate institutional or the broader historical and geographical context within which its texts are produced' (Crush 1995a, 6).

Various scholars have criticised postcolonial approaches because they neglect the material realities of global capitalism (Dirlik 1997; Ahmad 1995). Postcolonial studies have generally been accused of showing a 'culturalist bias' – that they undertake a 'critical analysis of literary and other discourses, of social mentalities and subjectivities, ideologies and symbolic practices' and thereby run 'the risk of concealing or neglecting the materiality of the social and political relations that make possible, if not inevitable, the reproduction of those discourses, ideologies and symbolic practices' (Santos 2010, 234). In light of the continuity as well as reconfiguration 'of the divisions in economic and political power created by the processes of colonialism' (Biccum 2002, 37), recent postcolonial approaches in development studies have, however, taken material inequalities and global power relations into account (Wainwright 2008). The continuity of colonial-era economic and political dependence has been noted in African countries in particular, where 'continuing economic hegemony . . . means that the postcolonial state remains in a situation of dependence on its former masters, and that the former masters continue to act in a colonialist manner towards formerly colonized states' (Young 2001, 45). Bill Cooke (2001), for instance, shows how the seemingly empowering agenda of participation is impossible in the context of economic and political asymmetries between the global South and North and how a disregard for these inequalities is subservient to donors' self-interest in development agendas. Instead of challenging dominance and hegemonic norms, the credo of participation thus rather 'masks and perpetuates social and economic structural inequalities' (Cooke 2001, 20). In this book, I attempt to take into account both development discourse and how it is 'articulated through concrete socioeconomic practices' (Wainwright 2008, 9), and the context of structural inequalities and global capital accumulation 'which both underpin and are sustained by . . . discursive representations' (Wilson 2012, 208).

Instability and Challenges

Postcolonial critics such as Homi Bhabha (1990, 1994) have suggested that power during formal colonial rule was inherently unstable. Scholars of development have also highlighted that colonial discourse in contemporary development is not monolithic and uncontested (Kapoor 2008; Heron 2007). For example, Eriksson Baaz (2005) takes into account questioning attitudes and criticism of development 'aid' in Scandinavian professionals' accounts of their work in Tanzania. When interventions do not yield the expected results, and recipients behave contrary to the development workers' expectations, this may arouse doubts as to the rationality of development 'aid'. Professionals involved in international development take different stances with regard to dominant discourses (McKinnon 2008). This means that established development discourses and power relations can be transformed by development professionals. Of course, 'aid recipients' or 'target groups' also challenge colonial power through their thoughts and actions (Yeboah 2006). Chapter 3 takes into account the effects of postcolonial and anti-racist critique on the field of DE, and chapter 4 pays attention to the progressive potential of billboard advertising and also to subvertising and adbusting. Furthermore, chapter 5 is attentive to the 'hidden transcripts' (Scott 1990) in development professionals' accounts of their work that highlight doubts and criticism and thus contest dominant conceptions of development.

DISPOSITIF ANALYSIS

Having laid out the theoretical framework employed to understand colonial power, this section briefly elucidates the methodological approach for the empirical study. Discourses are rarely consistent in themselves. In order to elucidate different and contradicting discourses, this book draws on James Scott (1990), who differentiates between 'public transcripts' and 'hidden transcripts' in analysing power. A hidden transcript 'contains . . . gestures, speech, practices . . . [which are] excluded from the public transcript by the ideological limits within which domination is cast' (Scott 1990, 28). Such transcripts may be found in interactions among peers and people in similar socio-political and professional positions. As mentioned in chapter 1, I accessed 'hidden transcripts' through interviews with German development professionals in Germany and Tanzania who regarded me as part of their 'culture'.

To explore colonial power, it is useful to conceive of power as dominant ways of thinking and their interconnectedness with the material world. A useful tool in this enterprise is Foucault's (1979, 1980) concept of power as dispositif, which is apt to grasp the interactions between discourses and non-discursive phenomena. The methodology of dispositif analysis can be understood as an extension of discourse analysis and permits an examination of the interrelationship of discourses with materiality and actors (Bührmann and Schneider 2008). Some critical development studies have sought to bring together an analysis of discourses, materialities and actors by referring to dispositif analysis (Brigg 2001; Ziai 2007). Inspired by these studies, the dispositif analytical methodology of this book explores discourses and their material manifestations as well as the agency of actors by way of combining archives data, documents, images, statistics, interviews and observation. This combination of resources and methods helps to provide a broad and differentiated picture of development policy because it addresses speech as well as practical interventions and agency. The approach must include sensitivity to different dimensions of power and to shifts in discourses and practices. It must also pay attention to actors' space to manoeuvre within discourses and challenge colonial power in current development.

Development policy is largely driven by the need for efficiency and achievement of tangible results, and this drive is mirrored in the focus on practical interventions in contemporary development studies (Bernstein 2006). This goal and target orientation entails a preoccupation with the future in international development and a neglect of its roots (Kothari 2011). However, history (in the sense of the past as well as of an academic discipline) is important as a resource of critical and reflective self-awareness regarding the nature of development as a discipline, its current focuses, the reasons why those focuses and not others have come to take their particular form in the present and how they differ from past motives and goals (Woolcock et al. 2011).

For development policy at home (chapters 3 and 4), this book builds on studies that analyse contemporary development from a postcolonial perspective without undertaking empirical historical analyses (Kapoor 2008; Kontzi 2015). It resorts to literature on the history of DE and billboard advertising to contextualise these fields of development intervention historically and otherwise relies on contemporary documents and imagery to understand the knowledge represented and produced, the practices proposed and undertaken and the agents constructed and invoked.

For development policy abroad (chapters 5 and 6), I draw on approaches which empirically examine colonial-era policies and empirically link these to contemporary development (Wainwright 2008; Deuser 2010). Inspired by Foucault (1979), I use what I would term *genealogical dispositif analysis* (Bendix 2013a). It combines the methodology of dispositif analysis with the approach of genealogy (Foucault 1977; Kerchner 2006). The genealogical approach, as used in this book, rests on an understanding of history as change from one situation of power to another, rather than on an understanding of history as a teleological, linear process. This allows for relating German colonial-era policy to contemporary interventions in issues of population and reproduction without examining the times between these two periods. This historical approach de-familiarises perspectives on policies and practices which, on the surface, appear to be given and self-evident. At the same time, such an examination of the field of population and reproductive health during colonisation makes it possible to grasp the specificity of colonial power in this sphere and to better understand contemporary policy and practice on this basis.

CONCLUSION

In this chapter, I have introduced the history of German colonialism and highlighted its reach beyond the relatively short period – if compared to other European colonising nations – of formal colonisation from the mid-1880s through the end of WWI. The specific treatment of the Nazi era in German post-WWII memory has had an extinguishing effect on the memory of colonialism: That era was considered an aberration from an otherwise civilised history, connections between colonialism and German fascism were seldom drawn and race and racism were commonly confined to the Nazi period only. Until today, colonial history is not perceived as particularly relevant for German society as a whole or for the field of development policy. German colonialism is either disremembered or remembered as having had little or positive effects on the colonised societies.

Development ideas and practice with regard to the colonised people in German colonies need to be understood as having emerged as early as the beginning of the twentieth century in attempts to reform colonial exploitation. Such changes towards a developmental colonial policy were embedded in a pan-European debate, influenced by domestic changes in the colonial administration, as well as by devastating wars fought in 'German East Africa' and 'German South-West Africa'. Post-WWII German development policy has – just like German colonial endeavours – focused on Africa. Government policy today tends to be more and more geared towards and open about neo-liberal strategies that benefit German corporate interests.

Through a review of postcolonial approaches to development, this chapter has suggested understanding colonial power as an analytic concept. Colonial power in development, as conceptualised for the purpose of this book, is characterised by various dimensions. These include, first, the establishment of colonial difference between (former) colonisers and (former) colonised, which may take different forms in different times and contexts but is always based on the idea of race. Second, colonial power in development is marked by the assumption of linear, teleological historical and societal 'progress' with the West at the upper end. Societies of the global South have been and continue to be transformed based on Western epistemology and modes of organisation. Third, these aspects of colonial power take effect in the context of global political and economic inequalities which have their origin in colonial-era conquest and exploitation. Finally, colonial power in development is not monolithic, and this allows actors to contest and challenge its articulations.

Methodologically, this book explores power as discourses that are fundamentally bound up with actual practices, institutions and the political-economic environment. At the same time, attention is paid to actors and their agency which is conceptualised as circumscribed by dominant knowledge configurations and material circumstances but not wholly determined by these. Colonial power takes effect in the present through the persistence of discourses that emerged during colonial conquest and their relation to material practices and structural political and economic inequalities. Such an understanding of the operation of colonial power allows for a reconstruction of colonial thinking and practice in contemporary German development at home and abroad. The following chapters explore empirically how and with what effects current German policy at home – in the realms of DE and billboard advertising – and abroad – in those related to childbirth and population – is shaped by colonial power.

NOTE

1. This is done 'by deducting from the overall net disbursements of ODA in 2011 the estimated level of imputed student costs . . . the estimated level of refugee costs . . . debt relief for 2011, 30% and 15% of the estimated tied and partially tied aid share per Member State, respectively and estimated repayments on ODA loans' (CONCORD 2012, 66).

Chapter 3

Development Education and the (De-)Stabilisation of Colonial Power

The white man's burden is not what you heard it is
It ain't about a mission to christian the heathens
But it's connected to that vision of us as superior beings
And the world's darkest history
His-story is my story it ain't no mystery
. . .
And I can carry the weight when we share the burden
Ain't nothing that's too heavy for my shoulders
We can conquer the hate we bring it up to the surface
And listen to what history done told us.

– White Swedish rapper Promoe, 2006

Development education (DE) in Germany aims at encouraging learners to participate in the shaping of a more just and sustainable world marked by solidarity (KMK and BMZ 2007). It takes place both in schools and in non-formal educational contexts. The actors include governmental agencies, kindergartens, primary and secondary schools, universities, adult education centres, vocational schools, faith-based organisations, non-governmental organisations (NGOs), international volunteer programmes such as *weltwärts* ('out into the world', by the Bundesministerium für wirtschaftliche Zusammenarbeit und Entwicklung [German Federal Ministry for Economic Cooperation and Development, BMZ]) and *kulturweit* ('culturewide', by the Federal Foreign Office) and many others. DE is supposed to enhance levels of knowledge to invigorate and turn people into responsible members of their society as well as responsible global citizens. However, quite contrary to its declared objectives, DE may serve to facilitate the perpetuation of existing hierarchies and strengthen certain societal or global spectra at the expense of others (Andreotti and de Souza 2012). Empirical studies in school contexts in

Germany have, for instance, ascertained a direct link between the portrayal of the global South in education material and, disturbingly, the prevalence of racism of white German students and teachers towards Black students (Marmer et al. 2010). This chapter explores DE as the one crucial realm of German development policy at home.

What is discussed under the label of *global citizen education* in the Anglo-US-American context is most commonly referred to as *education for sustainable development*, *global learning* or *development education* in Germany. Even though these approaches have different histories and, at times, use different focal points, they are also often used interchangeably as (near) synonyms. They are thus merged in this chapter under the term *DE*. Of all the OECD (Organisation for Economic Co-operation and Development) countries, Germany's spending on DE is the highest in absolute numbers (World University Service 2014). As a reflection of its financial contribution, German DE in general and its materials in particular serve as a point of reference not only for other German-speaking countries such as Austria and Switzerland but also for several Eastern European countries.

Lagging behind with regard to the UK and other national contexts (Andreotti and de Souza 2012; Andreotti 2011), German academics and educators have only recently started to conceptually discuss the possible contribution of postcolonial theory to DE (Danielzik, Kiesel and Bendix 2013; Castro Varela and Heinemann 2016; Bechtum and Overwien 2017). Here, María do Mar Castro Varela and Alisha M.B. Heinemann, for instance, call for the 'pedagogical aim of not degrading the global South to an object that is in need of Europe's aid, but to attack . . . the script of an imperialist education and to give space to "epistemologies of the South"' (2016, 21). Previous analyses of education in Germany inspired by postcolonial critique have examined school books (Marmer et al. 2010; Marmer and Ziai 2015), school partnerships (Steinwachs 2012), educational science (Albrecht-Heide 2005), North-South volunteering (Kontzi 2015) and fair-trade representations (Bendix et al. 2016). German DE policy as well as material has not yet come under much systematic scrutiny from a postcolonial vantage point. Studies in other country contexts of curriculum policies and school linking (Andreotti 2011) as well as educational materials (Mikander 2016) have ascertained the tendency in DE of reinforcing Western superiority. DE in Irish post-primary schools, for instance, primarily resorts to the framework of modernisation theory to explain issues of development: 'This perspective attributes few if any external "causes" for the continuing "underdevelopment" of majority world countries and thus offers limited scope for understanding how "global citizens" are implicated in global economic processes' (Bryan and Bracken 2011, 15).

This chapter explores the presence of colonial power in DE in Germany and the ways in which it gets challenged. As laid out in chapter 2, colonial

power takes effect in the present through the persistence of colonial discourses and, at the same time, impacts via disremembering. Just as with
chapter 4 on billboard advertising, I am also interested in the potential for
agency and transformation. This means that I zoom in on challenges to, or
shifts in, colonial power and interpret them in light of recent postcolonial and
anti-racist critique of DE in Germany. The concrete pedagogical practice taking place in classrooms and in extracurricular contexts is beyond the scope
of this book.

I examine key policy papers as well as selected DE materials. The production of materials in Germany is primarily financed by the development
budget of the federal state, the *Länder* (federal states) and the churches and
is dominated by a limited number of institutions and individuals (Steinbrink
2014). I employ

> the post-colonial as a critical mode of enquiry . . . to pose a series of questions
> concerning [the policy papers and DE materials] as 'sites of enunciation': For
> example, who are the agents of knowledge, where are they located, for whom do
> they speak, how do they conceptualize, where are the analytical silences, who is
> being empowered and who is being marginalized? (Slater and Bell 2002, 339)

This discursive sphere is read in the context of the evolution of, and relations
of force in, German DE as well as of socio-cultural and economic global
inequalities. First, I provide the history of DE in Germany and sketch the
recent debate on postcolonial perspectives in DE – in contrast to development policy abroad, both DE and billboard advertising (chapter 4) have
been subject to rather widespread postcolonial critique in Germany. Then
I put forward how DE deals with different topics (development, colonialism,
population); which courses for action it proposes; and how it imagines its
target audience. Here, I discern dominant perspectives and narratives and ask
whether they prove the existence of colonial power. At the same time, I hope
to stay attentive to changes that point to more postcolonial sensitivities.

THE HISTORY OF DEVELOPMENT EDUCATION
IN GERMANY

DE was conceptualised in the Federal Republic of Germany since the 1950s.
Its predecessors were, on the one hand, 'colonial pedagogy' that was initiated
at the beginning of the twentieth century to promote colonial policy in schools
and society at large and, on the other, pedagogy in the spirit of the League of
Nations or 'world pedagogy' aimed at 'communication in the global context'
(Scheunpflug 2012, 90; Scheunpflug and Seitz 1995, 183–88). According to
Annette Scheunpflug, the context was 'collective German guilt' after World

War II as well as reconstruction efforts from outside leading to 'the desire to give something back in return for received aid' (2012, 90). Germany's 'return to the international community' of the United Nations (UN) and processes of decolonisation also influenced the initiation of DE. According to Neda Forghani, returning development workers actually triggered the commencement of development pedagogy in the 1950s: They believed that, in addition to changes in the South, political structures and the perceptions of people in the North had to change (cited in Paschke 2011, 26). More generally, DE in the global North has from the outset been motivated by the 'imperative for governments, international institutions, and non-governmental organisations (NGOs) to ensure public approval for their "development aid" programmes' (InWEnt and BMZ 2007, 8).

Since the 1960s, and in debates on international solidarity, DE in Germany has experienced further politicisation and sought to provide pedagogical responses to questions of under- and overdevelopment (Scheunpflug 2012, 90). DE has further been developed since the 1990s with the aim 'to enable responsible action of students in vein of the guiding idea of sustainable development' (Scheunpflug 2012, 91). While the 'role of racism in development cooperation and "our" [Western] perspectives and their consequences' was already discussed in the 1990s with regard to the theory and practice of global learning, such 'suggestions did not have a wide effect' (Bechtum and Overwien 2017, 75–76). A decidedly postcolonial critique that focuses on power-knowledge complexes and includes a focus on racism in North-South relations has remained marginal until very recently (for a notable exception, see Jouhy 1985). One of the central differences between the 1990s and today's debate on racism and colonial continuities is the involvement of anti-racist networks. Even more importantly, individual and collective agents of Color have taken a central role in the debate. It can thus be said that, to some extent, the empire is finally striking back in German DE.

CONTEMPORARY DEVELOPMENT EDUCATION AND POSTCOLONIAL CRITIQUE

To understand the extent to which colonial power impacts German development policy at home in the case of DE, it is useful to familiarise oneself with the ways colonial legacies have been discussed in this field. Postcolonial theory entered DE in Germany about a decade ago. Authors and educators inspired by postcolonial critique and involved in anti-racist activism began to give talks, write articles and facilitate seminars and workshops (Berliner Entwicklungspolitischer Ratschlag 2007, 2013, 2016; Goel 2011). While the legitimacy of postcolonial critique itself is still discussed controversially (see later in the chapter), some governmental institutions and NGOs or volunteer-sending organisations now officially include postcolonial perspective in DE. Such institutions were initially reluctant, but change was brought about particularly by freelance facilitators, who were less prone to being incorporated by institutions, and by networks of critical educators – often Germans of Color and migrants (Flechtker, Stein, and Goel 2013; Autor*innenkollektiv 2016). Due to the pressure by initiatives and individual educators, workshops on topics such as 'racism in language and images', 'postcolonial criticism of volunteering and tourism' or 'postcolonial perspectives on development policy' were, for example, included into the pedagogical framework of pre- and post-departure trainings for international volunteers. Yet, when attempts were made to extend the criticism beyond the classroom setting of workshops to the institutional level, those active were often sidelined, silenced or even lost their jobs (Flechtker, Stein, and Goel 2013; Danielzik and Flechtker 2012). Few organisations have gone as far as to critically reflect on racialised institutional structures and their foundation in Eurocentric, developmentalist ideologies.

As part of our work at the political education collective glokal, Chandra-Milena Danielzik, Timo Kiesel and I undertook a postcolonial analysis of German DE materials (2013; 2015).[1] It drew on materials that were accessible as printed method booklets, as websites or as downloads and that are applied by NGOs, teachers and multipliers as guidance for their own educational work. From a wealth of material, we selected and analysed over a hundred sources and core documents dating from 2007 (in some cases, from 2002) to 2012 that reflected the breadth of topics, regional foci and authorship. The publication of our examination in 2013 caused lively discussions among DE stakeholders in Germany[2] and was cited as the key contribution to postcolonial DE in Germany in the authoritative German handbook on political education (Asbrand and Scheunpflug 2014, 405–6). A controversy ensued between advocates of postcolonial critique and those accusing this perspective of imposing a particular normativity and of pursuing an authoritarian agenda.

Well-established DE actors rejected the critique as ideological, totalitarian and racist – for example, because it named white people as profiteers of colonial legacies (Krämer 2013) or because it was allegedly marked by an uncompromising, polarising critical whiteness perspective and 'missionary zeal' (Overwien 2013, 41; Scheunpflug 2014, 31). Further responses to the documentation and accompanying articles mentioned criticised that it did not acknowledge the racism- and colonialism-critical works in DE (Overwien 2013), that it made unjustified generalisations regarding the whole field of DE (Scheunpflug 2014, 31) and that it underestimated the 'complexity of strengthening responsible subjects' (Steinbrink 2014). Furthermore, the danger of reinforcing Eurocentrism was voiced if critique centred around

European colonialism (Krämer 2013). Voices more sympathetic to postcolonial critique repudiated the counter-critique as 'the empire striking back' and
strongly emphasised the benefits of facing colonial legacies in German DE
(Ziai 2013a; Open School 21 2017).

Tellingly, even those critical of our study conceded that 'Eurocentric feel-
ings of superiority and the degradation of other peoples and cultures . . . still
exist today, also in development education' (Krämer 2013), and that 'the
examined materials in fact hardly show any approaches that can be understood as questioning current, historically evolved relations of power and
domination' (Steinbrink 2014). However, the fervent dismissal of established
DE educators and academics is indicative of a general discomfort with perspectives that seem to radically challenge the status quo of DE in Germany.

THE CURRICULUM FRAMEWORK AND 'DECOLONIZE CURRICULUM FRAMEWORK!'

The debate on colonial legacies resurged in the context of the reworking
of the curriculum framework (CF) for DE in 2014. In 2007, a CF had been
published by BMZ and the Kultusministerkonferenz (Standing Conference of
the Ministers of Education and Cultural Affairs of the *Länder* in the Federal
Republic of Germany, KMK) for the field of 'global learning' (KMK and
BMZ 2007). It was revised in 2014 and presented to the public in a draft
version. The final version with the title 'Curriculum Framework Education
for Sustainable Development' was published in 2015. It is the central policy
document and serves as reference and guideline for DE practitioners:

> In order for schools, school book publishers and all those in the education
> system who administrate and plan curricula to [face the challenge of preparing
> children and young people more effectively for topics involving global devel-
> opment, to impart an understanding of globalisation processes and give them
> the necessary skills to critically analyse this], they need an interdisciplinary
> approach and a concept. The *Cross-Curricular Framework for Global Develop-
> ment Education* offers this support. (KMK and BMZ 2009, 1–2)

According to BMZ and KMK, DE – referred to as *global development
education* or *education for sustainable development* in the CF – is supposed
to 'give[] students orientation in an increasingly globalised world' and 'aims
at developing basic competencies for shaping one's personal and professional
life, for actively involving in the transformation of society, and for accepting
shared responsibility on a global level' (KMK and BMZ 2015, 91). The CF
makes 'suggestions for the elaboration of competencies that students should

develop, thematic areas and contents that are important and suitable for developing these competencies, and performance standards to be achieved' in order to attain the 'educational objectives of the learning area' (KMK and BMZ 2015, 91). The competencies are divided into three domains: recognition, evaluation and action. The twenty-one thematic areas include 'diversity of values, cultures and living conditions: diversity and inclusion', 'history of globalisation: from colonialism to the "Global Village"', 'commodities from around the world: production, trade and consumption', 'global environmental change', 'demographic structures and developments', 'poverty and social security' and 'development cooperation and its institutions' (KMK and BMZ 2015, 104).

The working group of the CF invited academics, professionals and the general public to comment on a draft version. A group constituted of anti-racist, postcolonial, diasporic and Black organisations and scholars, including glokal and myself, got together under the motto of 'decolonize curriculum framework!' to formulate an open letter. It was addressed at the working group of the CF and signed by more than seventy initiatives, organisations and associations as well as numerous academics (decolonize orientier-ungsrahmen! 2014). 'Decolonize curriculum framework!' criticised the CF quite fundamentally: in terms of the composition of its authors (primarily white, German and male); discrimination in terms of imagined target group; adherence to hegemonic concepts and obscurity of the ideology behind the concepts used; content (not enough focus on power relations and historical as well as current epistemic and material violence); and courses for action (apolitical). All in all, 'decolonize curriculum framework!' criticised the draft version for not serving the aim of transformative education.

While some of those involved in the process of reworking the draft version dismissed the critique, others stated that it actually strengthened critical voices within the working group and circle of contributors.[3] The CF was subsequently reworked considerably and also saw some inclusion of points mentioned by 'decolonize curriculum framework!' (see later). The impact of the critique has not been acknowledged openly by those responsible for the CF. Nor are any racism-critical or postcolonial works cited or suggested as resources in the reworked version. In contrast, organisations and professionals active in the field of DE have been reprimanded by superiors – or from governmental bodies through which they are financed – for referring to or reiterating the critique.[4] That 'postcolonial positions (e.g. of the association Glokal e.V.) were integrated' in the process of reworking the 2007 version has only very recently been mentioned by one of the contributors to the CF in an academic article (Bechtum and Overwien 2017, 77). It could be said that at present we witness a phase in German DE in which silencing of postcolonial

critique goes along with partial acknowledgement, acceptance or incorporation of some of its perspectives – even by mainstream actors and at highest
levels of German DE governance. One aspect of colonial power in DE in Germany seems to be thus the incorporation of knowledge without acknowledging the creators of that knowledge or the struggles in which it was generated.

Whether colonial power is evident or challenged in the different versions
of the CF as well as in DE materials is analysed in the remainder of the
chapter. For the analysis of DE materials, I mainly draw on the empirical
material of the study by glokal mentioned previously. The exploration begins
with an inspection of different conceptions of development, then zooms in
on the place of colonialism, examines the modes in which population issues
are discussed (as a link to chapter 6 on population policy abroad), regards
the treatment of a diverse target group and concludes with a focus on the
proposed courses for action.

DEVELOPMENT QUA CAPITALISM, BOXED-IN POST-DEVELOPMENT AND THE DEPOLITICISATION OF INEQUALITY

To grasp the operation of colonial power in DE, it seems pertinent to first
of all look at how 'development' is conceptualised and how related themes
are treated. '[O]riented at national and international resolutions on sustainable development', the CF places this concept at the centre of its approach
(KMK and BMZ 2015, 20). 'Development' itself is broken down into four
dimensions: 'economic performance, social justice, ecological compatibility
and good governance' (KMK and BMZ 2015, 29). The CF mentions 'target
conflicts between the four dimensions of development' and is aware of the
context of a 'variety of cultural and socio-economic situations and interests'
(KMK and BMZ 2015, 29). However, perspectives that question the concept
of sustainable development as such are not mentioned centrally in the CF.
The 'international consensus' around the concept has, for instance, been
rejected because 'the visions associated with the concept did not break with
the hegemonic norms of economic growth and a capitalist property order'
(BUKO 2013) or with patriarchal structures (Bauhardt 2011).

In the CF's section on 'economic education', neither capitalism nor economic growth is brought up as systems or ideologies for critical debate. The
following quote equates the economy with capitalism and economic development with capitalist economic growth:

> In functional markets, behaviour that is based on the individual interest in
> maximising utility results in both efficient use of the factors of production and

resources (allocation) and, via the 'detour' of the profit motive, in a supply
of scarce commodities. . . . Permanent ability of economic performance as a
target component of sustainable development could for example be defined as
economic management, which both secures the natural capital stock over the
long term and builds up new possibilities of socially and ecologically appropriate income generation through investment. . . . Economists largely agree that
economic growth will ultimately be necessary in order to achieve this. (KMK
and BMZ 2015, 283–84)

The problem is not this orthodox economic and green growth perspective
as such, but that this perspective is not marked as ideological or proposed
as subject for discussion: Capitalism is thus not characterised as a particular
economic system but as quasi-natural law and quintessential for development. Furthermore, the section refers to 'industrialised, transition, emerging
and developing countries' in an affirmative manner; treats these as separate
entities; and does not relate the wealth of some people to the poverty of other
people – neither in the present nor in the past. Instead, the section argues that
'[e]conomic growth [in developing countries] is indispensable to overcome
poverty and to secure the supply of growing populations' (KMK and BMZ
2015, 285).

Rather than discussing the pros and cons of capitalism with regard to
development which some exceptional DE materials undertake (Informationsbüro Nicaragua 2011a), capitalist economic growth is thus put forward as
the natural response to development problems. Naturalising 'capitalism qua
development' and vice versa, the section cannot respond to important questions such as how 'the sublime absorption of capitalism into the concept of
development . . . created the effect that capitalism *is* development', or how
'development . . . reproduc[es] an imperial, and hegemonic, form of power
that governs the world' (Wainwright 2008, 12, 13).

In the rest of the CF, the link between growth and sustainable development
is less rigidly drawn. For example, the possibility for decoupling is doubted –
'an effective delink of economic growth from the consumption of resources is
not in sight' (KMK and BMZ 2015, 27); we learn that 'sustainable globalisation can only be designed with . . . [a] new understanding of growth' (KMK
and BMZ 2015, 27), and the authors state that '[s]ustainable development (as
key term) is not equated with growth but needs to be comprehended as sustainable development towards a quality of life for everyone, taking ecological
conditions into account' (KMK and BMZ 2015, 21).

While the CF otherwise gives little inspiration in terms of '[d]ifferent
ways of seeing the future, in non-developmental ways' (Santos 2012) – for
example, degrowth, eco-feminism, food sovereignty, solidarity economy or
commons – postcolonial critique seems to have led to at least one noticeable
change in the reworked CF. Post-development ideas were not mentioned in

the draft, but the updated version now includes a box on 'Buen Vivir and sustainable development' that states:

> Its present celebrity should serve as a reminder of its absence in the dominant development discourse where it should squarely belong as the central component of the now invisible cultural pillar of sustainability. In consequence, in the central Andes, Buen Vivier [*sic*] is tantamount to sustainable development. . . . As such it has mainstreamed in public consciousness the questioning of the belief that economic growth, tantamount to 'living better', necessarily leads to *Buen Vivir*. (KMK and BMZ 2015, 31)

Here, the words of Peruvian academic Jorge Ishizawa are merely reiterated. The concept itself is not taken up again in the CF – nor any other non-Western development concept – and thus appears to merely serve as an add-on to underline the willingness to take into account a variety of perspectives. It can be said to have been boxed into the CF.

It is striking that the CF does not discuss wealth and poverty as interrelated on a global scale – a perspective that would have meant taking colonial continuities in structures of global distribution of material well-being into consideration (cf. Lessenich 2016). The focus is either on poverty separately – as evident in the thematic area 'poverty and social security' – or on overconsumption and its ecological impacts. Wealth and prosperity are not discussed as an overarching problem. The debates in DE from the 1960s and 1970s on under- and overdevelopment seem to have been sidelined – here, DE is no exception in the trend of de-politicising inequalities in international development more generally since the 1980s (cf. Ziai 2011). The CF's chapter on history is a laudable exception in this regard. For the thematic area 'commodities from around the world: production, trade and consumption', it suggests the sample topics 'trans-regional trade networks from the antiquity to the present age (f.e. spices, cotton, silk, coffee, sugar, cocoa)', 'slavery', 'trilateral trade and colonial goods', 'industrialisation, imperialism and colonialism', 'international division of labour and global imbalances', 'change of consumption patterns' and 'fair trade' (KMK and BMZ 2015, 247). This compilation seems promising for reflections on the interrelatedness of the wealth of the global North (or the global consumer class) and the poverty of the global South.

But again, a lack of structural and/or political perspectives on poverty and wealth characterises the way in which the following DE materials attempt to critically bring up German students' consumption and mode of living:

> Imagine . . . You have flown to the paradise of your dreams and you are being pampered by people who like their job. Because they earn enough money to live on and are themselves able to once in a while go on holidays. Culture and

nature in this paradise are protected. Delicious regional dishes of high quality are available. Flying is more or less free from emissions, and, additionally, trees are planted to curb the effects. (Entwicklungspolitisches Bildungs- und Informationszentrum Berlin 2011, 1)

Departing from this quote, consumerism can hardly be discussed politically: wealth and poverty are not presented as related, deeply entrenched, global power relations, and clashes of interest seem non-existent. Instead this particular material exhibits a fantasy of sustainability according to which the West's present privileged lifestyle can be preserved without trade-offs and can even be extended to those far-away Others who are to date excluded and exploited. These should, however, stay as they are – 'culture' is 'protected' – to provide consumable, exotic authenticity (cf. Danielzik and Bendix 2016).

Critical debates on climate economisation or on neoliberal practices of sustainability and green capitalism are happily ignored with the approach evident in this material (cf. *PERIPHERIE* 2008). At the same time, and tellingly, the global division of labour remains untouched in this vision of a sustainable tourism industry. This sort of approach refrains from self-reflexivity or humbleness in light of the historical and present responsibility of wealthy societies and people in terms of ecological destruction and human exploitation. Here, DE in Germany does not but could hark back to perspectives that shift the focus on historicising wealth creation and acknowledging interdependencies: 'This European opulence is literally scandalous, for it has been built on the back of the slaves, it has fed on the blood of slaves, it comes directly from the soil and the subsoil of the underdeveloped world' (Fanon 1965, 95).

While German DE materials seldom explicitly invoke the actual term 'development', their representation of the global South and the implicit norm of the West is evident. The global South is associated with lack of economic performance, social justice, ecological sustainability, democracy and good governance, and so on. At the same time, it is often clear that the West – or the image the West cultivates of itself – serves as the benchmark. This becomes, for example, evident in the following quote from material that mentions accomplishments in Africa with regard to 'development':

[O]ne has to mention a certain, meagre process with regards to sub-Saharan Africa. Thus, child mortality . . . has gone down. The number of literate adults was 5% higher than in 1990. . . . Furthermore, the number of people with access to clean water is rising. . . . Some countries in Africa have now also become exporters of industrial products. . . . Exports, too, have clearly increased. . . . The number of internet users has risen drastically. (Gemeinsam für Afrika 2009, 12)

Here, 'sub-Saharan Africa' is characterised as 'on its way' but 'not there yet', and the global North obviously serves as the norm: low child mortality, literacy, access to clean water, export-orientated industrialisation and Internet usage are commonly associated with Western 'modernity'.

The previous quote buttresses the findings by postcolonial development studies that have discerned a tendency to perceive all phenomena in the global South in terms of the history of the global North (Kothari 2011). Here, the colonial-racist notion that societies 'develop' in a linear and teleological manner, that the West constitutes the epitome of 'development' and that other societies lag behind becomes apparent (cf. Dussel 1995). A recent analysis of social science textbooks commonly used in secondary schools also came to the conclusion 'that the "developing world" – and Africa in particular – is discursively constructed as inferior, as an anti-thesis to the "West", and as devoid of history and progress' and that this 'construction is thus essentially based on the same premises as colonial racism' (Marmer and Ziai 2015, 64). A study of students' perspectives furthermore found that these are dominated by classical development thinking that locates the problem of 'global inequality in endogenous development deficits' (Kleinschmidt et al. 2015, 28). Historical and colonial connections, the coming-into-being of current North-South relations and structures of power and exploitation are not taken into account (Kleinschmidt et al. 2015). Diagnosing a lack of 'development' – and particularly if it is portrayed as caused by endogenous factors – implies the prescription of ' "development" in the form of modernisation, transfer of technology and capital investments (in order to stimulate economic growth)' (Ziai 2007, 43). Just like the CF, DE materials rarely embed contemporary inequality in historical injustices or bring up anti-colonial post-development ideas as valuable perspectives (for laudable exceptions, see FairBindung and Konzeptwerk Neue Ökonomie 2013; Informationsbüro Nicaragua 2011b).

(DIS-)REMEMBERING COLONIALISM AND ITS EFFECTS

While DE tends to refrain from linking the issue of 'development' to colonialism, this section enquires whether and how colonialism is explicitly discussed in the field of development policy at home. In the CF – even in the earlier one of 2007 – the subject of colonialism features rather prominently. One of the potential themes suggested for DE is 'The history of globalisation: From colonialism to the "global village"' (KMK and BMZ 2007, 80). In the new CF of 2015, the theme of colonialism has been substantially elaborated on, especially for the subject of history. In the thematic area 'migration and integration', the sample topic 'changing images of the self and others in the context of transcultural processes of migration and integration (e.g. development of a European superiority feeling in the wake of the European expansion/colonisation)' is suggested (KMK and BMZ 2015, 248). Regarding the '[i]mplementation in school subjects and learning areas', the '[c]ompetency-oriented learning unit: the European colonial policy in Africa in the 19th century' is suggested for the subject of history (KMK and BMZ 2015, 250). Here, 'globalisation' is presented as encompassing 'a *precolonial, colonial* and the *current* phase' (KMK and BMZ 2015, 250).

While the history of colonialism is thus quite well covered in the CF, colonial continuities are not discussed as much, and, what is more important, colonialism is discussed only with regard to Africa and not other colonised regions and much less with regard to its effect on colonising powers. However, as rationale for the selection of the just-mentioned topic of European colonial policy in Africa, we now find the following statement in the new edition:

> The questions and tasks developed here focus on the change of perspectives by including sources which show the colonised peoples' views. They train critical media competency and inspire to discuss the colonial heritage in the context of the present globalisation process – with respect to African societies and in particular to the German society. They open the students' awareness for phenomena of racism in Germany and in other societies which are structural and relevant to everyday life, and they demonstrate the ethical claim to accept social responsibility today, based on historical facts. (KMK and BMZ 2015, 251)

This is in line with Bechtum and Overwien's demand that 'dealing with knowledge production and global entanglements . . . should be reflected more prominently in educational curricula and didactical materials' (2017, 73). The reworked CF shows signs of questioning the colonial legacy of Eurocentric knowledge production and calls for a critical reflection of 'the industrialised countries['] . . . views of the universal validity of their own living conditions and values . . . and have them review the existing models of development' (KMK and BMZ 2015, 44). It now has a box on 'Eurocentrism' – absent in the draft version – which reads sentences such as 'Are we aware that basic terms that we hardly scrutinise like *wealth, poverty, growth* and *progress* are almost totally eurocentric?' (KMK and BMZ 2015, 45).

The CF thus highlights the mental and epistemological effects of the colonial legacy on the (former) colonisers. In the newly inserted box, Eurocentrism is described as a 'complex phenomenon of modern times' that legitimised 'the expansion of power and dominion' and is 'linked to the intention to convince other cultures of the validity of the own ideologies' (KMK and BMZ 2015, 45). Yet, despite this promising attempt to reflect on the colonial legacy of liberal humanism and while considerable changes in terms of the discussion of colonialism are discernible, it is still not conceptually mainstreamed in the CF – as evident in the missing conceptual link between colonialism and development discussed earlier. And the mention of

Buen Vivir and Eurocentrism and the call for reflecting European ideas of
superiority in individual chapters (particularly history) contrast profoundly
to others such as the one on economic education and to the general disregard
for post-development perspectives and the colonial legacy of development
thought and practice in the rest of the CF.

In German DE materials concerned with contemporary issues, the history of North-South relations does not seem to play a central role. This is,
for instance, observable when the subject of globalisation is broached. In
the introduction to a special issue of *Politik & Unterricht*, a journal for the
practice of political education, published by the Regional Agency for Civic
Education Baden-Württemberg, the only information that is given regarding the history of North-South relations is the founding of the International
Monetary Fund and the World Bank in the post-WWII era (Weber 2003, 7).

The silence regarding colonialism in some materials is conspicuous. For
example, whole fifty-two-page-long manuals provide materials to discuss
issues such as global food crises (Landeszentrale für politische Bildung
Baden-Württemberg 2011) or globalisation more generally (Landeszentrale
für politische Bildung Baden-Württemberg 2003) without a single reference
to colonialism and its repercussions. Disremembering the global North's
and global South's shared history of colonialism can create a clear separation between an era of colonialism and an era of development. Despite the
fact that 'development as a framework of ideas and practices emerged out
of efforts to manage the social, economic, and ecological crises of the late
colonial world' (Hodge 2007, 2; Cowen and Shenton 1996; Koponen 1994),
development interventions can thus be marked as philanthropic endeavours
that have nothing to do with the all too often cruel realities of colonialism
(Kothari 2011, 66).

If colonialism is mentioned at all in DE materials, it is usually with regard
to Africa. Here, it is telling that the booklet *Learning to Understand Africa*,
published by the German Federal Agency for Civic Education, a federal
public authority 'providing citizenship education and information on political issues to all people in Germany' (Bundeszentrale für politische Bildung
2014), mentions that examining the colonial legacy is necessary for understanding the present conditions in Africa but does not apply this logic to
Germany or other former colonising nations in Europe (Bundeszentrale für
politische Bildung 2007). Their present situation seems to be understandable
without considering colonial involvement and its legacy. This is not merely
an elision but crucial for upholding the West's self-image as superior. '[S]itu-
ating colonialism outside Europe and the North Atlantic enables a division of
the world into modern/developed and traditional/under-developed societies'
(Gutiérrez Rodríguez 2010, 53), rather than understanding the exploitation of

the global South as constitutive for the global North's modernity, development and general position of global power (Rodney 2012).

Alongside the prevalent strategy to disregard colonialism altogether or to locate it outside the West, DE materials at times legitimise colonialism ex post. In the previously mentioned material by the Federal Agency for Civic Education, the following quote can be found – referring to the textbook *Post-Colonial Africa* by eminent German scholars Rainer Tetzlaff and Cord Jakobeit, who introduce it as an attempt at an 'honest evaluation' of colonialism:

> Accordingly, next to indubitable atrocities, societal destructions, economic structural changes and mental traumatisation, we find changes without which any development would have been impossible, such as the installation of school and health systems, infrastructures and the intrusion of the 'European mind'. (Bundeszentrale für politische Bildung 2007, 148)

In addition to a problematic, Eurocentric notion of development, the quote evokes the colonial-racist argument that Africa or the global South in general did not undergo any development prior to colonialism and that it would not have 'progressed' had it not been for the benevolence of the European colonial powers. In contrast, exceptional DE materials show that it is possible to tackle the issue of colonial discourse in development ideology head-on, for example, by analysing 'the influence of colonialism on the contemporary representation of former colonies in the media and PR' or by explicitly analysing images of development billboard advertising as well as 'adbusts' of charity advertisement for their reflection of colonial discourses (Welthaus Bielefeld 2014, 3; see also Informationsbüro Nicaragua 2011a).

The narrative just discerned echoes colonial-era legitimisations of colonialism according to which colonialism was supposed to be guided by a so-called dual mandate: colonisers were thought to have the task of exploiting the colonised territories' resources for colonial benefit as well as to contribute to the 'development' of occupied lands and the welfare of its people (Lugard 1923). To weigh negative – 'yes, there were massacres' – and positive aspects – 'but roads were built' (Adichie 2011) – against one another with regard to colonialism has long since been denounced as 'an act of the most brazen fraud' (Rodney 2012, 206; Césaire 1953). Such a 'balancing-out strategy' 'frees Europe of responsibility, of a significant and traceable connection to the African present and allows it the glow of charity' (Adichie 2007). Apart from the cynicism evident in such a profit and loss calculation, the function of colonial education, health and infrastructure is hardly ever taken into account. Infrastructure, hospitals and schools were first and foremost installed to further colonial interests (Rodney 2012). Education, similarly, was not 'designed to give young people confidence and pride as members of African societies, but one which sought to instil a sense of deference towards all that was European and capitalist' (Rodney 2012, 240–41). Such an 'education for subordination [and] exploitation' continues to stifle emancipatory processes in the global South and has been characterised as ongoing colonisation of the mind (Rodney 2012, 241; Nandy 1983; Thiong'o 1986). All in all and while changes and exceptions are observable, DE as German development policy at home proves the tendency to dis-remember colonialism and to downplay its relevance for the contemporary world.

DEMOGRAPHISATION OF POLITICAL ISSUES

As mentioned earlier, one of the thematic areas of the CF is 'demographic structures and developments'. A closer look at how this topic is dealt with is of particular interest for this book, as the issue of German interventions in population in the global South plays an important part in its argument (chapter 6). To begin with, it is quite striking that 'sexual and reproductive health and rights' are not invoked in the CF, that is, that the CF limits itself to demographics and population developments. Due to an alliance between women's health NGOs and organisations comprising the 'population establishment' (Hartmann 1997b), the outcome of the 1994 International Conference on Population and Development in Cairo (known as the Cairo Consensus) had shifted the focus of population policy on health and rights (Schultz 2010). The focus of the CF on 'demographic structures and developments' mirrors the observation by Susanne Schultz and me (2015) of a return to more explicit population control in German development policy abroad (see also chapter 6). A neo-Malthusian rationality is evident in recent German government policy and is reflected in the CF, particularly in its draft version of 2014 (see later in the chapter).

In the CF – as a whole and in particular in the sample topic for the subject of mathematics in the 2014 draft – the thematic area of 'demographic structures and developments' is approached for the various school subjects. In geography, it is suggested to deal with '[p]opulation policies in developing and industrialised countries' via the statements '"You shouldn't have any more children" – "You have to have more children"' (KMK and BMZ 2015, 233). More information on how to go about it and whether and how to depart from a theoretical perspective that acknowledges the classed and raced dimension of global as well as local pro- and anti-natalist policies is not provided. The description of the sample topic may lead to a critical discussion if the statements are discussed as related to power relations, inequality and utilitarian ideology but may also reinforce colonial representations of an overpopulated South if not. The decision of which of the ways to take is left to the individual teachers.

As sample topics for history, the CF puts forward 'depopulation and over-population in different historical contexts (e.g., Thirty Years War, industriali-sation/medical progress); changing population policy (e.g., family planning); change of the family, gender roles and age distribution (e.g., differences between industrialised, threshold and developing countries)' (KMK and BMZ 2015, 248). The concept of national population age structure evident in the third sample topic is nowadays used as the master frame in population policy in order to compare 'ageing' ('industrialised'), 'transitional' ('thresh-old') and 'high-fertility' ('developing countries') nations. Different economic potentials are then deduced from such categorisation. This perspective tends to abstract not only from intra-national diversity but also from social, eco-nomic or other power relation within and across different age groups and does not take into account how global capitalist relations define access to income and resources across the globe.

For history, the discussion of population recurs in the thematic area 'global environmental changes', which, inter alia, proposes the sample topic 'con-ditions and consequences of the global population growth in the past and presence' (KMK and BMZ 2015, 248). While not explicitly causally linked, the juxtaposition of the two sample topics associates environmental changes with population growth – and not, for instance, with capitalism or colonial exploitation.

These observations do not allow us to conclude that population is approached only through a positivist, demographic lens. Yet the sample topic for mathematics in the 2014 draft does so quite explicitly. One of the sample topics for the thematic area is '[p]opulation growth in different world regions' (KMK and BMZ 2015, 305), and it is sketched as a teaching example for educators. One of the success indicators mentioned is that students are able to use 'data and mathematical analyses to develop arguments and to show via the example of population development how they can employ their math-ematical competences to participate in a rational discourse on questions of global development' (KMK and BMZ 2014, 236). The rationale for the topic of 'global population development' reads as follows:

> The disparate development of the global population, its rapid increase in parts of the world, but also its decline and ageing in some countries, pose a serious challenge. The provision with food, drinking water, energy and basic consumer goods is not succeeding adequately despite considerable efforts. What is more, an increase in living standards is directly or indirectly detrimental to the natural environment and therefore to the basis for life. (KMK and BMZ 2014, 235)

While the first sentence presents population developments generally in an alarmist tone as a 'serious challenge', the combination with the second sen-tence reveals that the problem is seen in growing populations in the South, as only these can be connected to deficits in the provision of basic consumer goods. The third sentence highlights the critical issue of overconsumption, but it is not clear how this is connected to the perspective on decreasing and ageing populations (in the North). It thus is open whether the problem of rising living standards and their detrimental effects on the environment is attributed to growing populations in the South or to the lifestyle in the North or to both.

While a purely mathematical approach to population without a discussion of social factors and a reflection on demographic ideologies is problematic in itself, the statistics provided in the teaching example provide further cause for concern. A table on past and future developments of the world's population provides data for 2,000 years ago and then jumps to the year 1750 (KMK and BMZ 2014, 239). This is particularly problematic in the case of Latin America and Africa. In the former, about 90 per cent of the 80 to 100 million inhabitants were exterminated in the first five decades of colonisation by European weapons, forced labour and diseases (Plumelle-Uribe 2007, 5). The latter is the only continent whose population, due to the enslavement of millions of its inhabitants and to the societal disruptions this caused, stagnated between 1500 and 1900 (Michailof 2016, 45). Desegregated data that might, for instance, show that the indigenous population of Australia, Latin America and North America was decimated considerably, while the European settler population grew at the same time, is not provided. Colonial genocides disappear in such statistics.

The advice for designing the mathematics lessons on 'demographic structures and developments' in combination with seemingly neutral statistics allows an assessment of the ideological stance taken. Citing UN projections, this learning unit puts forward 'that even minor differences in the average number of children per woman can have a considerable influence on population development' (KMK and BMZ 2014, 242). It goes on to state that 'provided that the number of children per woman remains constant at current levels until 2100, the global population would increase to almost 29 billion until the turn of the century' (KMK and BMZ 2014, 242). Combined with a graph given on the same page that highlights that an increase in world population would mainly be due to population growth in Asia and Africa, it becomes evident – but tacitly, never open and explicitly – that the 'minor difference in the average number of children per woman' refers not to an abstract world woman but to women in the global South and particularly in Africa.

In this context, it is no surprise that the unit recommends the Berlin Institute for Population and Development – a private think tank with a neo-Malthusian agenda and strong links to the international population establishment – and the German Foundation for World Population (DSW) for data and other material (KMK and BMZ 2014, 242). DSW receives part of its budget from Bayer

HealthCare (DSW 2015 17), one of the world's main producers of contraceptives (see chapter 6). In the context of organising a high-profile population campaign for United Nations Population Fund's (UNFPA) 'Day of Seven Billion' together with BMZ and Deutsche Gesellschaft für Internationale Zusammenarbeit (German Agency for International Cooperation), it issued sensationalist population statements to the media, such as 'The number of people on earth rises by 2.6 per second, 158 per minute, over 225,000 per day, or almost 83 million per year' (Deutsche Welle 2012). In 2014, DSW also installed a 'World Population Clock' at the entrance of the Hannover Zoo.

The overall perspective in the CF can be understood as framed by the ideology of demographisation which renders almost any political or social problem demographic (Hummel 2006; Barlösius 2007). Demographisation points to a specific biopolitical epistemology that turns the size of a population or a specific population group – and not dynamic social and international relations – into the decisive variable and starting point for political strategies (Schultz 2015). Establishing a causal link between 'global resources' and 'growing population' and suggesting 'education' and 'family planning' as necessary interventions – evident in German development policy abroad (chapter 6) – are undertaken in an exemplary fashion in the following question formulated for students in the mathematics example: 'Which ways exist to exert influence on a rapidly growing global population with its consequences for global resources, for example? Discuss amongst others the impact of girls' and women's participation in education on family planning and the impact of the availability of family planning methods' (KMK and BMZ 2014, 244). The authors of 'decolonize curriculum framework!' (2014), of which I was part, criticised that the sample teaching guidelines 'put students into the position of omnipotence of pondering on ways of affecting fast growing populations in the global South and on methods of family planning for these'. While any influence of this statement can only be assumed, the reworked CF no longer includes this example. From the overall CF, it cannot be deduced how issues of population will eventually be discussed in the classroom – especially given that the sample topic for mathematics has been removed. However, it evidently does not invite facilitators to critically reflect on the problem of demographising social, political and economic issues of power and inequality.

In DE materials, we also find indications that population growth – particularly in Africa – is seen as problematic and that few children per woman are seen as a sign of 'development'. In a material for primary school children, it is stated:

Also in society as a whole, the education/training of girls and women leads to progress in the long term. Education, for example, slows down population growth indirectly, because women with formal education marry later and have fewer children. . . . If a woman from a developing country attends school for seven years or longer, she marries on average four years later and on average has 2.2 children less (in sub-Saharan Africa women have five children on average). (Gemeinsam für Afrika 2011, 25)

This perspective is typical of neo-Malthusian demographics: Population size is regarded as a variable that may be deliberately manipulated in order to influence social conditions and vice versa (Schultz 2006). Considering many children a deficiency that has to do with lack of education or emancipation and proposing small families have been criticised as 'reproductive Westernisation' (Frey 2007). And proposing birth reduction among the global poor as the solution to nearly every global crisis phenomenon – from poverty, economic recession, migration and patriarchal systems to ecological destruction – and thus blaming the poor instead of, for instance, structures and agents responsible for inequality are emblematic for the population control agenda. As we will see in chapter 6, these characteristics of development policy at home through education are mirrored by German policy directed towards so-called developing countries, particularly Africa.

MAKING THE CLASSROOM (IN-)SECURE

Having explored some central thematic areas of DE, I shall now look at how the target group within Germany is imagined and the role of colonial power in this regard. While students in Germany generally profit from the legacy of colonialism and ongoing colonial relations of exploitation on a global scale (cf. Lessenich 2016), they inhabit different positionalities within Germany society (Danielzik and Bendix 2013b). As bell hooks (1994) and scholars working on the German context (Malter and Hotait 2012; Mecheril et al. 2010) have pointed out, the classroom is a place where inequalities of race, gender, class and others are replicated. Many exercises in DE materials clearly rely on the authors' assumption that their primary target group is white: 'To see people with a different skin colour than one's own – most of the time a light colour – in school is not an everyday experience for many students, despite the high proportion of foreigners in the German population' (Lensing 2006, 8). The author of this material puts herself in the position of the target group and speaks of white or light skin colour as 'one's own' skin colour. She thus clearly imagines her target group to be white. The quote also evidences the assumption that 'normal' Germans necessarily have to be white or light-skinned. Whoever does not show these phenotypic characteristics consequently belongs to the group of 'foreigners'. It is quite striking in this context that to be a 'foreigner' is not related to the question of citizenship but explicitly related to bodily or external characteristics. Fatima El-Tayeb has argued that the hegemony of an internal German history that denies outside influences has led to the repression of the acceptance of plural positionalities in German society (2016, 45).

The following quote from a DE material authored by one of the most influential DE actors and stern critic of postcolonial or anti-racist perspectives provides argumentative assistance to teachers to incite interest in Africa:

> If we affirm that we want a political future for our world in which wars and violence do not dominate the agenda, if we want to prevent the pandemic AIDS from becoming a deadly threat to everybody and that more and more Africans without a future flood into Europe, then interference is a necessity. . . . If we become active here – as a state or individually –, we act in our own best interest. Of course there are also other, immediate, and emotional motivations for an interest in Africa. The enthusiasm for Africa's people, for their joie de vivre and courage to face life, for music, dance and outstanding sportive qualities can be part of that. However, Africa always also remains a moral challenge, even though most people would prefer not to be faced with this unease. (Gemeinsam für Afrika 2009, 22–23)

In this material, Afro-German or African students are obviously not envisaged as potential participants since they might have very different motivations for their interest in the continent. What is more, they run the risk of being associated with problems, on the one hand (cf. Marmer et al. 2010), and of being used as objects of exoticisation, on the other (cf. Danielzik and Bendix 2010). Ultimately, their mere existence is turned into a moral challenge. What must go on inside a child or teenager whose family migrated to Germany from Africa to hear that it is in 'true' Germans' best interest to prevent such migration from taking place? While such materials explicitly or implicitly question equal citizen rights or rights of belonging of non-white participants, white students profit as the myth of European, white superiority is upheld. It not only means that non-white students are not included as worthy addressees of DE but can also have other dramatic consequences for students of Color, as mentioned in the introduction to this chapter. When Africa is portrayed as deficient in school materials and teaching, this gets directly associated with students who are thought of as African and has emotional as well as physical consequences for these students (Marmer et al. 2010). They are connected to poverty, hunger and war by their fellow students, who themselves are convinced they are part of an intellectually and materially superior 'culture'.

In DE materials, participants are often given the task to put themselves in the position of those constructed as racialised others. To give an example, one exercise asks the participants to 'close your eyes now and put yourself in the position of the black person' (Deutscher Entwicklungsdienst 2006, 34; see also Mohio 2011). The material provides a cartoon in which a Black person tries to get in contact with two white people who look as if they are afraid of the Black person. The objective of this exercise is for the participants to develop empathy with the Black person. The increase in social and emotional competence is thus intended only for white participants, a fact which is, however, not stated as such by the authors of this material. They do not take into account that participants of Color might themselves experience such racist situations on a daily basis, and thus do not need to develop empathy, but rather are in need of empowerment to deal with such discrimination. In such educational exercises, they might also run the risk of serving as an object of learning for white students in the classroom.

Hardly any DE materials show sensitivity to the question of different (learning) needs depending on the social positioning and lived experiences of the participants, or even of the educators themselves. This insensitivity and lack of professional knowledge have recently been criticised by a network of educators who have responded by devising a 'racism-critical guide for reflection on existing and to-be-developed didactic teaching and learning materials for educational work in schools and out-of-school on Blackness, Africa, and the African Diaspora' (Autor*innenKollektiv Rassismuskritischer Leitfaden 2015). Neither the CF nor the DE materials really acknowledge – or put out the question for reflection in DE – that the classroom is per se not a secure space, as 'many students, especially students of Color, may not feel at all "safe" in what appears to be a neutral setting' (hooks 1994, 39).

The classroom could, however, be made more secure if inequalities were acknowledged and educators explicitly dealt with different needs and countered existing power structures with regard to race but of course also with regard to gender, class, ability and other intersecting systems of domination (Adams, Bell, and Griffin 1997). It could mean, for example, empowering students of Color to value themselves and to develop counter-strategies. This is undertaken by some exceptional materials such as 'Homestory Deutschland', developed by the Initiative Schwarze Menschen in Deutschland (Initiative Black People in Germany). Furthermore, racism by white students and instructors could be made visible and worked against, for example, through fostering the ability to 'retrace the itinerary of . . . prejudices and learning habits' (Kapoor 2004, 641). Here, the material on colonial continuities, mentioned earlier, that invites all students to critically reflect on their perceptions and prejudices, constitutes a positive example (Welthaus Bielefeld 2014).

(LIMITING) COURSES FOR ACTION

This final empirical section on DE turns to the crucial aspect of what the addressees of DE are supposed to actually do with their acquired knowledge and skills, and whether postcolonial inequalities are taken into account in this dimension of DE. Its third prime competency domain – in addition to 'recognition' and 'evaluation' – is 'action'. It is seen as

> the precondition for Global Citizenship and for the acceptance of shared responsibility in the 'One World', where not only understanding and tolerance but most of all solidarity in thinking and acting as well as the protection of basic values are needed in order to cope with developmental crises, human rights violations, terrorism, ecological disasters and other global challenges. (KMK and BMZ 2015, 85)

Looking at the more concrete proposals, the courses for action proposed seem rather limited. The CF's section on geography, for instance, reads as follows:

> Acting in the learning process can have an effect on the students' own lifestyle, for example on sustainable *consumer behaviour*. The Geography classroom is also fertile ground for perspectives, opinions and activities centred on remote regions (*partnerships* with other schools, *campaign participation*, and *aiding in development projects* or [natural] disaster help campaigns), giving students motivation for sustainable action. (KMK and BMZ 2015, 229; my emphasis)

This is similar to the limited options that Verband Entwicklungspolitik deutscher Nichtregierungsorganisationen (Confederation Development Policy of German NGOs, VENRO), the umbrella organisation of development and humanitarian 'aid' NGOs in Germany, suggests as in line with DE: 'school partnerships, charity runs, and information events, world music evenings and film screenings, international chats and online discussions, school-worldshops and climate schools as well as participation in various campaigns of development policy' (VENRO 2010, 4). It is evident that proposals for action tend to be aligned to 'development policy' or suggest exchanges and changes in individual consumption (worldshops are places in which 'fair trade' goods from the global South are sold).

In the CF's section on 'New foreign languages', the 'Competency-oriented learning unit: Adivasi Tea-project' is put forward. Here, one of the tasks for students is described as follows: 'As you want to help them keep and improve the quality of life, you have decided to design a campaign for your fellow students: "Support the Adivasi Tea-project"' (KMK and BMZ 2015, 177). And students are asked to 'work out strategies for taking action to help the Adivasi people effectively' (KMK and BMZ 2015, 177). The course of action is embedded in the logic of development 'aid', which is also highlighted by the recommendation 'to use the digitally offered material of Adivasi-Kooperationsprojekt e.V.', a project that 'is managed by volunteers and sponsored by the BMZ' (KMK and BMZ 2015, 181).

The glokal study mentioned earlier found that many DE materials' strategic focus lies on collecting donations for development projects and programmes.

This also has to do with the fact that materials are sponsored by development NGOs or have a direct link to the German government's development policy. Hence, a great deal of DE materials does not discuss development 'cooperation' critically but highlights successes and does not question global structures: 'The achievements of successful projects and programmes that provided the people with new prospects should not be forgotten. . . . What is pleasing about the described success? How many people benefit from the success?' (Gemeinsam für Afrika 2009, 17).

Even though the usefulness of 'development aid' has been a cause for debate for decades and its colonial legacy and Eurocentrism has been criticised repeatedly, materials still highlight its unquestioned beneficence and – what is more worrying – do not invite teachers and students to discuss its historical and epistemological fundaments. It is furthermore often reduced to charity and, for instance, not discussed as related to military, political or economic interests (cf. Ziai and Brämer 2015). The role of the Diaspora (an actor that is completely ignored in the CF) as key supporter of the global South is also not mentioned, even though the remittances are by far greater than the overall disbursement of 'foreign aid' (World Bank Group 2016).

An additional strategy in German DE is to propose activities that encompass getting to know the Other in the vicinity – for example, 'foreign children in the class' (KMK and BMZ 2007, 92) – or in the global South. Regarding the latter, school links are one of the favourite courses for action. Studies of such school links, however, doubt their transformative potential. In her study of German participants of school links with schools in African countries, Luise Steinwachs (2012) has found that these increase prejudices and a sense of superiority, that they increase the desire to 'help' the others while downplaying injustice, that the recognition of privilege goes hand in hand with the desire of safeguarding these and that instead of irritation of participants' self-conceptions these are stabilised. Similar findings have emerged with regard to the volunteer service *weltwärts* launched by the BMZ in 2008 which sends around 3,500 volunteers per year to 'developing countries'. According to Kristina Kontzi (2016), 'The program reinforces what has been characterised as ongoing colonisation of the mind that encompasses the internalisation of superiority and the idea of being in charge of criticising and teaching the Others'. Another course for action proposed in DE materials is critical consumption, which is well summarised by the slogan 'with chocolate against poverty' (Welthaus Bielefeld et al. 2012, 16). While the transformative potential of individual consumer choices can be doubted, the main problem with DE in Germany is that it does not put the question of, for example, the potentially de-politicising effect of critical consumption on the agenda.

CONCLUSION

The historical introduction illustrates that while colonial legacies had been a topic in DE in earlier times already, a decidedly postcolonial critique has entered the field only about ten years ago and continues to serve as a point of tension. Yet, it is noteworthy that significant and promising changes in DE policy and material are taking place. The examination of DE policy and materials shows that they sometimes reproduce and sometimes fail to question a particular euro- and capital-centric notion of (sustainable) 'development'. This notion is commonly posited as universally accepted and valid, opposing interests and alternative world views tend to be sidestepped and its connectedness with colonial-era relations of power is 'disremembered'. Following Vanessa Andreotti, instead of suggesting that '[w]e are all equally interconnected, we all want the same thing, we can all do the same thing', critical DE that is sensitive of colonial power would do well to discuss 'asymmetrical globalisation, unequal power relations, [and] Northern and Southern elites imposing [their] own assumptions as universal' (2006, 9).

The absence of a strong conceptual link between colonialism, modernity and 'development' (as process, practice and vision) within the German CFs for DE means to disregard it as a crucial structuring moment that continues to shape North-South relations. If colonialism is brought back into the equation, the concept of development would be unveiled as historically interwoven with racism and colonial exploitation, and its contemporary effect as supportive of a racist classificatory system becomes evident (cf. Kothari 2006a; Wilson 2012). Or, as Castro Varela and Heinemann put it:

> It is . . . politically wise and pedagogically essential to question the historical amnesia, so that the assumption of the colonial civilising mission – that an intervention into postcolonial countries is an ethical act – is not reinforced again and again. (2016, 21)

Notwithstanding the recent hesitant inclusion of post-development ideas and postcolonial critique, little room is provided for students to question dominant concepts of 'development' or to get to know alternative epistemologies.

If the history and present of (neo-)colonial exploitation is acknowledged, students in the global North turn out to be implicated. This may lead to a sense of insecurity as privileges and entanglements in power relations become apparent (cf. Jensen 2005, 52–58). Remembering colonialism in such a way may prevent 'disintegration and denial' and thus lead to 'responsible and "care-full" agency' (Raghuram, Madge, and Noxolo 2009, 10). This might also have consequences for the classroom setting. At the moment, DE material proves that not all potential participants with their different societal positions and learning needs are addressed; instead, learning at times takes place on the basis of and at the expense of the Others; non-white participants who are not regarded as legitimate or equal participants or citizens of Germany.

The narrative of development as an accomplishment of the West that is disconnected from exploitation and still needs to happen in the global South means that development policy abroad is proposed as the obvious solution (see chapters 5 and 6). Rather than destabilising the 'superiority complex' of white people and elites in global North and South (cf. Fanon 2008), the courses for action dominating German DE consolidate this structure. The propagation of a certain idea of development implies that 'assistance' and 'aid', rather than exploitation and oppression (or solidarity), are constructed as central to the relationship between global North and South.

Taking into account that it is difficult to make sweeping statements about the vast field of DE in Germany, this chapter has highlighted that German DE embraces concurrent and contradictory tendencies: On the one hand, ideas of Western supremacy are perpetuated, and on the other, it seems to hesitantly acknowledge fundamental postcolonial critiques that question the dominant concept of development and call for an actual recognition of diversity in the context of a continuous colonial present. All in all and taking into account both policy papers and teaching materials DE in Germany continues to (re-)produce or not fundamentally question colonial power – while cognisant of the necessity to do so. Whether this characteristic feature of development at home operates transnationally and finds its counterpart in German interventions abroad will be explored later on. First, let us turn to another crucial field of development at home, namely billboard advertising by development organisations.

NOTES

1. I would like to thank Chandra-Milena Danielzik and Timo Kiesel for allowing me to draw on our research for this chapter, and Juliane Juergensohn and Kristina Kontzi for their contribution to the initial research.
2. Chandra-Milena Danielzik also published articles in a well-known magazine on North-South relations (Danielzik and Flechtker 2012) as well as in the key German academic journal for DE (Danielzik 2013).
3. Personal conversation with one of the consultants and contributors to the CF in Spring 2015.
4. Personal conversation with two professionals in the field.

Chapter 4

Billboard Advertising and the Potential for Subverting Colonial Power

Today I am your conscience your nightmare your Massai
Only today do I devour clay with my small hands
Today I am your big heart of darkness
And ask you for the one Euro
That it costs you
To conceal your ignorance
For Thine is the power and the glory
The rigid finger on the ruler
That draws the borders
Whose names you don't know
. . .
Act now and secure a rice bowl of future for us
Today Africa and tomorrow who knows
Buy your way out of it, pale-face
for us
Who can help us
If you can't do it
Yours Friday

– Afro-German poet Philipp Khabo Koepsell
2010, 19–20; my translation

While development education (DE) is explicit in its educational thrust, and young students or adults will be aware of engaging in an openly educational exchange, billboard advertising of development organisations – just as any other advertisement – targets the unconscious to a much greater extent. It seems to be one of the central realms of indirectly educating the general public about 'development' or global inequality. By focusing on billboard advertising, this chapter explores colonial power in fundraising and public relations strategies of secular and faith-based non-governmental organisations (NGOs) as well as of the German government as the second aspect of German development policy at home.

Billboard advertising serves two main purposes: To generate funding for the work of charities and to influence the consciousness or behaviour of the public (Lingelbach 2007, 346). 'Aid' organisations are often acutely aware that their dual concern of awareness-raising and fundraising can be contradictory in practice (Darnton and Kirk 2011). This chapter is concerned with charity advertisements as an influential mode of political education: They confront the German public with questions of development. Whether advertisements are intended to educate or not, the effect is that the audience taking them in is affected by the images created and the truths put forward (Philipp and Kiesel 2011). They are 'subtle proposals as to how we should feel and act towards suffering' (Chouliaraki 2010, 110). I understand billboard advertising as both representative of societal or governmental ideas of poverty, global inequality and development as well as performative in this regard. Accordingly, this chapter reads billboard advertising with regard to the question of the stories it tells about development, colonialism or North-South relations – without delving into the 'practicalities' of charities advertising endeavours (see Rideout 2011).

This chapter is thus mainly interested in the dominant narratives evident in advertising for development in Germany (cf. Kiesel and Bendix 2010). However, it also takes interest in the advertisements' transformative potential. Without dismissing charity advertising as per se reactionary or colonial, it seeks to answer the question whether NGOs also 'provide an alternative representation of the Third World and a notion of development, in which the attitudes and practices of the First World are targeted, and the Third World is represented with dignity' (Rideout 2011, 40). It relies on the assumption that NGOs are crucial '[i]n their position as distributors of images to the public' and that the same applies to other agents who use similar formats to influence public opinion. Thus, this chapter goes beyond the 'public transcript' (Scott 1990) to include adbusting and subvertising as sites for speaking publicly about global inequality at home.

If one acknowledges the agency of the recipients of media images, the reception of advertising must be understood as a reflexive process (Fiske 1987). While billboard advertising aims, of course, at a dominant reading, Stuart Hall's (1980) concept of encoding/decoding suggests that the interpretation can also be negotiated, resistant or oppositional. Hall's and John Fiske's thoughts on the reception of media take into account the socialisation and social positioning of users. This thought is especially relevant for the section in this book that considers billboard advertising in a German society that is not solely white. The chapter looks at the dominant messages and assumes that the consumers of billboard advertising 'decode' imagery according to the way it was 'encoded' by the charity or the commissioned advertising company. However, it also undertakes negotiated or oppositional readings of posters. The production of adbusts and subvertising, in themselves, require an oppositional decoding in which dominant readings are commented on or turned on their head.

After introduction into historical changes of billboard advertising, I focus on the analysis of tropes evident in recent NGO billboard advertising. For that section, I draw on existing critiques of development advertising in Germany that are connected to the political education work of glokal (Philipp and Kiesel 2011; Kiesel and Bendix 2010; Kiesel and Della 2014). The chapter then turns to a particular event in 2013, when the German government launched its first and only development billboard campaign to date entitled 'The Big Five!'. This campaign sparked a short but intense debate on colonial-racist imagery in billboard advertising and on colonial power in German development policy. I then go beyond criticism and try to tease out the transformative, subversive potential of billboard advertising. The representativeness of the selected images is assured through communication with members of glokal who have closely monitored billboard advertising in Germany in the past decade and more. For each section, I have chosen images or campaigns that are exemplary for the particular tropes or narratives I identified.

THE HISTORY AND PRESENT OF
BILLBOARD ADVERTISING

In order to lay the ground for understanding colonial power in contemporary billboard advertising, this section sketches its historical precedents and provides some insights into recent debates on racism and colonial continuities in this field. Western humanitarianism vis-à-vis the global South dates back to the late eighteenth century 'when new forms of print media publicized the plight of far-off peoples' (Baughan 2015). Adverts for products from the colonies can also be regarded as predecessors of development advertising. The history of billboard advertising for development in Germany began in the early 1960s when the Catholic agency Caritas and the Protestant agency Diakonie sought to persuade members of the church to contribute to their activities in the 'Third World' (Lingelbach 2007, 353–54). At that point in time, West Germany had just overcome its own role as a recipient of 'aid' – primarily provided within the framework of the Marshall Plan but also by UK NGOs such as Oxfam – and become a 'donor' of development 'aid' and 'charity'.

The media coverage of the famine in the context of the Biafra-Nigeria war in the 1960s had established the 'hunger child' as a universal representation of human suffering and 'reduced the complexities of post-colonial politics to the image of a helpless, starving child, whose future rested not upon political self-determination, but Western aid' (Baughan 2015). In the late 1970s, and particularly in the 1980s – after the Ethiopian famine and charity initiatives such as Band Aid and Live Aid (founded in 1984 and 1985, respectively, and featuring mainly British musicians) – such representations became less acceptable. They were criticised not only by external commentators but also in internal debates that took place in the 'aid' community in Germany in the 1960s and 1970s and were marked by both ethical and pragmatic motivations (Lingelbach 2007).

Debates on racist representations in everyday culture in general, and in development 'assistance' more specifically, sprung up in Germany over the years, for instance, in the 1970s around the book and exhibition *The Third World in Children's Books* (J. Becker and Rauter 1978) and in the 1990s through the project and publication 'Partnership and Dominance' by the organisation Weltfriedensdienst (1999). The latest, more profound phase of criticism was initiated about ten years ago with the widely disseminated publication *On Drummers and Helpers. Contributions to Non-Racist Development Education and Project Work* (Berliner Entwicklungspolitischer Ratschlag 2007) published by several networks of development NGOs of German federal states, and the dissemination of a 'Checklist to Prevent Racism in PR for Development Policy' (Berliner Entwicklungspolitischer Ratschlag 2010). It was enriched by the documentary film *White Charity* (Philipp and Kiesel 2011) as well as various exhibitions, discussion events and open letters. ISD and other anti-racist initiatives (2013), for instance, publicly raised the issue of racist representations to the development NGO umbrella organisation Verband Entwicklungspolitik deutscher Nichtregierungsorganisationen (Confederation Development Policy of German NGOs) and the Deutsches Zentralinstitut für soziale Fragen (German Central Institute for Social Issues) which awards seals-of-approval to donation-soliciting charities. I found myself in the midst of this as part of my work with glokal, having contributed to the publication *On Drummers and Helpers. Contributions to Non-Racist Development Education and Project Work* and its updated and extended second edition *Develop-Mental Turn*, commented on the rough cut of the documentary film *White Charity* and, together with one of the filmmakers, authored an essay that supplemented that film (Kiesel and Bendix 2010).

The 1989 Commission for Images in the UK pointed out that 'the problem of images and perceptions cannot be separated from the methodology of intervention' (cited in Chouliaraki 2010, 113). In 'aid' circles, the discussion on the relationship between the characteristics of imagery and the nature of actual interventions added another dimension to the critique of imagery as dehumanising and objectifying. For example, the context in which 'aid' advertising in part turned away from ' "shock effect" appeals' to ' "positive image" appeals' was 'the new spirit of interventionism in the humanitarian project, which goes beyond relief and aspires to transform the economic and political structures that can support a better life for vulnerable others' (Chouliaraki 2010, 113). The partial transformation towards more positive, allegedly empowering images of people from the global South has been confirmed for the German context (e.g., Lingelbach 2007). The relationship between representation at home and intervention abroad is of particular relevance for this book as it attempts to understand colonial power in the interrelationship of internal and external development policy.

THE 'WHITE SAVIOUR INDUSTRIAL COMPLEX'

In this section and the following two sections, I focus on the 'public transcript' of development imagery in contemporary German billboard advertising, that is, on what constitutes the dominant narratives with the aim of finding out whether colonial power is effective in the portrayal of development issues at home. Here, it becomes immediately evident that racialisation plays an important role. Its effect has been described in a rather personal account by the artist Rajkamal Kahlon: 'When I moved to Germany, I was somehow shocked by these charity billboards displayed in the public sphere. In the American context you receive this kind of fundraising as brochures by mail in your private homes. I notice that there is an extreme exposure of Black or Brown bodies in these images' (2016, 18). Non-white people tend to be used to symbolise the 'recipients' of 'aid' or the global South more generally. If white people are depicted at all, they nurture the Other or tell us how gratifying it is for them to help. Skin colour and other racialised attributes convey 'visual "evidence"' (Wollrad 2005, 123) of the dissimilarity of a 'developed' and an 'underdeveloped' world. At the same time, it is not in tune with the realities of Germany's society, which is neither solely white nor necessarily German. Nor does the depiction of white Germans as providers of 'aid' correspond to global realities, in which remittances by migrants to the global South are about three times as high as 'foreign aid' (World Bank Group 2016).

The relatedness of national belonging and whiteness, on the one hand, and of foreignness and Blackness, on the other, is particularly stark in the German context (El-Tayeb 2016). All in all, whiteness in German billboard advertising is used to symbolise superiority, civilisation and charity, while Blackness is associated with deficiency (poor, ill, uneducated), closeness to nature, in need of help, passiveness, voicelessness and childlikeness. Teju Cole (2012) has defined such tropes as 'White Saviour Industrial Complex', a complex that has little to do with justice but a lot with the provision of 'a big emotional experience that validates privilege'.

Infantilisation and the Perseverance of the 'Hunger Child'

As pointed out earlier, the link between Blackness – constructed as symbolic for the global South – and deficiency is central in billboard advertising; and in the past this mainly encompassed depictions of misery. While this and particularly portrayals of the 'hunger child' have received much critique and have often been replaced with seemingly more dignified representations, the imagery itself has not vanished. To give an example for this trend, the Welthungerhilfe ('World Hunger Aid') (2015) initiated a billboard campaign with the hashtag '#EsReichtFürAlle' ('#ThereIsEnoughForEverybody'). One picture shows a naked, emaciated, dirty child. Over it is written 'It's enough! For everybody. With your help. Donate now and save lives: welthungerhilfe. de'. Neither the name of the child nor the geographical location is given. However, skin colour and hair suggest that the viewers locate it in Africa. The child, sitting on the ground, hides its face and has an empty tin bowl at its side. The children in billboard advertising in Germany are systematically shown alone – set aside from any social or cultural context – or together with an often faceless woman that cannot take care of the child without the help of the Western donor.

To exacerbate this positioning outside human society, children – and characters in advertising more generally – are often placed in nature or rural surroundings. Of the 200 advertisements in Germany that the project *White Charity* analysed, only one was set in an urban context (Kiesel and Bendix 2010, 483). While that tendency persists, slight changes have occurred in the course of the past years. For instance, the Christian organisation Kinder-nothilfe ('Supporting children in need') started a campaign entitled 'Heaven and hell. Life in the city is no child's game' ('Heaven and hell' is the name of a well-known German children's game). On its three billboards, one girl in school uniform skips rope in the middle of a city ruin, another girl blows soap bubbles in front of derelict houses and a boy stands lost in a rubbish dump (Kindernothilfe 2017a). Yet, even in these urban pictures, the children are shown as alone, beyond social embeddedness. The isolation of children on billboard advertisings together with their frequent depiction as naked or half-naked intensifies the image of a global South and – in particular – Africa as beyond civilisation and as the exact opposite of the West: 'Naturalising and infantilising societies and people in the global South are fundamental for the perception that the global North should develop them and, in practice, prevent an equitable international cooperation' (Danielzik and Bendix 2013a, 37).

While the presence of white or Western people in billboard advertising is often implicit – invoked as obvious counterpart to the misery of the South or addressed through slogans as potential donors, they are also at times explicitly displayed. An advertisement by the International Catholic Mission Society missio, the German branch of the Pontifical Mission Societies, that has decorated German streets and train stations from 2011 onwards, exemplifies this. It shows a child in the arms of an elderly white woman in the attire of a nun under the heading 'His mother died of AIDS. But he found new courage to face life' (missio 2011):[1]

> In the missionary iconography it is the missionaries who occupy the central and dominating position. . . . representatives of the native population are excluded. . . . Hence we see the missionaries and nuns operating in capacities traditionally performed by the local culture: as transmitters of knowledge, as healers, as authority figures, usually surrounded by children rather than adults. (Nederveen Pieterse 1992, 71)

In a replay of missionary ideas of colonial times, the white nun in the advertising, Sister Raphaela Händler, takes up the role of guardian, healer and saviour; African actors are written out of the story. During my research in Tanzania on reproductive health policy, I interviewed German professionals working at the Ndanda Mission Hospital in the Southeast of Tanzania, where Raphaela Händler has been active for decades. German professionals there reiterated the narrative of mending dysfunctional social relations in Tanzania through Christianisation (see chapter 5).

Other German 'aid' campaigns do not make use of pictures of people to represent misery but of metaphoric ones. The development and relief agency of the Protestant Churches in Germany, Brot für die Welt ('Bread for the World') (2008), for example, has published a poster of a bowl with a few grains of rice, with the caption 'weniger ist leer' ('less is empty') since 2008 until today – a pun on the German saying 'weniger ist mehr' ('less is more'). Another one by Kindernothilfe (2017b) has displayed the map of Africa as a dark hole surrounded by white pieces of chalk for some years now, thus evoking the idea of the 'dark continent'. Its accompanying scripture, 'We close gaps in education', lumps together the whole of Africa and relegates the continent to lack and disaster. The depiction of photographs of misery or destitute children has become less prevalent, but the message of a helpless and destitute South persists. And it has been found that – even if actual children are not shown – the public still thinks in exactly such images when asked about charity advertising (Kiesel and Della 2014).

As Kate Manzo observes, 'The iconography of childhood expresses institutional ideals and the key humanitarian values of humanity, neutrality and impartiality, and solidarity', but '[w]hen read as a metaphor for the majority world, the iconography of childhood reproduces colonial visions of a superior global north and an inferior south' (2008, 632, 636). Africa and the global South more generally have long since been infantilised (Hegel 1822). This evokes 'tropes of innocence, dependence and protection' (Manzo 2008, 636) and suggests that its people cannot live without the help, guidance and trusteeship of the parental colonisers or developers (Fanon 2008). The colonial representation of the global South in billboard advertising as analysed in this section for the case of German NGOs 'invite[s] the white West to be "parents" to people in need' (Baughan 2015). It thus calls for, and legitimises, development interventions abroad to help people out of their allegedly miserable conditions.

Feminisation and Semi-Empowerment

In her empirical study of fundraising and advocacy messages in the UK, Nandita Dogra found that 72 per cent of the characters shown were children and women in general, and mother and child in particular (2011, 335). This tendency is not any different in German billboard advertising (Kiesel and Bendix 2010, 489). Children and women, particularly mothers, are used in humanitarian advertising because they are seen not only as the incarnation of helplessness but also as emblematic of innocence, 'and, unlike adult men, removed from the complexity of politics' (Baughan 2015). Adult men are hardly ever represented in billboard advertising (cf. Dogra 2011). For Germany, in the past ten years I have only come across one image showing a group of men with missing legs on crutches playing football, one of an old man advertising education and one of a grateful young man who found education (for the latter two, see later in the chapter).

Healthy young men, particularly from Africa, are commonly – and more particularly since the recent so-called refugee crisis – perceived as threats to peace and security in Germany (e.g., Dietze 2016). They are also symbols of the public, political sphere; do not serve as harmless, deserving recipients of our 'aid'; and are thus not suitable objects of charity appeals. The centrality of mothers and children in billboard advertising is paradoxical. It evokes not only the notion of universal values of motherhood and womanhood but also the threat of 'the overcrowded [majority world], with its over-reproductive women' (Dogra 2011, 336). Colonial continuities in interventions into motherhood will be examined in chapter 5, and the question of overpopulation will be taken up in chapter 6.

As mentioned before, humanitarian communication has long since resorted to images of seemingly dignified, empowering representations (Chouliaraki 2010; Lingelbach 2007). In these, people are not only shown as victims but also as happy, grateful receivers of 'aid'. Brot für die Welt, for instance, showed a Black smiling woman in colourful attire and combined this with the sentence 'Your help bears fruit'. In a similar vein, empowerment dimensions can be found in the before-and-after billboard campaign by Welthungerhilfe that was carried out from 2004 through 2007. One of the posters depicts a man on the left-hand side whose expression shows sadness and desperation. On the right-hand side of the billboard, the same man is pictured with a much more positive outlook. The poster explains that Welthungerhilfe helped James O. Etole from Kenya, who is deaf, to attend school and to become an instructor at a school for deaf people. The text ends with the appeal to donate 'to give life and development opportunities to people like James O. Etole'. The campaign reiterates this arrangement, showing people before and after the reception of 'aid'. Here, as in most of the representations of so-called empowered characters in billboard advertising, the focus is on the positive effects of the donations and the promise that contributions improve the situations of people in need. These billboard images accompany – and are representative of – a general turn in development policy: from a concentration on problems towards a focus on the result of 'aid' (exemplified by, for instance, the 2005 Paris Declaration on Aid Effectiveness).

A recent campaign by Misereor that started in 2015 focuses on the creativity and agency of people in the South without stressing prior destitution (Misereor 2015a). One of the images shows an elderly woman sitting in front of her produce of fruits and vegetables, beaming. The heading reads: 'My business plan: Urban growth that one can eat'. The text at the bottom of the billboard explains that the woman, Júlia Machado Amaral, successfully grows and sells fruits and vegetables in the big city Belo Horizonte. The viewer is asked to help people help themselves and to visit Misereor's website to discover many more 'exciting projects'. Another image of this campaign shows Aminata Compaoré from Burkina Faso with the caption 'My start-up does not provide full profits, but full people'. The third advertisement of this series shows an elderly man in Vietnam and is entitled 'My ingredient for a future in Vietnam: Vocational training'.[2] While the representations in this campaign are devoid of the overt colonial narratives mentioned earlier and highlight activities already taking place, such billboard advertising invokes neoliberal entrepreneurialism as the state of the art of modern economics. It is indebted to the neoliberal governance of 'helping people to help themselves' but does not mention the responsibilities of the respective governments to provide social security or education. At the same time, global or national economic structures, their political dimensions and their colonial legacy are not highlighted for the viewers of the billboards – and thus written out of the story. The depiction, particularly of women, in billboard advertising as economically active but not politically involved as agents of structural change has been analysed as characteristic of the neoliberal agenda more generally (Dogra 2011, 339–41).

In most of the 'empowering' images, the characters are shown as doing something – picking coffee, using a well, selling fruits, learning or teaching – and it could thus be said that they are presented as people with agency. This is, however, as pointed out in the documentary film *White Charity* (2011), a 'restricted agency'. The people who are displayed in this type of billboard advertising would not be able to turn their life around and gain agency without the help and guidance by the Western benefactors, that is, the individual donors as well as the 'aid' agency. The images suggest that people's empowerment – and in a way their mere existence – depends on the goodwill of donors. It is the North that seemingly activates them, and if they themselves become supporters of other people, this is also traced back to development 'aid'. In such billboard advertisings, people from the global South are hardly ever set in a broader context of social activity or political engagement. The restriction of agency to non-structural dimensions not only pertains to the characters depicted as representatives of the global South, but it is also somewhat reflected in the role ascribed to the potential individual donors themselves. They, too, are not called upon to get involved in broader societal changes: In her study on 'post-humanitarian communication', Lilie Chouliaraki points out that contemporary 'aid' advertising 'foregrounds the power of personal rather than collective action in making a difference in the lives of vulnerable others' (2010, 121).

The analysis of the 'public transcript' of billboard advertising by German NGOs thus far provides evidence that despite some critique of representative practices and obvious changes, the colonial construction of the global South – often with recourse to infantilisation and feminisation – as destitute, helpless and in need of charity and guidance persists. Even if agency of people in the global South is evoked, this tends to remain limited to the private sector and entrepreneurial at the most but never political or concerned with broader economic structures. Agency seems further contingent on the willingness of the (white) German public to provide help. At the same time, interrelatedness of the global North and global South beyond development 'aid' is not highlighted. The lack of acknowledgement of the discursive and material colonial legacy that connects the global North and global South is striking.

COLONIAL-RACIST IMAGERY IN A GOVERNMENT CAMPAIGN

In spring 2013, the BMZ launched a billboard advertising and Internet campaign entitled 'The Big Five!'. In the following, I shall concentrate on this campaign as an example of how the German government directly – that is, not only via funding of development education, for example – devises and undertakes 'development at home'. The fact that it was the only ever billboard campaign by the BMZ makes it rather central for questions of representation in German development at home; and the BMZ's responsibility for most German development endeavours abroad makes a closer analysis especially worthwhile.[3] The poster – displayed across Germany several thousand times – shows images of an elephant, a lion, a leopard, a rhinoceros and the silhouette of a buffalo (see figure 4.1). In the background, we see a map of Africa. Short slogans are written next to each animal: 'Protecting human rights – promoting democracy', 'fighting poverty – fostering growth', 'promoting education – creating opportunities', 'safeguarding [or securing] resources – sustainable economy' and 'preserving biodiversity – visiting Kaza'. Above the huge heading 'The Big Five!' a smaller heading reads: 'The new German development cooperation'. At the bottom of the poster lies a photo of the then German BMZ minister Dirk Niebel (Freie Demokratische Partei [Free Democratic Party]) who is shown with a QR code (allowing for direct access to the BMZ's website via smartphone) and the question, 'Which animal are we looking for?' The spectator is challenged to identify the anonymous animal shown as a white outline.[4]

Figure 4.1. 'The Big Five!' poster by BMZ (www.whitecharity.de).

The poster provoked a debate among German NGO and activist circles. A coalition of individuals and development NGOs wrote an open letter to the minister criticising the poster and stating that the poster 'reinforces colonial, discursively conveyed patterns of thought' (EPIZ et al. 2013). The minister was asked to end the campaign. Other NGOs and associations disseminated a press release and lamented the 'discriminating depiction of Africa':

> This campaign for 'the new German development cooperation' is disrespectful and absolutely unacceptable. The German government reduces a whole continent with more than 1 billion people to a national park for wild animals. It thus directly links up to the dichotomy constructed during colonialism of European 'culture' and 'civilisation' vs. African 'nature' and 'wilderness'. The ministry is obviously far from appreciating African people and cultures and from the 'partnership at eye level' it continues to postulate. (AfricAvenir International, Berlin Postkolonial, and Tanzania-Network 2013)

People involved in anti-racist work or sensitised to representational issues in development obviously decoded the billboard in a way not intended by the BMZ or the company that designed it. Concerted criticism of this billboard from civil society and in the media also concentrated on the slogan 'The Big Five!' as a colonial term for big game hunting and on the choice of imagery and its use of animals to speak about Africa (e.g., Stielike 2013). 'The Big Five' refers to the five animals which were thought to be most dangerous and difficult to hunt on foot. Today, the term is often used for the same five animals but in the context of tourism they have become the animals that tourists need to see and hunt down ('shoot') with their cameras.

That Africa is mostly associated with negative phenomena in the general German public and that the 'heart of darkness'–'white man's burden' couplet is always latent are implicit in 'The Big Five!' campaign: Germany positions itself as the necessary player to help Africa get rid of its problems referenced by the five dimensions of Germany's activities. This correlates with the findings of studies on the representation of Africa in the German public more generally (Poenicke 2001; Ndumbe 2006) that a one-sided racist image prevails in which Africa is reduced to 'sub-Saharan Africa', depicted as a homogeneous entity, associated with backwardness and related to topics such as war, catastrophes, HIV/AIDS, hunger, oppression of women, underdevelopment and dependency on 'aid' from outside/the West. Yet, the imagery vis-à-vis Africa in Germany not only includes barbarity and negativity but also always includes the other side of the racist coin: Africa as close to nature, as nature per se. This exoticising dimension of anti-African racism is fulfilled by the choice of animals for this billboard campaign.

The initiation of the Ministry's campaign needs to be situated and understood in the context of another event initiated by the BMZ: the 'German

Development Day'. About a month after the inception of the poster campaign, on 25 May 2013, the German government as well as several development institutions and NGOs organised this day to promote the ideas of development 'cooperation' within the German public. It took place in sixteen cities and several other venues across Germany and cost at least €3 million. Parliamentary elections were due in September 2013, and so the German Development Day as well as 'The Big Five!' campaign were presumed to be part of Minister Niebel's personal election campaign (Jentzsch 2013).

As it happens, the day of the German Development Day, 25 May, is also, first and foremost, 'Africa Day' – the annual commemoration of the founding of the Organisation of African Unity in 1963, the predecessor of today's African Union. On this day, celebrations are held in many African countries as well as in the Diaspora. The year 2013, incidentally, was the African Union's fiftieth anniversary. The Afrika-Rat (2013) – a network of organisations, associations, initiatives and people of the African Diaspora – pointed out that the BMZ's choice of this day for their own Africa event was a sign of impertinence:

> In this year of all years, in which the 50 years of existence of African unity are celebrated, the Ministry for Economic Cooperation and Development (BMZ) has decided to not put emphasis on the dignity of those Africans who were active in the liberation movements and in the development processes on the continent and in the Diaspora, but to celebrate itself and other actors imprudently.

The Afrika-Rat as well as supporters of its press release called for the minister's resignation in light of his disrespect for African people. Disregard for African agency and expertise was also evident in the programme of the German Development Day. The roles were clearly defined and distinguished along racial lines, which is why the headline of the article in one German newspaper read 'black artists and white experts'. This newspaper reported that, for example, a Senegalese man present at the events said, 'I am ashamed that my children have to witness this . . . since I have arrived, there were only German [and white] discussants on the podium and then you have Blacks and they make the music' (Tomic 2013).

There are two more aspects that should be added to the critique of colonial-racist imagery uttered so far. First of all, it is telling to look at the way the African map is depicted. Africa is reduced to 'sub-Saharan Africa' or to what is often referred to with the racialised term of 'black Africa' in German, as the top (as well as the bottom) is slightly cut off and the animals are invariably placed in the sub-Saharan region. Frantz Fanon pointed out the functionality of creating a 'black' Africa:

> Africa is divided into Black and White, and the names that are substituted – Africa South of the Sahara, Africa North of the Sahara – do not manage to hide

this latent racism. Here, it is affirmed that White Africa has a thousand-year-old tradition of culture; that she is Mediterranean, that she is a continuation of Europe, and that she shares in Greco-Latin civilization. Black Africa is looked on as a region that is inert, brutal, uncivilized, in a word, savage. (1965, 160)

Blackening a particular part of Africa and whitening others as well as Europe serves two purposes: On the one hand, it perpetuates the myth of the counterpart of a white Europe that has only recently started losing its homogeneity (cf. El-Tayeb 2011). On the other hand, North Africa (as well as the 'emerging country' South Africa) is awarded an honorary place in the occident which – given that Greek 'civilisation' was heavily influenced by North Africa – is a necessary move to uphold the idea of Europe's supremacy and Africa's inferiority (Bernal 1987). As mentioned in chapter 2, such hierarchy between the 'West and the Rest' is central to the idea and practice of development 'cooperation'.

A second noteworthy aspect lies in the significance of the colours used to paint Africa in the billboard: red, gold and green. Whether this was intended or not is hard to tell, but these Pan-African colours are found on the national flags of many African nations and are inspired by the colours of the Ethiopian flag. The three colours are widely referenced in Rastafarianism, where red is said to signify the blood of martyrs, green the vegetation and beauty of Ethiopia and gold the wealth of Africa (Murrell, Spencer, and McFarlane 1998, 134). In this light, the fact that German development 'cooperation' occupied 25 May as the day to celebrate the 'white man's burden' of developing Africa and the global South takes on a whole new dimension. The company which devised the campaign has not explained its use of imagery, text and colours, but it can be read as a de-radicalising appropriation of African and African diasporic struggles for freedom from colonial oppression. The points raised thus far underline the necessity to pay attention to the presence of colonial-racist stereotypes in German development at home. However, they do not yet address the material relations and structures created and perpetuated by German development policy.

Neocolonialism and the Daily Neoliberal Grind of Development Policy

The reactions to the BMZ's billboard and Internet campaign 'The Big Five!' were a necessary anti-racist and anti-colonial critique, but they paid little attention to the neoliberal and potentially neocolonial agenda of German development policy. Colonial power takes effect through the interrelationship of colonial discourses and political and economic structures and processes. Some of the criticism has in fact broached economic dimensions and taken the content of the advertisement seriously. According to the Afrika-Rat, for example, the fact that Africans and Africa are not portrayed as actors but as passive objects raises the question whether the BMZ is interested in cooperation or rather in 'the implementation of a neocolonial agenda through which Africa is kept in poverty and dependence' (Afrika-Rat 2013). One commentator reiterated the charge of neocolonialism:

> What is new about the Germans wanting to 'fight poverty in Africa' and to 'secure resources' and foster their growth at the same time? That they are of the opinion that they can 'preserve biodiversity' through hunting and photo safaris? What is new about Germany wanting to export its ideas about 'democracy' and its models for 'education'? What is new about Europe talking about the 'protection of human rights', while denying African refugees that protection? (AfricAvenir International, Berlin Postkolonial, and Tanzania-Network 2013)

Here, it is useful to take a closer look at the agenda articulated in the billboard advertising and to embed it in Germany's policy towards Africa. 'Fighting poverty – fostering growth' and 'safeguarding [or securing] resources – sustainable economy' could be understood as meaning that German development policy supports African countries in fostering growth and protecting their resources for their own sake; however, it can also be perceived as referring to Germany's interest in investments and securing access to resources on the African continent.

As mentioned in chapter 2, since Minister Dirk Niebel of the Liberal Party took office in 2009, the BMZ has emphasised cooperation with the (German and other countries') private sector more and more and explicitly voiced Germany's self-interest in development 'cooperation'. In this respect, the German ministry was quite frank and outspoken. In an interview with the leading German tabloid *BILD* in 2013, Dirk Niebel outlined his approach to development 'cooperation' as follows: 'If we pursue smart development policy, we raise money for Germany. With every Euro spent for development cooperation, two Euros flow back to us in the long run. . . . Through business contacts. It is by far cheaper to engage in trade with peaceful countries than to fight hostile ones' (Niebel 2013).

Perceiving African countries not as a recipients of charity alone but also as useful 'partners' for Germany is well illustrated by the development ministry's 'New Africa Policy' entitled 'From a continent of crises to one of opportunities', in which Africa is presented as 'the continent of unexploited assets, potential and opportunities' and in which Africa's resources are mentioned (BMZ 2014b, 17). The focus on Africa as a place for investment, outlet market and provider of natural resources has become even more evident in recent months through the 'Marshall Plan with Africa' by the BMZ and the German Federal Ministry of Finance's 'Compact with Africa' as one of Germany's initiatives that are part of its G20 presidency (Bernau 2017). Germany today seems above all interested in 'integrating' Africa into a 'free'-market economy, and German finance minister Wolfgang Schäuble (Christlich Demokratische Union [Christian Democratic Union]) made it clear in Durban in 2017 that '[i]n Europe, we have come to understand that Africa represents one of the most important issues for the growth and stability of the global economy' (Handelsblatt Global 2017).

A network of African civil society organisations criticised the potential directions the German initiatives could enforce:

> The outlook could possibly be mainly how to integrate Africa into the global division of labour, at the terms of German/European outlook, with Africa playing the same old role of raw materials provider. . . . At a time when Europe is barricading itself against illegal immigration, a logical consequence of neoliberal policies and wars, it is easy to believe that the real motivation remains the exploitation of African natural resources, without the guarantee of getting the local populations out of poverty. In short, there is reason to fear that slavery and colonization may strongly come back. (AFRODAD and Africa Development Interchange Network 2017, 2)

The representation of Africa as nature per se on the billboard can thus be understood as finding its equivalent in a German Africa policy geared towards incorporating allegedly hitherto unexploited African economies into globalised capitalism to the advantage of German business. Given Germany's colonial-era exploitation of Africa (see chapters 2, 5 and 6), the novelty of this approach – beyond the change in capitalist policy from direct exploitation to neoliberal profit maximisation – can be doubted. According to the German-African Business Association (2015), a foreign trade association founded in 1934 representing German companies and institutions with an interest in Africa, German companies generated an annual revenue of €31.6 billion in Africa in 2014, and German-African export trade has increased by 35 per cent to €42.8 billion within five years.

German development policy seems to be about transforming countries of the global South – through particular ideas of democratisation, education, health care, legal reforms and environmental policy, and so on – so that these countries may serve as places for German investments, as consumer markets and – ever more evident since the Valletta Summit on Migration in 2015 – to prevent Africans from migrating to Europe. The following quote from an interview with a desk officer at the BMZ is marked by such logic and will be taken up in more detail in chapter 6. I had asked the interviewee about Germany's interest in reproductive health and population policy in the global South:

> I think it just becomes clear that it is one building block to create functioning, long-term functioning societies. . . . So, here it is the case, we have an interest in stable countries, in stable partners. . . . I mean the countries that function,

where the people then also have purchasing power, that will in the long term also be of benefit to the former, still export world champion. (Interview 6b, 15 January 2010)

What is crucial is that the economic rationality evident in this quote is intertwined with racialised depictions of particularly African societies: Germany considers population growth in the global South detrimental to 'creating functioning societies' and links high fertility rates to backwardness and traditionality (see chapter 6).

Another policy suggestion evident on the billboard states 'saving biodiversity – visiting Kaza'. As a footnote to Kaza, the bottom of the billboard explains, 'Kaza is the biggest national park on earth in Southern Africa'. The 'Kavango-Zambezi Transfrontier Conservation Area', also known as Kaza, is situated in a region where the international borders of Namibia, Angola, Zambia, Botswana and Zimbabwe converge. The billboard thus encourages the German spectators to spend their next holiday in this national park. This is a classist request that presumes that any German can naturally afford to go on a pricy holiday. More importantly, it suggests that one can protect the environment by stepping into an airplane. According to the website www.atmosfair.com, the emissions for a return air flight from Berlin to Harare alone, for example, are more than five times as high as the annual carbon emissions in Zimbabwe per capita and more than twice as high as what has been calculated as the 'climate compatible annual emissions budget for one person'.

Furthermore, conservation politics and national parks are often a colonial heritage and cater to the pleasure of tourists and the economic interests of national and global elites (Adams and Mulligan 2003). To take an example with German involvement and in the 'recipient country' context focused on in chapters 5 and 6, the Selous Game Reserve in South Tanzania, one of the largest faunal reserves of the world, was first designated a protected area in 1896 by the governor of 'German East Africa' Hermann von Wissmann and became a hunting reserve in 1905. The subsequent (and related) Maji Maji War against the German colonisers from 1905 until 1907

resulted into an appalling ecological disaster across southern Tanzania. These parts have not yet recovered from this trauma. Selous was expanded to the detriment of people's livelihood. Germans were to ban African hunting in South East Tanzania, since it was found to have caused the Maji Maji War. But the banning was for other reasons than those, since elite sports hunting paid more to the government coffers than African taxes. Over the years, Germany, through GTZ has been spending millions of money in conservation measures. These measures resulted into the harassing and beating of the poor men, women and children of Southern and Southern East Tanzania on the pretext that they were poachers and illegal arms owners in 1989. GTZ had devised a 'participatory' method of benefits sharing for the people around Selous – in terms of getting a share of a hunt once in a while. The Selous game reserve remains very important for elite hunting and it is quite profitable for the hunting companies that have blocks in the game reserve. (Chachage 2006)

As Danielzik (2016) argues, international tourism policy as part of development 'cooperation' is marked by the intertwining of colonial-racist and neoliberal economic rationalities. Thus, suggesting tourism as a panacea for 'development' issues disregards the fact that tourism from the global North to the global South is historically and contemporarily based upon racialised cultural and economic exploitation of people in the global South. Zooming into the policies suggested in 'The Big Five!' campaign and contextualising them in Germany's political and economic agenda towards the global South in general and Africa in particular have thus far brought to light how routine German neoliberal policies are intertwined with racialised discourse.

As an alternative to the agenda evident in 'The Big Five!' advertisement, some commentators have suggested that 'the African continent does not need development "aid" but economic partners with whom it cooperates at eye level. It is time that the BMZ thoroughly reconsiders its principles of cooperation with Africa and adapts to the zeitgeist' (Afrika-Rat 2013). Yet, as pointed out earlier, contemporary German development policy takes the Ministry's addendum 'for Economic Cooperation' seriously and asserts a neoliberal agenda. The latest initiatives by the BMZ and Ministry of Finance push exactly for such an idea of African countries as economic partners. This, however, seems to be much harder to question than obvious racism. Limiting criticism to colonial-racist stereotypes neglects that we are in the midst of what Hall calls the 'neoliberal revolution', in which 'neoliberal ideas, policies and strategies are incrementally gaining ground globally, re-defining the political, social and economic models and the governing strategies, and setting the pace' (2011, 708). As has been shown until now, a scrutiny of development policy needs to incorporate a critique of colonial discourse in billboard advertising as well as a scrutiny of the respective political-economic structures and agendas – and what is most needed: a critique of the intertwining of different systems of oppression (Wilson 2012). In this light, one needs to be careful not to remain on the level of criticising colonial-racist picture language if this means overlooking how the fundamentally capital-friendly and neocolonial policies of German government policy rest upon, perpetuate and are interrelated with colonial-racist representations.

NEW DIRECTIONS IN NGO BILLBOARD ADVERTISING

While the chapter thus far has focused on how colonial legacies are present in billboard advertising, it now turns to the question of whether traces of a non-racist, non-discriminatory practice are also discernible or whether advertising even confronts colonial power in development. In terms of reflecting on development institutions' public relations and advertising work, SAIH (The Norwegian Students and Academics International Assistance Fund), with its first campaign 'Africa for Norway' and its well-publicised Rusty and Golden Radiator Awards, is rather successful. The Golden Radiator is awarded annually to the best charity adverts, with the Rusty Radiator given to the most harmful example. The aim of SAIH's (2014) work and campaigns is 'to end stereotypical and pessimistic communication in fundraising campaigns'. While SAIH condemns the portrayal of people and societies in the global South, it implicitly maintains the assumption that it is these people and societies that are deficient and have to change – rather than, for instance, the interrelation between the safety and wealth of a few and the insecurity and poverty of many. Thus, the awards tend to perpetuate the classical development discourse – albeit in the empowerment version discussed earlier. Speaking with Vanessa Andreotti (2012), if billboard advertising really is to make a difference with regard to global justice, it should

> help people in the task of learning to 'go up the river' to the roots of the problem. . . . Going up the river means asking questions such as: What creates poverty? How come different lives have different value? How are these two things connected? What are the relationships between social groups that are over-exploited and social groups that are over-exploiting? How are these relationships maintained?

That it is in fact possible to produce non-racist, non-discriminatory advertising as critiques of fundamentally unbalanced power structures in a policy field so deeply entrenched in the colonial history and present has been shown by the organisations Brot für die Welt and Misereor criticised earlier. In 2013, Brot für die Welt launched a campaign that highlights the problem of speculation in food commodities. One image shows a hand of a white person holding a banana in the manner of a gun and the headline reads 'Speculation with food: a murderous game' (Brot für die Welt 2013a). At the bottom of the billboard, a statement claims that those who speculate on food products gamble away the lives of human beings. Another one shows a bowl of soup with dices on a spoon and the written message similar to the first one (Brot für die Welt 2013b). These billboards bring criticism of capitalism on the agenda, which none of the other pictures analysed thus far do. They furthermore connect wealth-creating activities taking place in Germany – in this case speculation with food – with poverty and destitution in the global South. While a big step from images of starving children, the images still enable the common viewer to stay detached from the issue at hand. Food speculation is not something that the usual German is aware of being implicated in – most are probably ignorant of the fact that many banks, insurance companies or pension funds are involved in such speculation (Hachfeld, Pohl, and Wiggerthale 2012).

Another rather widespread and prominent campaign by Misereor (2011) can also be taken as an unusual example of bringing up questions of inequality. It encompassed more than 100,000 posters with at least eight different themes, all of them pictograms set in black and white with the text beginning with 'Courage is . . .'. They acknowledge, for example, the work of people in Southern Africa supporting AIDS orphans and those acting for refugees in Africa. They ask for donations to help Misereor in supporting the 'courageous ones in Sudan' who 'fight weapons with words' and 'build new schools in Sudan after 50 years of civil war', and the 'courageous ones in Latin America who fight against judicial arbitrariness'. This campaign is noteworthy, as it is one of the few that actually acknowledges agency in the South beyond the restricted version mentioned earlier. One poster shows a tiny boat with one person inside in front of a huge boat and asks us to, for instance, support the struggle of small-scale fishermen in West Africa against poverty in the face of foreign fishing fleets. People aware of historical connections and contemporary African-European relations may also decode the poster of the fishermen's social struggle as scandalising neocolonial and neoliberal economic conditions. They may also become aware of 'our' responsibility for forcing former or potential fishermen from West Africa to undertake the dangerous journey to Europe. Other posters of this campaign explicitly call for support of those who struggle against mining methods that cause diseases, or scandalise land grabbing. While this campaign does not connect prosperity and patterns of consumption in Germany to conditions in the South as explicitly as Brot für die Welt's campaign, it can be read by viewers as highlighting political agency while pointing to an 'imperial mode of living' (Brand and Wissen 2013), that is, Germany's economic, political, social and cultural configuration that upholds unsustainable levels of consumption of fish, precious metals or bio fuels.

Medico international, a German NGO that has generally refrained from typical development 'aid' practices and says that it follows the maxim 'defend, criticise and overcome aid', has trodden new ground in terms of politicised advertising. Its campaign against exploitation in the textile industry pointed to the responsibility of the German discounter KiK for working conditions and the deaths of many people in fires and collapses of factories (medico international 2015). One image depicts a man during what seems like a press conference or an interview with the header line 'the plaintiff'. Below the image a text explains that the man, Mohammed Hanif, 'survived the fire in the factory in Karachi. Supported by medico he sues the discounter KiK for compensation, together with three co-plaintiffs'. A quote follows that seems to be by him: 'Such an accident should never happen again! We have to hold those who are responsible accountable'. Another billboard shows a demonstration of women and is entitled 'the trade unionists' and explains that the image shows the protest of the National Garment Workers Federation after the collapse of Rana Plaza and lists their demands. This campaign brings together the aspect of political agency in Misereor's campaign with that of global interconnectedness and inequality in Brot für die Welt's but goes further in as far as it explicitly names specific agents and their organisations. Thus, people in the South no longer appear as a homogenous mass of destitute or aided people but as political subjects: German people can, if they share the cause, support their struggles – and think about whether they want to continue buying clothes at KiK.

Billboard advertising can hence bring up issues of global inequality and address complex questions that highlight the interconnectedness of poverty and wealth, of exploitation and our complicity. They can stress political agency in the South and the possibility for solidarity with struggles against injustice. However, it is noteworthy that both Misereor and Brot für die Welt have again resorted to more classical advertising in the aftermath of the campaigns examined here. Maybe the campaigns focusing on global inequality and the implication of the target groups of the billboard advertisings did not yield the expected fundraising results.

THE SUBVERSIVE POTENTIAL OF ADBUSTING AND SUBVERTISING

The more progressive campaigns analysed in the previous section have not explicitly connected anti-racist or anti-colonial struggles (also with regard to representation) with issues of material inequalities and neocolonialism. This is on occasion undertaken by people who engage in adbusting: 'A subvert [or adbust] is a satirical version or the defacing of an existing advert, a *detournement*, an inversion designed to make us forget consumerism and consider instead social or political issues' (Barley 2001). A(i)dbusting functions in line with this definition and uses existing billboards to amend them in such a way that it subverts or changes their logics of development 'aid'. Playing with the images and stereotypes that we are accustomed to and turning them around are a manner of providing food for thought on questions of development and inequality. A(i)dbusters evidently decode and deconstruct the images they amend in a negotiated or oppositional way, reconstruct them and present their newly encoded version to the public. While the adbusts and subverts explored here have not been widely disseminated, and their substantial effect on German society can thus be doubted, they point to a subversive potential.

The artist Mansour Ciss Kanakassy from the Laboratoire Déberlinisation reacted to the campaign 'The Big Five!' by replacing the five animals with famous African anti-colonial thinkers and fighters such as Thomas Sankara. This subvertising criticised the colonial-racist imagery in an attempt to stay true to the special day of the fiftieth anniversary of the founding of the Organisation of African Unity. It did so by highlighting that African liberation is not in the former colonisers' hands. In another less artistic, rather illicit style, a group calling itself DIANOKIE (2016) – invoking the previously mentioned Protestant agency Diakonie – changed the Welthungerhilfe's poster series 'It's enough. For everybody. With your help', analysed earlier. It replaced it with 'It's enough! Enough racist advertising'. The poster by Misereor mentioned earlier that calls for support of those in Latin America who stand up against judicial arbitrariness have also been amended by adbusters to draw attention to issues of injustice and racism within Germany. Somebody changed 'Latin America' to 'Dessau' and added 'Oury Jalloh, that was murder'. This brings forward the case of a Sierra Leonean man who was in all likelihood burnt to death by the police in the German town of Dessau in 2005.[5] The United Nations' Working Group of Experts on People of African Descent (2017) during its official visit to Germany in 2017 regarded this particular case as representative of the widespread 'failure to effectively investigate and provide justice in cases of racial discrimination and violence against people of African descent by the state, in particular by the police'.

Other adbusts take up questions of material relations. The poster by Misereor on those in Sudan who 'fight weapons with words' has, for example, been amended in such a way that the depicted chalk board now reads 'Made in D' instead of 'A B C', and the text says: 'German weapons and German money are responsible for war and destruction around the world. And who profits? We support political resistance here and globally' (see figure 4.2). This adbust points to the fact that German companies sell weapons and related technology all over the world – Germany is the world's fourth-largest exporter of large arms and the second-largest exporter of small arms (Stockholm International Peace Research Institute 2015, 10). An adbust of the same Misereor campaign now carries the headline 'Courage is to fight modern colonialism!' and the name of the NGO is changed to 'misery' ('Misere'). Below, the adbust quotes Fanon with 'the material wellbeing and progress of Europe have been built with the sweat and the corpses of the colonised' and demands 'more anticolonial education in German universities!' All in all, it becomes evident that adbusts and subverts in the context of development billboard advertising are an interesting strategy to irritate the 'development gaze' (Escobar 1994, 155), to make observers reflect on racism in the representation of the global South, or to put questions of poverty into the context of historically developed relations of exploitation and injustice.

Figure 4.2.   Adbust of a billboard advertising by Misereor – 'Courage is to fight weapons with words – German weapons and German money are responsible for war and destruction around the world. And who profits? We support political resistance here and globally!' (www.whitecharity.de).

CONCLUSION

All in all, the analysis of billboard advertising in German development highlights two problems: First, there is limited recognition of the colonial legacy that connects the global North and South discursively and materially; second, perspectives and political agency from the global South remain conspicuously absent. While classic racialised images of poverty and deprivation are less prevalent in development advertising in Germany today – due inter alia to postcolonial critique – they can still be found alongside those of the happy, empowered Other. At the same time, billboard advertising continues the trope of the white man's burden, is based on an understanding of Germany as white and reproduces a corresponding self-image of a homogeneous non-migrant society. While governmental and non-governmental development policy in Germany – at least rhetorically – aims at partnership with the global South and at curbing global inequality, the hegemonic narratives of billboard advertising and fundraising strategies in Germany reinforce the colonial discourse of a superior North and an inferior South in need of trusteeship. This operation of colonial power is particularly problematic if billboard advertising is acknowledged as one of the key ways of educating the German public on questions of 'development' and global relations. On the other hand, some isolated, more recent campaigns actually tackle issues of inequality and colonial legacies head-on. They portray global injustice in a more complex manner and seem to be well aware of the political implications of advertisements and the historical-political context in which their work is situated. Adbusting further shows the possibilities of billboards' role in educating the public, as they criticise both the colonial present in North-South relations and racism in billboard advertising and in German society more broadly.

The billboard advertising by faith-based and secular NGOs displays a particular obsession with images of children. As a rule, their plight is decontextualised, and the global South thus appears not only as childlike but also as unable to care for itself. Northern trusteeship, donations and development interventions are the quasi-natural consequences. If the South is not associated with children, it is represented through women. They are used as non-threatening and non-political victims of their societies. At the same time their prevalence and depiction as mothers who cannot take care of their children invoke visions of an overpopulated South. As will be examined in chapters 5 and 6, the evident concern of 'development at home' about the societal position of women as related to childbirth, fertility and child-rearing was common in colonial times and continues to take centre stage in German 'development abroad'.

With regard to the governmental campaign 'The Big Five!', it became evident that, while a critique of representation continues to be necessary, it is not sufficient. If criticism concentrates on colonial-racist imagery only, it runs the danger of overlooking the neocolonial and neoliberal directions of German 'development abroad' and the centrality of colonial-racist ideas for the perpetuation of such development policies. The intertwining of colonial discourse and racialisation, actual interventions on the level of Southern bodies and societies, and the furthering of economic interests will be further dealt with in the subsequent chapters on German development policy abroad.

NOTES

1. While this advert very much replays colonial representation, other images of the same series also depict non-white nuns helping non-white children.

2. On the website we learn that this man, Francis Van Hoi, acquired skills as a cook in Germany and now applies these standards to his school in Vietnam. Invoking the colonial dichotomy of Western mind/rationality and Southern body/emotion, Misereor (2015b) breaks down the concept as follows: 'German training + Vietnamese energy = Perspectives for 110 poor youth in Ho Chi Minh City'.

3. A few months before this campaign, in December 2012, the BMZ had placed an ad in various newspapers with the heading 'Merry Christmas Africa', a picture of a

hut at night with lighting in the form of reindeers, sleighs and Father Christmas, and the quote by Minister Niebel below saying: 'We have achieved a great deal already. With your help we can do even more'. This has been criticised as racist and perpetuating the idea of the white man's burden (Ziai 2013b).

4. This animal, the African Buffalo or Cape Buffalo, used to be (and still is) known as *Kaffernbüffel* in German. This translates to 'kaffir buffalo' – 'kaffir' being a derogatory, racist term used for Black South Africans during Apartheid, a term still in use today to dehumanise Black people (the word is derived from the Arabic term *kafir*, which means 'unbeliever').

5. The interpretation of billboard advertising cannot be controlled, and its decoding by adbusting does not necessarily need to be progressive. Here, I have also come across Misereor's poster on judicial arbitrariness being used to transport the revisionist agenda of right-wing radicalism. Somebody had written 'Dresden 250,000' on the poster to point to the alleged number of Germans who died in the bombing of the German city of Dresden by Allied forces. The figure is estimated to be at the most a tenth of this (Müller, Schönherr, and Widera 2010, 49). Remembering the bombing of Dresden is one of the key events for neo-Nazis in Germany and is also a site of considerable anti-fascist protests.

Chapter 5

Transforming Childbirth-Related Care in East Africa and Challenges to Colonial Power

These experts bring with them
the marks of their origin!
Prejudices, lack of confidence
in the peoples' ability;
to think, to want, to know
They thus run the risk
of falling into harmful generosity
Whereby they believe,
They must be the executors
of the transformation.

– Tanzanian poet B. R. Nchimbi 1977, 163

Focusing on the realms of development education and billboard advertising, chapters 3 and 4 examined how the public in Germany is socialised into ideas and practices of development, and how colonial power takes effect or is dealt with in these areas. This chapter and chapter 6 now turn to German 'development abroad'. German development policy is particularly appropriate for an analysis of policy implementation abroad as – in contrast to other 'donors' – it favours a multi-level approach that also entails the deployment of actual practitioners on the ground. Here, development policy on childbirth-related practices lends itself to an analysis: It was a prime target of colonial policies for transforming the colonised people in the name of civilisation and modernity (Ram and Jolly 1998; Vaughan 1991). German colonial interest in this realm – sparked by a colonial 'reformist' agenda after the turn of the twentieth century and entrenched in concerns of a 'population decline' (Colwell 2001) – is striking, and 'maternal health' and 'pregnancy and delivery' are priority areas of BMZ's endeavours. Given Germany's concern with birthing in East Africa in the colonial past and today, this case provides a unique lens through which to explore whether colonial power is alive in contemporary Germany development policy abroad.

This chapter draws on scientific and government publications, archival sources of the German colonial administration and documents of German development policy. Between 2009 and 2011, I also conducted semi-structured interviews with fifty-nine mainly German professionals in Germany and Tanzania involved in reproductive health in Tanzania (for a list of cited interviewees, see appendix). As mentioned in chapters 1 and 2, my position-ality as a white German with experience in German development policy and settings such as being hosted in development professionals' private homes helped to create an atmosphere in which my respondents seemed com-fortable enough to also share uncertainties regarding their work. I should stress here that this chapter and chapter 6 focus on German perspectives of development 'cooperation' and do not account for the perspectives of Tanzanians.

The chapter begins with an introduction to German colonisation of East Africa and contemporary German-Tanzanian development 'cooperation', which also provides the context for chapter 6. In each of the following three empirical parts, I first review the colonial period, then turn to contemporary German development policy and conclude by comparing the two periods in order to shed new light on the present. The first part analyses the manner in which childbirth-related practices in East Africa were generally perceived by German professionals and institutions and the interventions proposed today and during colonisation. The second part addresses health care planning and management. The third explores the manner in which German commentators in both periods raised the issue of attitudes in obstetric care.

GERMAN COLONISATION OF EAST AFRICA

To understand Germany's contemporary development interventions in Tanzania, it is indispensable to go back to the history of its presence in this area. In the mid-1850s, before the private German East Africa Company (in 1884) and the German Empire (in 1890) occupied the territories which they then referred to as 'German East Africa', German Protestant and Catholic missionaries had already arrived there (Köhler 2000). However, Germans had been involved in colonialism in East Africa even prior to this. In 1505, German commercial agents Hans Mayr and Balthasar Sprenger accompanied Francesco d'Almeida in his attack on and occupation of Kilwa, in the south of present-day Tanzania (Bruchhausen 2006).

Opinions vary as to when 'German East Africa' was effectively established and when it ended (cf. Colwell 2001). Colonial imposition formally lasted from the mid-1880s until around 1920. Between 1889 and 1896 more than fifty wars of resistance were fought against German colonial rule (Kjekshus 1996). Only around 1904 was the German Empire able to fully bring the territory and people under its control, with great brutality and ruthlessness, and this was again challenged in the Maji Maji War (1905–1907), in which approximately 300,000 Africans died (Boahen 1996). 'German East Africa' constituted the largest German colony and, in contrast to the so-called settler colony 'German South-West Africa', served as a 'plantation colony', facilitating economic exploitation via agricultural enterprises. German 'settlers' (in contrast to administrators, entrepreneurs and missionaries) played a relatively marginal role in 'German East Africa', compared to their role in 'German South-West Africa', and were mainly confined to the area around the Kilimanjaro and the Usambara mountains (Marx 2004). In 1913, there were 882 German settlers in 'German East Africa', of a total of over 4,000 Germans, including military personnel, traders, government officials, missionaries, nurses, doctors and their families, and a total white population of 5,336 (Friedrichsmeyer, Lennox, and Zantop 1998).

Systematic health policy by European colonising nations was initiated at the turn of the twentieth century, when colonial administrations established the discipline of 'colonial medicine' in order to protect the colonisers against diseases and climate previously unknown to them. Germany was no exception to this trend. Colonial health policy by European nations followed a similar pattern: Western health care and medicine were first brought to the colonies to ensure the well-being and survival of colonisers; later on, colonised people employed or forced to work by the colonisers were cared for as well; the third stage was the inclusion of the colonised people in general as objects of Western medicine, 'hygiene' and health care (Worboys 2000). This chapter and chapter 6 focus on the third phase, which Michael Worboys specifies as 'missionary activity, modernization, and protection of the health and welfare of indigenous peoples' (2001, 207).

Matters of health and medicine were administered by the Medizinalreferat des Reichs-Kolonialamts (Medical Department of the Imperial Colonial Office) in Germany and by the Medizinalreferat des Kaiserlichen Gouvernments von Deutsch-Ostafrika (Medical Department of the Imperial Government of German East Africa) in Dar es Salaam. In addition to government involvement, missions had always included medical care as part of their proselytising activities. As from 1905, they began to form specific medical missionary associations to intensify their involvement in this sphere (Beck 1977). The German colonial government also subsidised missions in order to provide medical services in rural communities (Masebo 2010).

With the advent of reformist agendas after the turn of the twentieth century, and especially after the Maji Maji War, the German colonial administration in 'German East Africa' became particularly interested in questions of population and reproduction. 'Population decline' was identified as a problem; the official German statistics of the number of offspring per family confirmed a 'very low reproduction' rate and a 'decline' in population for some areas (Medizinalreferat in Daressalam 1914, 440–41). A perceived depopulation and low reproduction rate was a common point of departure for many scientific and government publications (see chapter 6). Recent studies, however, suggest that actual 'population decline' probably never occurred in 'German East Africa' and that the 'depopulation', which the German colonisers claimed to have observed, instead had to do with labour migration and people moving away from the sphere of influence of the colonial administration (Koponen 1994). Nonetheless, as will be expanded upon in chapter 6, colonial administrators, missionaries, physicians and scientists cautioned against a 'population decline', and East Africans were considered a resource in need of 'protection', 'preservation' and 'enhancement' (Stoecker 1991).

As focused on in detail in this chapter, German missionaries, physicians and administrators showed great concern for East African obstetric care and child-rearing. This concern was part of a larger European project of discussing and intervening into maternity and reproduction of colonised people (cf. Vaughan 1991; Hunt 1999; cf. Hesselink 2011). Before German colonisers began to be worried about East African birthing, obstetric care in 'German East Africa' had female colonisers such as the wives of German settlers, missionaries and administrators in mind. Once doctors, missionaries and the colonial administration began to take an interest in child and maternal health, they evaluated and assessed practices of midwifery and infant care. Moreover, in order to control the sphere of reproduction, they were committed to identifying the prevalence and methods of induced abortions.

POST-WORLD WAR II GERMAN DEVELOPMENT POLICY IN TANZANIA

After Germany had lost World War I, the UK was mandated to administer parts of the territory of 'German East Africa' conferred to it by the Supreme Council of the League of Nations in 1919. What was formerly 'German East Africa' was reduced in size to today's Tanzania and renamed Tanganyika. Ruanda-Urundi was awarded to Belgium, and the Kionga Triangle to 'Portuguese East Africa'. During British colonial rule, the British Medical Administration felt it was important to '[e]liminat[e] the cultural superstitions and practices surrounding childbirth and child rearing as well as educat[e] mothers in proper nutrition and sanitation practices' (Allen 2002, 20–21). By the late 1920s, the 'issue of medically assisted births and the training of native midwives in Tanganyika received much attention from colonial administrators' (Allen 2002, 27). In the 1940s, British colonial policy emphasised 'development' more and more in order to maintain legitimacy. Funding of social services was increased, particularly for education, housing, water and health (Schneider 2006). Apparently, by the 1940s, women in Tanganyika had begun to make more and more use of the colonial medical facilities to give birth (Allen 2002). However, in the late 1940s and early 1950s – due to economic and personnel constraints – the Medical Services in Tanganyika suggested focusing more on prenatal and postnatal care (with hospitalisation reserved for complicated deliveries), refraining from expanding institutional midwifery services, and encouraging home births for normal cases (Allen 2002).

In a press release on the occasion of fifty years of Tanzanian independence, the German government stated that 'Tanzania is one of Germany's most important and oldest cooperation partners, with development "cooperation" between the two countries going back to the early 1960s' (BMZ 2011d). It has been one of the focal countries of German 'aid' since the 1970s (Bohnet 2000). Total 'aid' commitments from 1962 through 2011 amounted to about €2.6 billion (Köhler 2000; Open Aid Data 2017). From 2015 to 2017 the volume of German development 'cooperation' with Tanzania was about €160 million (BMZ 2017c). In terms of per-capita 'aid', only Israel has received more 'aid' than Tanzania over the course of the past decades (Köhler 2000). Development 'cooperation' is focused on three priority areas: health care, water supply and sanitation, and decentralisation and local government (Embassy of the Federal Republic of Germany, Dar es Salaam 2012, 7). In accordance with Tanzania's 'national development strategy', most bilateral 'aid' is given in the form of direct budget support (BMZ 2012). Development 'assistance' further includes the deployment 'of development workers and government subsidies for development cooperation measures conducted by the German churches, non-governmental organisations and political foundations active in Tanzania' (German Federal Foreign Office 2012). Moreover, non-governmental organisations (NGOs), faith-based and church organisations also channel 'aid' to Tanzania. For example, hundreds of German congregations, associations and groups maintain bilateral relations with parishes of the Evangelical Lutheran Church in Tanzania (Köhler 2000).

In Tanzania, the German government has established its largest health programme in Africa, the Tanzanian German Programme to Support Health (TGPSH). Virtually all German development agencies are involved in this programme. At the time of my research, this programme included four main areas of intervention: 'sexual and reproductive health and rights, including HIV/AIDS prevention', 'health financing and social health insurance', 'human resources and capacity building' and 'decentralised health services' (German Federal Foreign Office 2012). While only one area is explicitly categorised as 'reproductive health', activities in the other three areas address reproductive health issues as well. According to interviewees, reproductive health, especially family planning and maternal health, constitutes the key focus of TGPSH. German 'aid' considers the general health situation in Tanzania highly problematic; it is seen as 'precarious with a generalised HIV & AIDS epidemic, high maternal mortality ratio, high fertility rate and a high unmet need for family planning' (evaplan 2009, 13; BMZ 2017c). According to TGPSH, the situation with regard to obstetric care is grim and had shown no change since 1996 (TGPSH 2009b). That regarding the use of 'modern family planning' was described as equally bleak, having shown little improvement in recent years (TGPSH 2009a), and 'population growth of around three per cent a year' is regarded as one of the Tanzanian health sector's many challenges (BMZ 2017c). At the same time, the health system is suffering from a severe lack of qualified personnel.

Other German endeavours in the area of population and reproductive health in Tanzania include activities by NGOs such as the German Foundation for World Population mentioned in chapter 3. German mission hospitals are also active, such as the Ndanda Hospital, founded more than 100 years ago during German colonial rule and run by the Benedictine Sisters and the Congregation of St. Ottilien (see chapter 4 for a billboard image of one of the central figures of this mission hospital). Relations between German congregations and Tanzanian churches also typically involve health care.

'GIVING BIRTH IN THE WHITE PEOPLE'S MANNER'

The following sections empirically investigate how contemporary German 'development abroad' in the specific case of childbirth-related care is marked by colonial power. The chapter does so by relating the colonial past to the present. It proceeds by first scrutinising general German perceptions and interventions, then looking at the issue of health care planning and management and finally closing with an investigation of the role German interveners accord to questions of attitudes in health care. Historical studies have also alerted us to the fact that Western intervention into birthing and child-rearing began during colonial occupation (Hunt 1999). Class-based policies in many European countries and in North America were mirrored by projects in the colonies (Jolly 1998). Experiences of motherhood, birthing practices and obstetric care in the colonies – just like healing and therapeutic practices in general – were transformed by missionaries and colonial state policies. In the

'Belgian Congo', for example, missionaries and colonial government officials tried to medicalise African reproductive practices by founding health
facilities, training Africans to be nurses and midwives and promoting childbirth in hospitals (Hunt 1999). Scholars of health and medicine have pointed
out that colonial-era interventions were based on a hierarchical categorisation of bodies, societies, systems of thought and practices along the lines of
colonial difference (Ferzacca 2003). Colonial government and missionary
health interventions 'played an important part in constructing "the African"
as an object of knowledge, and elaborated classification systems and practices which have to be seen as intrinsic to the operation of colonial power'
(Vaughan 1991, 8). While a range of analogies to European gender and class
hierarchies were expressed in health policies during colonial rule, so were
'distinctive features of the colonial poetics of pollution', which meant that
colonisers drew lines that 'traced more explicitly than in Europe the boundaries of race' (Anderson 2000, 236).

Just like their European colleagues in other colonial contexts, German
physicians, missionaries and administrators after the turn of the twentieth
century proceeded to assess the practices they encountered in 'German East
Africa'. Some were deemed functional, others inappropriate. Commentaries
such as the following by a senior staff surgeon in Kilwa give evidence of such
estimations of East African midwifery:

> In cases of lateral or posterior positions, a correction is undertaken through hand
> pressure and massage; one also drinks a medicine in such cases. . . . In case of
> premature bleeding during the pregnancy, one also applies dawa – medicine –
> internally, bed rest is also prescribed; in serious cases . . . the mother dies
> unsalvageable due to exsanguinations, since they do not know internal interven-
> tions. . . . In case of strong contractions, she [the midwife, DB] massages the
> body with both hands, stroking from the chest towards the abdomen. In case of
> lateral positions, mother and child die unsalvageable; the people do not consider
> it possible to bring help in such cases. (Peiper 1910, 461–62)

This German doctor acknowledged certain practices as useful, while
maintaining that the East African midwives were unable to deal with serious complications. Most of all, however, German commentators accentuated
perceived deficiencies (Feldmann 1923; Reichs-Kolonialamt 1913; Ittameier
1923). Evaluations at times amounted to positing a complete 'lack of pregnancy and maternity protection' (Peiper 1920b, 19). Supposedly harmful
standards of 'hygiene' were also underlined by German agents (e.g., Peiper
1910). While some commentators referred to 'native midwives' and thus
acknowledged the existence of women who specialised in midwifery (Axenfeld 1913, 12), others stated that East Africans did not know of midwives 'in
our sense' or referred to 'women assigned to the midwifery task'; 'elderly,

experienced women' (Peiper 1910, 461); or 'mothers-in-law' (Sister Nikola, cited in Walter 1992, 304), thereby doubting their knowledge and skills.

Yet German colonisers did not always speak with one voice. For example, a mission superintendent considered midwifery among East Africans fairly developed (Axenfeld 1913), and the Medical Reports of the German Administration explained the limited use of German hospitals for childbirth as partly due to the fact 'that the native midwife is quite skilled, knowing the manipulations necessary for all eventualities, so that the European physician is only a last resort' (Reichs-Kolonialamt 1915, 233). Hermann Feldmann, editor of the journal *Medical Mission*, and staff surgeon in Dar es Salaam even mentioned that in some 'tribes . . . quite a number of really useful midwives exist, who stand out in skilfulness and a certain empirically acquired expertise, so that they were even asked to carry out deliveries of European women in some especially favourable cases' (1923, 129). Here, Feldmann refers to so-called native midwives, as opposed to East Africans trained as nurses in mission hospitals. All in all, however, the claim that 'the native midwife is quite skilled' was marginal in the broader debate. The emphasis in those quotes which were more favourable towards East African obstetric care suggests that acknowledgement of knowledge and skills did not counteract the conviction of East African inferiority to what commentators took as their benchmark, that is, the standards of German midwifery.

In order to improve the situation of pregnant and delivering women and to transform obstetric care, the German colonial administration, physicians, missionaries and colonial 'reformist' lobby groups made numerous suggestions. These included increasing the number of German medical doctors and midwives, training East Africans in nursing and midwifery, building health facilities and propagating Christianity in order to root out the influence of what they called 'pagan mothers-in-law' (Feldmann 1923, 142). The call for an increase in 'European trained sanitary personnel' entailed dispatching German physicians and nursing staff 'in their thousands' and 'training . . . nurses for the service of the native population, particularly in the area of midwifery and infant care', on the one hand, and qualifying East Africans as nurses and midwives while discouraging their existing practices, on the other hand (Feldmann 1923, 128–29). Some commentators also considered recruitment and training of those East African women who 'stand out due to their ability and certain empirically acquired knowledge' (Feldmann 1923, 129). The Deutsche Gesellschaft für Eingebornenschutz ('German Society for the Protection of the Natives') and the Deutscher Frauenverein für Krankenpflege in den Kolonien ('German Women's Association for Nursing in the Colonies') were convinced that lack of 'delivery institutions for natives' was responsible for a poor obstetric situation and pressed for the inauguration of 'institutions for the education of native midwives, nurses, and nurse aides as well as the

founding of delivery homes for natives' (Deutsche Gesellschaft für Eingebornenschutz 1914a, 132; Deutscher Frauenverein für Krankenpflege in den
Kolonien 1909).

Calls for transforming obstetrics and health care in 'German East Africa'
were matched with practical interventions: More government physicians and
medical officers were in fact hired, mission societies sent midwives and the
training of 'adequate native women as midwives' started just prior to the
demise of German colonial occupation (Reichs-Kolonialamt 1914; Feldmann
1923). Interventions also included behavioural advice for pregnant women
via dissemination of leaflets. The Medical Administration, for example,
printed a leaflet with advice on how to raise children and what to do in cases
of complications during pregnancy:

> To avoid miscarriages, the mother should already be careful during her preg-
> nancy, should not carry heavy loads and should not hoe on the field extensively.
> If blood shows, she should lie down in bed until the blood is gone. If the child
> and mother are ill, they should immediately consult a European doctor for his
> advice, who will gladly tell them what to do. (Cited in Peiper 1912, 259)

Ten thousand such leaflets were printed and distributed throughout 'German
East Africa' at the beginning of 1911 by the respective district administrations (Eckart 1997).

As an example of concrete interventions into birthing, the issue of delivery
positions is noteworthy. German physicians introduced a specific type of
birthing on a stretcher in the supine position which was the widely accepted
practice in Germany at the time (Dziedzic and Renköwitz 1999). According to German reports, East African women often preferred other positions
(Peiper 1910; Axenfeld 1913). While my research did not yield evidence of
physicians introducing the supine birth position in 'German East Africa',
interviews with German development professionals currently working in
Tanzania (Interview 31, 8 June 2010) and the documentary film *Der lange
Weg ans Licht* (*The Long Way to Light*) on midwifery in Germany and
Tanzania (Wolfsperger 2005) indicate that German colonisers must have
advocated the supine birthing position in 'German East Africa'. A colonial-
era report from a German medical doctor in Togo also mentions that 'the
seating of the woman in labour in a supine position on a clean . . . sheet was
made obligatory' in order to lessen the risks for mother and child during
delivery (Rodenwaldt 1912, 275). In some areas of Tanzania, to give birth
in this position is, still today, referred to as *kuzaa kizungu*, which can be
translated as 'giving birth in the white people's manner'. A German medical
doctor also mentioned that – when she asked why her Tanzanian colleagues
resorted to the supine birth position – she was told 'this was how you taught
it to us back in the days' (Interview 31, 8 June 2010). The interventions into

childbirth-related matters may be understood as a part of what Pascal Grosse has framed a 'comprehensive medicalisation of the female part of the population' (2000, 142).

AMBIVALENT HOSPITALS

Having explored German perceptions of, and interventions into, childbirth-related practice during colonial occupation, I now examine German interventions into obstetric care in Tanzania in the present to explore the prevalence of colonial power today. Tanzania was no exception to the trend in many newly decolonised nations: Independence did not entail a turning-away from the Western biomedical model, but rather an expansion thereof 'as a result of the growing dependence of developing nations on Western aid and the parallel growth of international health and development agencies . . . which work within a Western biomedical paradigm' (Packard 2000, 97–98). In 2010, at the time of my research in Tanzania, its maternal mortality rate was 460, which put it in twenty-third place worldwide (CIA World Factbook 2014). Maternal deaths account for 17 per cent of all deaths of women between age fifteen and forty-nine (National Bureau of Statistics and ICF Macro 2010). Provision of reproductive health care for women is generally marked by poor, unaffordable treatment at health care facilities, where staff are underpaid and must pursue additional income-generating activities (Allen 2002). Only about half of births take place in health facilities and are assisted by 'health professionals'. The remaining home deliveries are assisted by '[t]rained and traditional birth attendants' and 'relatives or other untrained people' (National Bureau of Statistics and ICF Macro 2010, 135–36).

Contemporary German development policy finds obstetric care in Tanzania to be lacking and commonly relates this to restricted 'access to skilled birth attendants and to good obstetric care' (BMZ 2008, 9). Germany and other international donors have until recently supported the training of 'traditional birth attendants' (TBAs) in biomedical health care, but the desired effect of lowering maternal mortality has not materialised. As a consequence, maternal health policy today generally does not include TBAs. The BMZ 'Initiative for Voluntary Family Planning and Maternal Health' thus also aims at increasing the number of 'medically professionally accompanied deliveries' (BMZ 2011c).

Ongoing German development 'cooperation' links high maternal mortality and poor maternal health in Tanzania to a high prevalence of home births, especially among poor women; according to a staff member of the German Development Bank, five out of six poor women deliver at home, and even among wealthier women, only 60 per cent make use of biomedical health facilities for delivery (Interview 14, 18 March 2010). German development professionals regard giving birth to be risky because TBAs, who often assist home births, are perceived as unskilled and reliant on 'experiential' or 'traditional' (Interviews 02, 08, 10 and 28) rather than on 'Western-based, evidence-based medicine' (Interview 08, 14 February 2010). The stated aim of German development 'aid' is to have all deliveries performed in biomedical health facilities. In line with Tanzanian government policy, German development 'aid' strategy in Tanzania does not include any cooperation with TBAs. German development professionals also commonly voiced their opposition to such cooperation. They generally construed a dichotomy between home births by unskilled TBAs, on the one hand, and deliveries in biomedical facilities by skilled birth attendants, on the other. The former is associated with high risks and discouraged; the latter is propagated as desirable and associated with lower risks for mothers and infants.

At the same time, German development policy points out the insufficient quality of obstetric care in those facilities. Their deficiencies are highlighted as one of the reasons why Tanzanian women avoid official health facilities. In the following quote, a German doctor working in a missionary hospital mentions problematic medical and hygienic conditions in one of Tanzania's biggest hospitals: 'Well, delivery ward here, that is . . . if you are lucky, there are only three beds in one room, merely separated by curtains. . . . And, but also from the medical standpoint, it is just . . . well, I don't know, well, from the, from the cleanliness, from the medical, it is . . . no, no' (Interview 31, 8 June 2010). Aside from mentioning lack of privacy (see later, 'Post-Modern Birthing'), this doctor considered the medical and hygiene standards disastrous. In the interviews, Tanzanian hospital staff were characterised as badly educated and lacking know-how and capacity (e.g., Interviews 18, 35, 43 and 53).

A German doctor working in a large Tanzanian hospital explains how she perceives nurses' deficiencies:

> there are some, that's a catastrophe, a real catastrophe. They don't do anything. But I think that it's not wickedness, but rather that the people just don't get what it's about. That might have to do with their training. You can pose any question from the schoolbook. And you get a whole page rattled out by heart. But in a concrete situation . . . no consequence whatsoever, no inkling what kind of situation one faces and what is to be done. (Interview 35, 22 June 2010)

This professional regards nurses as unaware of the fundamentals of obstetric care. According to several German physicians and nurses I interviewed, Tanzanian hospital nurses were unable to implement their acquired knowledge in practice and were merely capable of mechanically reproducing what they had learned by heart.

This perception is particularly evident in the way German professionals talk about the use or non-use of the partograph, a tool for monitoring progress of delivery. If filled out correctly, the partograph allows nurses or doctors to determine at what stage a medical intervention such as a Caesarean section is called for. This procedure is widely regarded as a sine qua non in biomedical obstetric care. Many of the German health workers with whom I spoke reported that Tanzanian nurses commonly did not fill it in at all or did so incorrectly, or that nurses did not take the appropriate actions on the basis of a filled-in partograph (Interviews 08, 29, 37 and 39). A professional of the German Development Service (DED), specialised in obstetrics and gynaecology, who worked in a Tanzanian district hospital, reports German development policy's experiences in propagating the use of the partograph:

> And this lady [his German development 'aid' colleague, DB] was training this partograph for five years now, and still, every time she went to the hospitals, the same people did not understand the partograph. And she explained again and she said: because I think this is the best way to deal, and in a very simple way, of how to deal with delivery and how to detect problems. But it did not get . . . nobody uses it. (Interview 08, 14 February, 2010)

Thus, the inability of the Tanzanian hospital staff to use the partograph properly despite repeated training is met with disbelief by this development professional.

The DED professional also asked himself what to do in the face of the reluctance by Tanzanian professionals to use the partograph:

> Is this because this is our system, our idea? This is Western-based medicine, this is evidence-based medicine, but it doesn't work somehow. So we sometimes say: If it doesn't work, why try to continue with it, why try to . . . teach and implement this thing. . . . Who are we, who are we as white doctors to say, this is the best one? (Interview 08, 14 February, 2010)

This doctor raised the point of possible incompatibilities of Western and Tanzanian medical paradigms. He considered giving up the transfer of health knowledge to Tanzanian hospitals but did not consider alternative paradigms or ways of teaching health care. In the follow-up to this excerpt, the same interviewee brushed off his uncertainty by pointing out that if he began to doubt his ability to bring about positive change, he would have to question the whole project of international development cooperation and quite literally 'go home'.

As during colonial rule, the issue of birth positions remains a German concern. Several German physicians and nurses complained of the almost exclusive use of the supine birth position in Tanzanian health facilities. They considered it the worst birthing position, 'right after a handstand' (Interview 29, 8 June 2010), and said it was a way of exerting authority over the women giving birth. Consequently, the German physicians working in obstetrics in Tanzania said that they tried to introduce other birthing positions (see figure 5.1).

Notwithstanding the general perception of deficient skills and knowledge of Tanzanian health care staff, some German professionals acknowledged that they considered some nurses and doctors highly skilled. For example, one interviewee said she had 'fantastic colleagues, really, who think, act and plan exactly as I am used to . . . from back home' (Interview 29, 8 June 2010). This remark evidences that standards associated with German hospitals are conceived as the desirable norm but are fulfilled only by a few. According to my research, one can ask whether German professionals can only imagine Tanzanian health professionals catching up with them if they work just like them or whether there might not be a possibility for them to work differently without this being perceived as inferior.

Figure 5.1.   Stills from the documentary film *The Long Way to Light* (*Der lange Weg ans Licht*; Douglas Wolfsperger Filmproduktion 2005).

RELATING THE PRESENT TO THE PAST

During formal colonial rule, the colonisers attempted to replace 'traditional' East African midwifery with 'modern' European biomedical practices. German practitioners today no longer establish difference by opposing 'modern' biomedicine to 'traditional' practices. Instead, they differentiate fully fledged biomedical obstetric care as practised in Germany from its deficient adaptation or the maintenance of outdated biomedical practices in Tanzania. Yet in contemporary German development policy, biomedically trained Tanzanian health personnel are depicted in a similar manner as were 'native midwives' during colonisation: lacking skills and knowledge. Thus, despite the hegemony of biomedical health care in Tanzania today, the 'dichotomizing system' (Mudimbe 1988, 4) introduced by Germans during colonisation between correct German obstetric care and deficient Tanzanian practices is rearticulated. In both periods obstetric care is measured against German midwifery, and differences are considered deficiencies. Rearticulating the assumption of linear progress of obstetric care with German standards as the epitome of 'development' (despite the obvious non-linearity of changes in 'truth' as evident in the case of birth positions) can be considered colonial in contemporary German interventions today.

Notwithstanding the general devaluation of East African obstetric practices during colonialism, German professionals partially acknowledged East African practitioners' knowledge and skills. This might be explainable by the fact that obstetrics in Germany had not yet fully entered the sphere of the hospital and the all-male medical profession; home births with the help of female practitioners were still the norm at the time (Major 2003). Moreover, there was no significant medical advantage of a German physician assisting deliveries through 'Caesarean sections . . . in the pre-antibiotics era in the tropics' (Colwell 2001, 101). Given that maternal mortality was significant in imperial Germany (Bundesinstitut für Bevölkerungsforschung 2014), a sense of superiority must have been harder to uphold. Today, German obstetric care fares so much better statistically, with a maternal mortality rate sixty-six times lower than in Tanzania (CIA World Factbook 2014), which in part explains German development policy's assumption of superiority.

It is striking that commentators in both periods never mentioned the knowledge, skills or functions of East African midwives that were less reconcilable with German biomedicine, such as use of herbs, charms, spiritual powers and communication with 'nonhumans' (cf. Langwick 2011). Today, German professionals also do not take into account that nurses and nurse aides in Tanzanian health facilities often mediate between 'modern' biomedical and 'traditional' healing (Langwick 2011). They also tend to disregard the fact that TBAs often occupy a much broader societal role than merely assisting with birthing (World Health Organization 2005). The colonial-era devaluation of 'non-professional' female knowledge and practice is thus echoed in contemporary German development policy, and the disregard for East African alternative knowledge and practice evidences a colonial legacy in contemporary German development policy.

INSTALLING A HEALTH CARE SYSTEM
FOR EAST AFRICANS

The following sections turn to the specific aspects of planning and attitudes in German 'development abroad' in the area of childbirth. In publications and reports from the colonial era, there is little mention of planning by East Africans in obstetrics or, more generally, health care. German commentators sometimes explicitly stated that they thought Africans were unable to organise their lives. A staff surgeon mentioned East Africans' 'hand-to-mouth life' and 'lack of foresighted planning', which would make it difficult for them to endure the fight for survival (Feldmann 1923, 139). This as well as the general silence regarding East Africans' capacity to plan ahead and organise their lives is revealing as it is grounded in the century-old racist assumption that Africans are people without history and incapable of building a future and that Africa's capacity for progress and development is minimal (cf. Mudimbe 1988). The construct of East Africans as passive and unambitious allowed the German colonising endeavour to assume trusteeship: to 'educate' East Africans to become good Christians, good workers and proper housewives; and to guide them in health matters (cf. Conrad 2004; Akakpo-Numado 2007).

Since East Africans were not seen as capable of planning, thinking about the future or progress, the German colonisers made it their task to look after them. Consequently, the role attributed to colonial health professionals was to 'standardise the living and working conditions of the native workers' masses' (Eckart 1997, 60). As mentioned in chapter 2, the maxim among colonial 'reformists' after the turn of the century was to employ 'theoretical and applied science' for the task of colonisation (Dernburg 1907, 9). Planning and management were fundamental to Germany's colonial endeavours. German doctors, nurses, missionaries and administrators meticulously established statistics (see figure 5.2), planned intervention, discussed infrastructure and financing, and reported on cases of sickness and operations in a lengthy, detailed manner in scientific and government publications. For example, the Medical Department of the Imperial Government of German East Africa implemented a thorough survey of the number of offspring per women, causes of death and so on (Medizinalreferat in Daressalam 1914). Examples of the most comprehensive examinations, documentation and

Familien- (Nachwuchs-) Statistik der Eingeborenen.

Lfde. Nr.	Sanitätsdienststellen	Stamm	Frauen unter 45 Jahre	Aborte	Verstorbene Kinder unter 1 Jahr m	w	Summe	über 1 Jahr m	w	Summe	Lebende Kinder m	w	Summe	Frauen über 45 Jahre	Aborte	Verstorbene Kinder unter 1 Jahr m	w	Summe	über 1 Jahr m	w	Summe	Lebende Kinder m	w	Summe	Todesursachen
1	Oberarzt Dr. Schönebeck (Kilwa)	Wamatumbi, Wangindo, Wayao	62, Alter 24 Jahre	9	?	?	9	?	?	21	18	12	30	42, Alter 41 Jahre	5	—	—	—	16	11	27	16	29	45	Darmkatarrh, Malaria, Framboesie, Lebensschwäche.
2	Derselbe	Desgl.	21, Alter unbekannt, da †	5	—	—	—	?	?	14	17	12	29												
3	Stabsarzt Dr. Schumacher (Mahenge)	Wapogoro	218, Alter 26 Jahre	69	?	?	270	?	?	33	?	?	185												Darmkatarrh, Malaria, Pocken, Framboesie, Erkältungen.
4	Mission Kwiro bei Mahenge	Desgl.	39, Alter 17 Jahre	16	?	?	20	?	?	1	?	?	35												Darmkatarrh, Fieber, Erkältungskrankheiten.
5	Sanitätsunteroffizier (Ssongea)	Wangoni	45, Alter 23 Jahre	40	10	15	25	5	4	7	29	26	55												Durchfälle.
6	Stabsarzt Dr. Penschke (Usumbura)	Warundi, Wawira	21, Alter 31 Jahre	13	12	15	27	6	2	8	20	14	34				1								Darmkatarrh, Fieber, Schlafkrankheit.
7	Stabsarzt Dr. Neubert (Bukoba)	Waiambo	15, Alter 38 Jahre	2	?	?	13	?	?	8	?	?	11	23, Alter 63 Jahre	5	?	?	35	?	?	2	?	2	29	Syphilis, Dysenterie, Pocken.
			441	154			364			92			479	65	10			35			29			74	

Figure 5.2. Statistics of offspring of East African women (Reichs-Kolonialamt 1915, 182–83).

planning undertaken by the German colonial rulers are the Medical Reports on the German Protectorates. These were annually published from 1903/1904 through the end of German occupation by the Colonial Department of the Foreign Office and its successor, the Imperial Colonial Office, with input from the respective administrations in the colonies and included statistics, reports, challenges and plans for the future.

The colonial administration also undertook censuses of the population in 'German East Africa'. The final census, published in 1913, was the most comprehensive and 'still resurfaces in Tanzanian demography as anchor for current population projections' (Colwell 2001, 121). Moreover, a flurry of local demographic and health surveys was undertaken after 1909. The most comprehensive health survey was solicited in 1912 and 1913 by Hugo Meixner (1914), chief medical officer for 'German East Africa', in order to identify the reasons for infant mortality. Meixner requested that all district medical officials submit statistics; the results, based on interviews with 46,503 women, were published in 1914. In order to survey public health issues and make recommendations to the administration, the governor of German East Africa (Gouverneur von Deutsch-Ostafrika 1913) also decreed the establishment of health commissions for each station in which a German physician was deployed. Medical population planning was deemed essential for the growth of the African population. Ludwig Külz, government physician for Togo and Cameroon and an influential commentator on colonial health and population issues, demanded exhaustive gathering of vital data as well as periodic censuses of African populations so that the German colonial administration could properly plan intervention into economic, cultural and medical issues (cited in Schäfer 2007). Physicians developed quantitative demographic methods to monitor disease prevention and population growth (see also chapter 6).

IMPLANTING A 'PLANNING CULTURE'

In my interviews on German development policy today, German professionals often claimed that the poor state of obstetric care in Tanzania was caused by Tanzanian professionals' deficient sense of planning, forethought and management skills. The perception of a deficit in planning is voiced with regard to government departments, individual health facilities, physicians and nurses, and also expectant mothers and their families.

On the national level, German professionals lament a lack of organisation and systematic planning. According to them, the Tanzanian government lacks capacity and is unable to manage the health system (e.g., Interviews 04, 08 and 32). For example, a former manager of the TGPSH 'district health and

quality management' area points to the problems he sees in Tanzania by rais-
ing the issue of drug procurement: 'It cannot be magic to say we need this
and that drug; these 50 drugs should be available in every health centre at all
time. That's not possible, you know. . . . It doesn't work. And it hasn't been
possible for 20 years, for 30 years' (Interview 04, 14 January 2010).

In other interviews, chaos and lack of coordination were brought up.
German professionals regarded administration and management by the Tanzanian government to be chaotic, complicated, bureaucratic and slow (e.g.,
Interviews 18, 19 and 20). For example, a German development professional
advising the Tanzanian government on health financing on behalf of KfW
stated that she needed 'great persistence' to constantly push her Tanzanian
counterparts so that they would work properly (Interview 18, 20 May 2010).
When she received a Tanzanian government department report that she considered to be of high quality, she assumed that it must have been compiled
by Western consultants (Interview 18, 20 May 2010). It seemed to her to be
out of the question that Tanzanian government bodies could deliver what she
considered high-quality work.

Correspondingly, German development professionals invoke the conviction that Tanzanian hospital managers or administrators are not competent
in management, administration or planning (e.g., Interviews 37, 38 and 43).
This estimation is extended to most areas of hospital management, such as
budgeting, organisation, drug procurement, storage, equipment maintenance.
Several of the interviewees working in Tanzanian health facilities mentioned
that there was no proper monitoring of work shifts or planning of operations
and that they had initiated changes in this direction (e.g., Interviews 08, 37,
38 and 43). The following statement by the aforementioned DED physician
who worked in a district hospital addresses the deficits perceived by German
development 'aid' in Tanzanian health care:

> But it is not only how to deal with the medical problems, it's also how to deal
> with administration. How do you write everything in a file, how do we store
> these files. I mean it was a big mess in the hospital. . . . If a patient was coming
> to the hospital, was discharged one week ago, all the files were missing because
> there was no proper storage. So we had to sit together and think of how to deal
> with that. Make a duty roster, who works this night, who works the other night,
> who works in the weekend. Before I came it was quite often the case that there
> was nobody in the hospital. (Interview 08, 14 February 2010)

This quote shows that the German development professional perceives
himself to be instilling order amid chaos. Correspondingly, a former senior
manager of the German health programme for Tanzania mentioned that
German development 'cooperation' was about creating a 'planning culture'
which entailed teaching how to systematically plan and implement projects

(Interview 10, 21 April 2010). Some interviewees considered expertise in 'methods' and 'instruments' for planning to be a specific strength of German 'aid' as compared to other donors (Interview 03, 14 January 2010).

The view of a Tanzanian who used to work as a hospital manager and for German development policy sheds a different light on the matter. He said that many German professionals would almost instantly begin by telling Tanzanian colleagues what they did wrong and what they should change (Interview 52, 30 July 2010). According to this Tanzanian professional, 'development workers' should learn to support existing structures and habits of working: 'You cannot turn our health system into a German health system; you cannot change our management system and want a completely new one'. He suggested that 'development workers' needed to be instructed prior to their deployment that they were going neither to the 'jungle' nor to work with people who did not know anything.

German physicians involved in clinical work or 'capacity building' in hospitals generally complained of a dearth of documentation, systematic thinking and planning. A physician working in a district hospital for DED summarised German 'development cooperation's' difficulty in changing this situation with the phrase that 'it's easy to change the hardware, but hard to change the software' (Interview 43, 9 July 2010). According to him, it was much more difficult to improve Tanzanian staff's knowledge and skills than to, for example, make amendments to hospital infrastructure.

The following excerpt from a conversation with a German nurse working in a hospital as well as a training centre for midwifery in Tanzania is a telling example of how German professionals try to make sense of the problems they see in obstetric care. The frequent use of 'they' in the quote is indicative of the binary form of othering – 'them' and 'us':

> Well, I slowly try to figure out what actually is the problem. I believe that the problem is partly that documentation is tedious, you know. Well . . . because . . . time-consuming . . . I discover that, if they actually write something down at times, they wrote down novels. . . . There is somehow no sense of priorities whatsoever. Then they forget half, which also has to do with the utterly unsystematic story that the nurses write down. That means, I may be able to teach it to them and we have gone through the partograph five times, and now during the exam, I see . . . they still don't know it. And I think that it has to do with the fact that they just don't . . . after I have gone through it with them . . . that they don't see it in practice, that the nurses don't fill it in themselves. That's a problem of time, that . . . we have nine beds in the maternity ward, they are actually always and continuously overcrowded, yes, well, it means you do a birth, then you go to the next, and the next, and then you should actually be writing in between. And I always say the way we learned it, you have to write it down promptly. . . . But that also means that I have to look at the watch. This

way of systematic association, that's missing somehow. And then, I think, they also don't consider it important. I believe they don't see a connection between documentation . . . and the actual outcome. (Interview 29, 8 June 2010)

In this interview extract, the German health worker perceives the ability of young nurses to use the partograph as deficient. An absence of nurses who could serve as role models as well as overcrowding in hospitals and workload are mentioned as factors for deficient documentation. This reference to lack of staff corresponds to official statistics regarding Tanzania's health staff situation. According to the World Health Organization, Tanzania has 'less than half the workforce . . . require[d] to meet essential health needs adequately' (2006, 19). However, other German professionals argued that lack of staff was not really the problem in the institutions of their respective deployments, but rather that Tanzanian staff were not managed well and did not work efficiently (e.g., Interviews 35, 37, 38 and 43). For example, a German CIM (Centre for International Migration) doctor working in a regional hospital in Tanzania said that the area of the hospital for which he was responsible worked well because he properly planned and supervised (Interview 53, 31 July 2010).

   In the previous quote, the German development professional showed some understanding of the deficiencies in organisation when she refers to the time-consuming workload and documentation. However, aside from these structural factors, she mentions that nurses write long narratives ('novels', 'stories') instead of concise information concerning relevant data of the patients. This German professional perceives a lack of ability to think systematically and logically and to transfer technical knowledge to a concrete situation in which action is required. While aware of the 'political incorrectness' of her statement, her overall diagnosis is that Tanzanians (or, even more broadly, Africans) somehow naturally do not have the capacity to think and plan ahead, or to anticipate and consider options:

Well . . . that sounds really racist now perhaps what I'm saying [interviewee laughs], sorry, but, I believe, it has to do with a lacking, well, to do with time, and a . . . not . . . prospective . . . prospective thinking, you know, well, the way we and I mean, I believe, this debate has always existed, how, well, Africans, sense of time, there are also ethnological studies regarding this somehow, that you, that they don't plan, yes. Planning means you are here now and this is your outcome, that's what you want . . . whether it is about, what do I know, that you want to achieve something personally, or as in this case, you want to achieve that the child is doing well and the mother is doing well, and that you . . . contemplate beforehand how you can actually get there. And, I believe, we are like that, that we do not only think of one way, but possibly also the other way and the other way and the other way, and that is sort of like making several plans beforehand. And that is basically what diagnosis signifies; to make a diagnosis means: Where are we now? And then you make a prognosis, i.e. something that comes later in time, now what significance does this have? And then there is the differential diagnosis. And, I have the feeling here that they are always sur- prised . . . you understand, of course all children get born somehow, yes. But . . . they . . . do not think . . . ahead. (Interview 29, 8 June 2010)

First of all, it must be noted that such statements were probably voiced so openly due to my positionality as a white European. We spoke at length several times, and finally carried out a recorded interview sitting in a bar in a posh hotel. She considered me part of the 'we' as opposed to the 'they'. The German nurse tried to understand her nursing students' behaviour through the racialised categories of Africans ('they') and Europeans ('we'). In the quote, it becomes evident that Tanzanians were perceived as living in the present only ('they are always surprised') and lacking foresighted thinking. This allegedly makes them fundamentally incompatible with the biomedical health model which requires abstract thinking and anticipation of different possible outcomes. Other interviewees also assumed that Tanzanians some- how naturally did things differently and had a different sense of planning (e.g., Interview 30, 8 June 2010) and that 'Tanzanians cannot think logically' (Interview 32, 20 June 2010). Tanzanians appear as a homogeneous group incapable of systematic thinking.

Interestingly, such reasoning was also expressed in relation to health- seeking behaviour of expectant mothers and their family members. One inter- viewee who worked as a consultant for BMZ and GTZ and as researcher on reproductive health in Tanzania claimed that Tanzanians, especially in rural areas, had a 'different perception of risk' (Interview 03, 14 January 2010). According to her, 'our' understanding of risk, especially in the epidemiologi- cal sense, had to do with 'probability calculation' and thinking of options, an 'if-then' thinking. She did not find this in Tanzanians and related the perceived deficit to a 'low educational background' and 'traditional beliefs'. Deficits in or nonexistence of planning capacities are thus either explained by socioeconomic circumstances such as educational infrastructure or poor pay, or related to the character of Tanzanians and Tanzanian/African 'culture'.

RELATING THE PRESENT TO THE PAST

Today, German professionals do not necessarily take the task of planning and management into their own hands but attempt to teach Tanzanians what they consider proper planning. While devaluing the knowledge and skills of other people cannot per se be considered colonial, the tendency to relate perceived planning deficits to Tanzanian learning ability or Tanzanian/African 'culture' is racist in that it binds specific (inferior) traits to people grouped together on the basis of origin (cf. Memmi 2000). It relies on the assumption that Africa's capacity for progress and development is minimal. Perceived deficiencies are at times also explained by structural factors, such as socio-economic conditions and educational systems. Even then, the German professionals I interviewed tended to propose universal solutions and stuck to the aim of changing the 'planning culture' so that Tanzanian obstetric care would one day resemble that of the global North. It was portrayed as unable to function properly without trusteeship of German development. Other approaches, as proposed by the Tanzanian hospital manager cited, seemed unperceivable.

At the same time, some German professionals doubted their own usefulness and legitimacy. The Tanzanian health workers' seemingly inexplicable immunity to reform profoundly unsettled their confidence to effect change. Colonial discourses and practices of trusteeship seemed to be undermined. Despite such doubts, German professionals did not seriously question their superior knowledge, the superiority of Western medicine and health care and the need for development intervention. In her study on former Canadian 'aid' workers, Heron points out that the work of development professionals is 'contingent on positioning the Southern Other as available to be changed, saved, improved, and so on, by us, thereby ensuring our entitlement to do so' (2007, 44). However, at the same time, colonial discourse tends to operate on the thesis that 'African culture is not susceptible to change' (Heron 2007, 45). In the case of the policy field under scrutiny here, when intervention fails, Tanzanian society (whether because of structural reasons or the 'nature' of Tanzanians) is held accountable for the failure of German professionals to induce change.

THE 'BITTER STRUGGLE BETWEEN DARKNESS AND LIGHT'

This final part of the chapter looks at how German professionals bring up the question of attitudes with regard to the quality of childbirth-related care in East Africa. Again, it first examines the colonial period and then turns to the present in order to understand the legacy of colonial power in this sphere. The archival material evidences that particular attitudes were considered crucial for quality childbirth-related care in the colonial past. Three issues were highlighted by German commentators with regard to East Africans' attitude towards health matters: timidity, superstition and carelessness. These aspects were continually mentioned by administrators, physicians and missionaries to explain the supposedly poor health situation of mothers and their children in 'German East Africa'.

First, they held that women's 'suspicion and timidity' made them fail to consult German health practitioners; they would only do so in the 'most dire' circumstances (Ittameier 1923, 56, 50). German hospital statistics from the colonial era confirm the reluctance of East African women to attend German health facilities. In the Medical Reports on the German Protectorates of 1903/1904, 1909/1910 and 1911/1912, only 0.12 per cent to 0.19 per cent of the diagnoses issued by government physicians for African patients were for 'female disorder and obstetrics' (cited in Colwell 2001, 89). Influence of elderly women and the persistence of 'customs' of giving birth at home served as explanations for non-attendance (Gouverneur von Deutsch-Ostafrika 1909). Anne Stacie Colwell (2001) understands the argument that East African women were too timid and too culture-bound to consult German health facilities as a strategy – 'the trope of the timid tribeswoman' – to blame African women and their 'culture' for their lack of attendance of European health facilities, rather than the dearth or lack of facilities to accommodate women. This allegedly allowed the German administration to legitimise its reluctance to invest in curative health services for East Africans, especially for women. According to Colwell, East African women kept their distance from the colonisers' health care because German government facilities did not cater to women in their infrastructure (lack of wards and beds) and because of stories of women who had gone to deliver in the facilities and had died or lost their babies. This argument implies that women (or their families) would actually have wanted to attend the hospitals, had they been more efficient and accommodating. Colwell's reasoning is grounded in her assumption that East African women actually consulted mission health facilities to a larger extent than those of the colonial government because they were more accommodating to East African women. However, I find no indication in Colwell's study or elsewhere supporting the hypothesis that large numbers of women attended mission hospitals specifically for birthing. On the contrary, Bernita Walter's (1992) analysis of the mission archive of the Benedictine Sisters of South-East Tanzania and Walter Bruchhausen's (2006) study of health and medicine in Tanzania point to the fact that mission facilities had significant problems attracting East African women for pregnancy-related issues and delivery. For example, a German mission annalist from Kwiro wrote in 1911 that '[o]ur young women would have none of the help of the midwifery sisters. They rather stick to the desturi [customs, DB] of their elders' (cited in Walter 1992, 312–13). German missionaries put a lot of effort into drawing East African women to their facilities (Walter 1992) and were probably aware that 'African "midwives" . . . exercised a large degree of social and moral control which had to be broken if Christianity was to succeed' (Vaughan 1991, 66). The complexity of birthing practices and their embeddedness in societal and political life among many East African societies are well documented (Green 1999; Blystad 1999). It thus seems more plausible to assume that East African women did not consult German health facilities, be they missionary or governmental, because the whole process of birthing was too important for the social and cultural reproduction of East African societies to be opened up to and controlled by German missionaries, doctors and the colonial administration.

German commentators explained poor obstetric health conditions for East African women also by pointing to their alleged superstition and indifference. The following quote by a staff surgeon is an example of such a position. He argued that a transformation of people's 'psyche' through schooling and mission was necessary:

> You the increase of purely intellectual education, as conveyed by the school, one can, of course, already achieve a considerable part of this [cultural, DB] elevation; superstitious beliefs can be pushed back through such an instruction, their effectiveness can be eliminated, and a certain degree of positive knowledge in child care and care of the sick can be conveyed through schools. . . . However, considerably more valuable are the impacts of mission work, if it leads to a heightened sense of responsibility towards children and for hygienic aspects in general. . . . Since the basis of the pagan treatment of the ill – animism, dread of ghosts and raw selfishness – relies on fear, a sensible care of the ill and of children can only be achieved by the destruction of that basis and new directions for the psyche of the natives. This task is first of all one for the mission. It is basically a bitter struggle between the darkness of the pagan being and the light of Christian insight and charity whose instrument is the mission. The institutions behind the mission work are capable of restricting and eliminating the fatal influence of pagan mothers, grandmothers, mothers-in-law as well as sorcerers. (Feldmann 1923, 140–42)

Superstition was seen as defining characteristics of East African health care. German professionals held people's belief in 'spirits and magic' accountable for inadequate responses to diseases (Ittameier 1923, 54). The quote evidences that it was women in particular who were seen as disseminating and perpetuating superstitious beliefs. This brings to mind the way 'wise women' and their knowledge and influence were deemed dangerous in the European Middle Ages, resulting in their persecution, torture and murder, and in the eradication of invaluable knowledge (Becker, Bovenschen, and Brackert 1977). That German colonisers in East Africa resorted to the dichotomies of Christian/pagan, rational/superstitious, hygienic/dirty and (en)light(ened)/ dark to understand East African maternal and child health care mirrors British colonising efforts in Africa in which Western ways of birthing were similarly represented as the epitome of 'sanitary virtue and enlightenment' (Nestel 1998, 267). The means by which a change of mindsets was to be achieved was first and foremost seen in the 'patient, educational work' of Christian-isation and schooling (Feldmann 1923, 127). Christianisation was seen as a means to instil not only 'enlightened' rationality but also the values of 'char-ity' and compassion. Other practices deemed to be pagan such as infanticide and abortions were prosecuted by more forceful means.

German commentators during colonisation did not only deplore 'supersti-tious beliefs', but they also accused the colonised people of carelessness and indifference regarding health care and childbirth-related care in particular. In the previous quote, this is evidenced in the reference to a low 'sense of responsibility' and 'selfishness'. East Africans were said to be inaccessible to advice and training (Feldmann 1923) and indifferent to proper infant care (Reichs-Kolonialamt 1913). According to a letter by Mission Superintendent Karl Axenfeld (1907), 'the afflictive health conditions are . . . particularly caused by the Negro's lethargy'. Some observers even stated that certain peoples ('tribes') almost completely disregarded children (Van der Burgt 1914). Portraying mothers as careless was not specific to German colonisa-tion of East Africa but common in many contexts in which colonisers were concerned about population decline after the turn of the twentieth century (Jolly 1998).

POST-MODERN BIRTHING

In contemporary German development policy, professionals also refer to Tanzanians' mindset and attitudes in order to assess health care around child-birth. Here, two important issues emerge: motivation and compassion. In my interviews, several German development professionals characterised nurses, and also doctors and the political elites working in the health field, as indif-ferent, 'apathetic', 'unmotivated', 'idle' and 'not enthusiastic' (Interviews 29, 37, 28, 54 and 53). Many German development staff mentioned a lack of initiative of Tanzanians working in the health sector (e.g., Interview 43, 9 July 2010). As long as everything was provided by donors, things would happen, but as soon as the flow of money stopped or a little extra effort was required, activities would stop immediately. This was regarded as running across different levels – the individual Tanzanian health worker, hospital management and political decision-making. For example, according to a doctor working for DED in a Tanzanian district hospital, nurses did not find it problematic to be ignorant and refused to criticise colleagues for wrongdo-ings (Interview 37, 25 June 2010). During training workshops they would allegedly reproduce inert knowledge, that is, present what they had read or heard without being aware of what they were talking about. Without showing any sign of embarrassment, nurses would engage in 'PowerPoint karaoke', by which she meant that they read out PowerPoint slides without understanding their content. None of the attending nurses would ask questions afterwards. This German development professional explained what she perceived as indifferent and inappropriate attitudes by referring to a general lack of accountability and public scrutiny of civil servants in Tanzania, to a 'culture' of not thinking independently and voicing criticism and to an intrinsic indifference of Tanzanians.

In the following excerpt, a German physician speaks of the way pregnant women are treated by Tanzanian nurses in the hospital in which she is deployed:

> You just have the feeling that every patient who enters is perceived as a source of irritation, who interrupts the nurses drinking tea. . . . If you come from outside and, moreover, you have a European head on your shoulders, you find some things really horrible. I fetched the hospital director a week ago, because I really could not bear it any longer. They let the people give birth on a wooden board in the toilet. And next door there are two wonderful delivery beds, but these wonderful delivery beds are reserved for when somebody from the family or the staff comes. (Interview 35, 22 June 2010)

Several interviewees complained of the absence of empathy for pregnant women and mothers. Tanzanian nurses allegedly did not care about the psychological or emotional well-being of their patients and sometimes even resorted to verbal as well as physical violence in order to assert their authority. Here, German health professionals saw it as their task to convey compassionate midwifery, which, according to them, meant looking patients in the eye, massaging expectant mothers and generally taking the needs of patients seriously. Compassion among Tanzanians was allegedly only reserved for their next of kin (Interview 35, 22 June 2010). Midwifery in Tanzania was perceived as highly 'programmed' and not very 'interpersonal' (Interview 15, 21 April 2010). This interviewee compared such attitude to practices in Germany thirty years prior and criticised it as too 'modern' in the sense of too mechanistic and not sufficiently sensitive. Here, 'modernity' ironically means backwardness. She contrasted this to the current state of the art in Germany, where midwives have 'become a little bit more generous' and regard giving birth as something 'individual'. German professionals reported that the supine position was favoured in Tanzania because it allowed practitioners to exert maximum control over birth processes and women in labour. They claimed that Tanzanian nurses or doctors would not consider squatting down because it would question the hierarchy between patients and staff. Here, Tanzanian hospital staff is construed as authoritarian and insensitive, and the German professionals consider it professional to squat down with patients and disregard and overcome differences in status and class. For the German health workers I interviewed, professionalism apparently includes empathy and compassion. They perceive themselves not only as enhancing Tanzanian health workers' technical skills but also as improving the interpersonal level of health care. A DED development worker in a Tanzanian district hospital, for instance, explained to me how he had made sure to separate delivery beds with boards and curtains so that women giving birth had more privacy (Interview 43, 9 July 2010). Crude, mechanical Tanzanian midwifery is thus differentiated from caring, sensitive, post-modern German midwifery providing the 'clients' with privacy and room to express their individuality freely (cf. Ahrendt 2012).

There is, however, a striking contrast between this concern for privacy and empathy and the way I was often shown around hospitals by German professionals. They commonly offered to lead me – a 'white' male without a function in the hospital setting – into full maternity wards. After I mentioned that I found it disturbing to just be led into a maternity ward without the patients' consent, several of my German interviewees stated that this was not a problem in Tanzania and that people's bodies were generally much more public (Interviews 29 and 53). It was striking that the physician who had applauded the visual separation in maternity wards invited me to put my ear to the belly of a woman and to listen to the heartbeat of her embryo. From the reaction of the delivering woman, who only just managed to cover her breasts and pubic area, it was clear that she was uncomfortable with this and that my (male) interview partner had not asked her permission. The fact that I complied and actually tried to listen to the heartbeat still troubles me today. Her body was not public because people's bodies in Tanzania were inherently more public than in Germany, but it was made public by two white men who encroached upon her privacy despite the fact that one of these men had earlier on boasted of improvements initiated by German development 'cooperation' to increase patients' privacy.

RELATING THE PRESENT TO THE PAST

In ongoing development policy as well as during German colonial rule, matters of attitude serve to construct difference and hierarchy between German and East African obstetric care. In the characterisation of Tanzanian health practices in current German development policy, superstition does not play an important role. Instead, Tanzanian professionals are described as unmotivated, rude and lacking compassion. There is some common ground here, however: Germans in both periods constructed East Africans as inactive, relating their inactivity to backwardness (cf. Mbembe 2001). Today, however, structural factors are sometimes also invoked as explanations for problems in health care. As mentioned before, this cannot be considered colonial thinking as such. Yet, Tanzanians' attitude is also related to a specific 'culture' of indifference and carelessness and thereby racialised.

Comparing contemporary with German colonial-era intervention indicates a noteworthy shift. In colonial times Tanzanian health care was perceived as not modern enough and insufficiently medicalised, a view that can be explained by the fact that state bodies and doctors in Germany tried to regulate and medicalise midwifery as much as possible at the turn of the twentieth century (cf. Szász, Stiefel, and Tschernko 2012). Today, midwifery in Tanzania is regarded as too regulated and lacking in compassion. Since the 1980s, medicalisation of birthing has been increasingly criticised in Germany, and home births and 'family-oriented midwifery' have become popular again (Szász, Stiefel, and Tschernko 2012). Given that medical knowledge and practice constantly advance, the shifting German notions of quality obstetric care are not surprising. Yet to establish one's own knowledge – regardless of its provisionality – as universal norm and to project it onto the lives of people in the global South, without being interested in or capable of interacting with the others, bear traces of colonial power.

CONCLUSION

The focus on the policy field of childbirth-related care and its implementation in the specific context of German-East African relations has allowed for a detailed understanding of whether colonial power affects contemporary development policy abroad. It became evident that German professionals continue to establish a fundamental hierarchy between themselves and East Africans in their assessment of Tanzanian childbirth-related practices. However, the ways in which German professionals make sense of Tanzanian midwifery are complex. If perceived deficiencies are explained with reference to social factors such as education or lack of public scrutiny, this cannot be considered colonial.

That is the case, however, when estimations are based on race, which is the case when professionals relate perceived deficiencies to notions of an intrinsic Tanzanian character, 'culture' or even 'Africanness' (cf. Kothari 2006a). From the perspective of German professionals in the past and today, childbirth-related practices in East Africa have always lagged behind, and East African alternative knowledge and practice is disregarded. German interventions into childbirth-related attitudes throughout are justified with reference to Germany's construct of itself as epitome of progress. Accordingly, what Germans considered the norm was projected onto East Africa: professionalism, rationality and Christianity during colonialism, and rational planning, empathy and sensitivity in the present. In addition to positing teleological developmentalism, German professionals have thus always regarded themselves as having to guide East Africans towards German standards of birthing. This shows that the practice of trusteeship – imposing Western epistemology and modes of organisation – on the global South is ever-present.

Despite the observation that contemporary German development policy on obstetric care in Tanzania tends to re-articulate racialisation, developmentalism and trusteeship, interventions today are marked by considerable hesitancy and realisation of ineffectiveness. Frustrated by the lack of success, some development professionals have to make an effort to keep up their self-image as able to mould the world (cf. Dyer 1997). The manner in which they dealt with their frustrations substantiates the finding that 'representations in the development aid context are characterized by hesitancy and a degree of self-reappraisal over time, which co-exist . . . with the location of the problem in Africa and the solution in the West' (Eriksson Baaz 2005, 164). While uncertain about the value of their work and approaches, German professionals eventually located the problem in Tanzania and could not imagine other ways of teaching midwifery. All in all, it can be said that while colonial power is alive in contemporary development policy abroad in the specific case under scrutiny, the sense of entitlement to change Tanzanian practices is fractured due to practical experiences of development professionals in their day-to-day work.

Chapter 6

Controlling Population in East Africa

Why should experts behave otherwise!
Are they the salesmen of white ideas,
The creators of demand for their countries' products.

– Tanzanian poet B. R. Nchimbi 1977, 167–68

To further examine colonial power in Germany's development abroad in yet more depth, this final empirical chapter turns to the field of population policy and again traces contemporary endeavours back to the colonial past. As mentioned in chapter 5, the German colonial administration had been concerned about 'population decline' in 'German East Africa'. In contrast, current German government and non-governmental organisation (NGO) development policies in Tanzania are worried about population growth. Colonial fears of 'depopulation' have transitioned into fears of 'overpopulation'. As discussed in chapter 2, development policy on 'Sexual and Reproductive Health and Rights' (SRHR), particularly since the Cairo Conference in 1994, is commonly perceived as people-centred and human rights-based and no longer aimed at population control. However, studies suggest that population control agendas have not disappeared from contemporary international endeavours in the global South and that these tend to reproduce racialised views on women in the global South (Wilson 2017). Scholars have also argued that intervention into population and reproductive health tends to serve the political and economic interests of the global North (Bandarage 1997). Building on these critiques and focusing on the specific case of German interventions into population in Tanzania today and in 'German East Africa' in the past, this chapter continues the exploration of colonial power in current German development policy abroad.

First, this chapter introduces ideas and practices regarding issues of population with regard to colonialism and international development, as well as Germany's particular involvement in this realm. The next two sections scrutinise the explanations provided by German actors for population decline during colonialism and for population growth during German development 'assistance', as well as the practical interventions which have been proposed and carried out in order to control population size. The following two sections examine the justification German actors have provided for intervening in population and reproductive health matters in both periods under scrutiny. The analysis of legitimising strategies for German intervention is complemented by an examination of whether German population control policies and practices in both periods have been interconnected with political-economic interests. Just like in chapter 5, this analysis is based on scientific and government publications as well as archival sources of the colonial administration from ca. 1905 through the formal end of German colonial rule and on documents of contemporary German development 'cooperation' as well as semi-structured interviews with German development professionals. I should stress here again that this examination focuses on German perspectives of colonial rule as well as development 'cooperation' and does not account for the perspectives of East Africans.

THE HISTORY OF POPULATION POLICY, COLONIALISM AND DEVELOPMENT

European thinking on population has its origin in the seventeenth century (Foucault 1979). The eighteenth century witnessed the advent of increasing academic work on population and reproduction (Ferdinand 1999) – with Robert Malthus's famous 'An Essay on the Principle of Population' published in 1798. This was situated in the context of mercantilism, and the development of capitalism would not have been possible without the adjustment of population to economic processes. According to Barbara Duden, conceiving 'people' as 'population' reduced 'persons to bloodless entities that can be managed as characterless classes that reproduce, pollute, produce or consume, and for the common good, call for control' (1997, 149). People were henceforth conceived in terms of indicators such as birth rate/fertility, mortality, health that need to be statistically measured and regulated in order to align with capitalism.

The emergence of policies by countries of the global North with regard to population and reproduction in the global South is commonly dated to the 1940s and 1950s, when population growth in colonised and newly independent territories began to be viewed as problematic, and birth control was propagated as necessary (Hartmann 1997a). The first period post-World War II (post-WWII), ending in the late 1950s, was dominated by the fear of overpopulation which was thought to threaten global resources and national security (mainly of the USA). The dominant demographic transition theory centred on the relation between economic growth and population size. It was strongly influenced by the ideology of modernisation, holding that capitalist 'development' would naturally lead to a decline in birth rates. This theory was joined in the 1960s by the so-called orthodox position that 'holds that lowering population must be achieved directly by supplying modern contraceptives to people in the Third World' (Halfon 1997, 128). The 1960s and 1970s constituted the high point of population politics. In the 1980s, new topics such as environment and migration emerged on the international population policy agenda (Schultz 2006). Some demographic approaches put forward a causal relationship between natural resources and population, which implied that less people would mean less resource consumption and environmental degradation (Hummel 2007). The more sophisticated idea of a 'carrying capacity' acted on the assumption that the number of people; characteristics of ecological space; and social, cultural and spatial forms of organisation are interrelated in a non-causal, complex manner (Hummel 2007). International development agendas have continued to be shaped by the demographic transition theory, the orthodox position, concerns about the environment and migration (Halfon 1997).

While the change in approach towards reproductive health in the context of the Cairo Conference 1994 is widely regarded as radical, scholars have pointed to the persistence of demographic goals after the Cairo Conference (Rao and Sexton 2010). According to Schultz (2006), a compromise between the contradicting paradigms of demographic control and people's right to freely decide on their number of children was achieved through promotion of individualised, neoliberal politics. Thus, international organisations, states and NGOs grant women the right to have as many children as they desire but focus on 'educating' them on the health risks and economic disadvantages of having 'too many' children and having them 'too early' and 'too close to one another'. With reference to women's responsibility for their own well-being, child-bearing is thus discouraged and use of contraceptives encouraged. Rather than challenging demographic goals, the Cairo Consensus thus resulted in their persistence and a dilution of originally radical feminist stances against population control (Sexton and Nair 2010).

As pointed out in chapter 5, discussions by colonial administrations regarding population decline had already been initiated at the beginning of the twentieth century in the context of colonial reforms towards 'rationality' and 'efficiency'. Colonised people were perceived in economic terms as part of the wealth of colonising nations, and European colonial reformists began to discuss ways of increasing population growth (Grosse 2000). Rather than beginning the story of population politics of the North in the South in the 1940s, this chapter thus suggests the need to examine the emergence of the Northern developmental concern with population size and reproductive practices of colonised societies at the turn of the twentieth century. At the heart of German discussions on population and reproduction in 'German East Africa' were birth rates; induced abortions, miscarriages and premature births; and infant and child mortality. In addition, aspects such as migration, housing and diet were blamed for unfavourable health conditions. The primary aim of the colonial administration was to supply German economic endeavours with a male workforce.

Following WWI, the British colonisers of East Africa continued to be concerned with 'underpopulation' (Allen 2002). After independence in 1961, the Tanzanian government rejected the international population control agenda for two decades (Richey 2008). The 1980s witnessed a gradual acceptance of dominant international health and population policy as a result of pressure by UNFPA, World Bank and USAID (Richey 2008). Especially since the mid-1980s, in the light of Structural Adjustment Programmes, state health service spending has been considerably reduced, and private clinics, NGOs and development projects have proliferated and replaced many functions formerly provided by the state (Lugalla 1995; Chachage and Mbilinyi 2003). The Tanzanian health sector is heavily dependent on donor money: for example, for the fiscal year 2011/2012, 41 per cent of the health budget was provided by donors (Policy Forum 2012).

Contemporary German development policy generally evidences the rhetoric of the post-Cairo agenda. At the same time, population growth in some countries, particularly on the African continent, is seen as still too high. While this is not put forward as the only reason for development problems, it supposedly 'impinge[s] on development progress' or 'hamper[s] . . . development' (BMZ 2014a, 3–4, see also BMZ 2008, 5). In the past years, the integrated concept of SRHR seems to have lost influence, and one can observe a stronger focus on isolated family planning once again (Bendix and Schultz 2018). UNFPA and the U.S. Agency for International Development (USAID) expanded their spending on contraceptives between 2006 and 2013 considerably – UNFPA from US\$ 74 million to US\$ 152 million and USAID from US\$ 63 million to US\$ 98 million (UNFPA 2013a, 41; 2014, 52). The German government invested US\$ 142 million in population programmes in 'developing countries' in 2015 (OECD 2016). In terms of contraceptive procurement, German spending has seen an increase in recent years: In 2013, it reached a new peak when KfW invested US\$ 29 million in contraceptives (UNFPA 2013a, 41; 2014, 27). This trend seems to be reinforced by Germany's latest commitments within the international Family Planning Initiative

FP2020 programme. In 2016, the German government announced that it would commit at least €514 million until 2019 to reproductive health and family planning, with 'twenty-five percent of its bilateral funding . . . likely to be dedicated directly to family planning' (FP2020 2016). Two German companies – Bayer and HELM Medical – are among UNFPA's biggest suppliers. Bayer generated more income from contraceptive commodities in 2012 and 2013 than any other pharmaceutical company (UNFPA 2012, 2013b).

POPULATION DECLINE, THE 'NEW ERA' AND THE SOCIETAL POSITION OF WOMEN

Let us now turn to the empirical examination of German interventions regarding population and begin with a scrutiny of colonial times. During German occupation of East Africa, German colonial reformists did not consider the number of births 'sufficient . . . for the survival or even growth of these African peoples' (Ittameier 1923, 7–8). 'Population decline' was, first of all, associated with a transformation in economic and social organisation due to labour migration and consequent disintegration of rural communities (Van der Burgt 1913; Deutsche Gesellschaft für Eingebornenschutz 1914b). While they did not condemn colonisation as such, several German physicians and missionaries criticised the carelessness of the colonial administration, entrepreneurs and farmers with regard to the way East Africans were exploited as labour. The following excerpt is an example of such a stance and refers to the effects of labour migration and exploitation of East Africans:

> The youngest and strongest individuals, i.e. those most suitable for procreation, are removed from these areas. Their huts decay, agriculture is reaching a low, family ties are loosened, adultery and polygamy increase, the number of children – already low in polygamist marriages – becomes fewer and fewer. Besides the dissolution of marriage and family ties which formerly, in the primitive state, were strong, there are other negative consequences, among them concubinage, prostitution, abortion, reluctance to give birth and have children, venereal diseases and high child mortality, and an increase of women and child labour. . . . The emergence of a proletariat which is inevitable in the case of such concentrations of people has negative effects on fertility. (Peiper 1920a, 433–34)

Otto Peiper, a senior staff surgeon in Kilwa from 1908 to 1911, relates the colonisers' removal of able-bodied men from their homes to work on plantations and in other colonial enterprises to the destruction of subsistence agriculture, the transformation of family organisation and generally the formation of a proletariat. Such socio-economic changes were regarded as reasons for a

declining birth rate, high prevalence of abortions and infant and child mortality –
in short, factors inhibiting population growth.

Furthermore, colonial reformists at the beginning of the twentieth century
were concerned that the imposition of European 'culture' might destroy the
colonised communities. Living conditions perceived by the colonisers to be
primitive were allegedly thrown out of balance by the 'new era' (Vohsen and
Westermann 1914, 66). The German Society for the Protection of the Natives,
for example, warned that the 'flood of new life' – 'unfamiliar, incomprehen-
sible beliefs, hitherto unknown wants and desires, and the means to satisfy
them' – transformed and threatened East African people's living conditions
and led to a halt or decline in population growth (Deutsche Gesellschaft für
Eingebornenschutz 1914b, 2–3). These estimations were based on the concept of the 'extinction of the primitive peoples' that was formulated by liberal
anthropology in the mid-nineteenth century (Grosse 2000). European anthro-
pologists had argued that the transformation of living conditions as a result of
colonisation endangered the survival of colonised peoples. These ideas resur-
faced in the phase of colonial reform at the turn of the twentieth century. East
Africans were seen as living in 'primitive', 'natural' conditions which were
disrupted by contact with the allegedly complicated, 'sophisticated' German
'culture'. Such deliberations were based on a distinction between a static
'traditional' situation in East Africa and a complex, flexible, moving German
'modernity' (cf. Mbembe 2001). Detrimental effects of 'modernity' were
similarly discussed within Germany with regard to the domestic situation.
Since the end of the nineteenth century, a decline in births among the 'lower
classes' had become an issue of public debate: 'proletarianisation', 'break-up
of families' and the spread of venereal diseases and abortions were discussed
and interpreted as negative consequences of 'modernity' (Sauerteig 2001).

In addition to the idea that colonial occupation and exploitation caused
population decline, German professionals pointed out problems they saw as
inherent to East African societies. The following statement by Carl Ittameier,
physician for the Leipziger Mission Society in Moshi, is a good example of
such a perception which links 'miscarriages' (one of the reasons given for
'population decline') to women's societal roles:

> the position of women in the social body . . . has to be regarded as low. Women
> are more or less without rights. Without going too far, one may say that the
> workforce of women is being exploited to the extreme. In the light of the heavy
> work which one sees women do, it is not surprising that this burden is one of the
> principal reasons for miscarriages. (Ittameier 1923, 25–26)

In addition to hard labour (here, referring to work on the family homestead
rather than in German enterprises), German reformists highlighted male polygamy, abusive sexual relations of older men with young girls and other alleged

'customs' as reasons for women's low social position, which harmed their health, led to spontaneous and induced abortions and caused low fertility as well as a high rate of child mortality (Peiper 1920a; Van der Burgt 1913). Pointing to repressive gender relations among colonised people was a common strategy used in colonising nations in order to establish racialised difference between colonisers and colonised and to legitimise colonial imposition (Oyèwùmí 2005; Spivak 2003). German colonial stakeholders' discussions of population decline in 'German East Africa' established a racialised hierarchy between themselves and East Africans on the basis of 'cultural' difference, particularly through reference to allegedly oppressive gender relations in East African societies.

Having ascertained a birth decline in East Africa, German reformists deduced that 'a strong advocacy for the protection and advancement of the coloured people has never been more necessary than today' (Deutsche Gesellschaft für Eingebornenschutz 1914b, 3). They sought to improve the situation of the colonised and to fight population decline 'through all available hygienic, social and similar means, especially to increase the birth rate and to lower child mortality' (Reichs-Kolonialamt 1914, 78). Research into the issue of 'birth decline' and measures to counter it were encouraged. The eminent colonial entrepreneur Eduard Woermann and his company, for example, donated 6,000 German Marks to encourage ideas promoting 'increase of the birth rate and a reduction of infant mortality in the native population' (Der Professorenrat des Hamburgischen Kolonialinstituts 1913, 567). The two winners, Carl Ittameier and Hermann Feldmann, both based their studies on 'German East Africa', where they had worked as physicians. Their proposals and those of other commentators ranged from strict regulation and control to those which sought to 'civilise' or 'modernise' East Africans through less explicitly forceful means. In the following quote, colonial physician and scientist Külz, who had led a demographic-medical 'expedition' to 'German New-Guinea' for the Reichs-Kolonialamt in 1913 and 1914, mentions interventions relying on regulation through force (he refers to the German 'tropical colonies' as a whole):

> [The increase of the birth rate through the containment of all harms, DB] entails all measures for a protection of Negro mothers as such: through surveillance and restriction of coloured prostitution, fighting the excesses of polygamy . . . sparing of women or complete containment from porter services; particularly, however, intervention against abortions, which have become rampant in many places. (Külz 1913, 327)

This quote provides evidence that East African women were paternalistically constructed as needing protection from East African men, from exploitative colonial practices such as 'porter services', and from their own practices of abortion.

The recruitment of East Africans for labour on plantations and elsewhere was regulated by decrees by the governor in 1909 and 1913 and included a ban on enlisting women (Gouverneur von Deutsch-Ostafrika 1913). 'Prostitutes' (as the taken-for-granted cause of the spread of venereal diseases) were required by law to register with the local 'inspection of the prostitutes' (Colwell 2001, 92). Missionaries, physicians and administrators advocated for legally restricting polygamy or discouraging it through taxes, but this was not put into effect. Furthermore, German commentators were unanimously in favour of prosecuting those responsible for abortions (Van der Burgt 1913; Ittameier 1923).

While anti-abortion laws were never codified, the following quote indicates that abortions were persecuted by German administrators responsible for upholding colonial rule in the districts in 'German East Africa': 'The punishment that the government sets on these things [abortions, infanticide etc., DB] may prevent the effectuation of a number of these customs' (Feldmann 1923, 110). In light of the fact that it must have been extremely difficult to actually punish people carrying out abortions – a situation similar to that in Germany at the time (Seidler 1993) – there are no indications in the archives (or in recent academic studies) that such punishments actually took place in 'German East Africa'. However, the German staff surgeon Wolff noted that 'now and then barks and small pieces of wood, which are allegedly used for abortive treatments, are taken away from native doctors' (cited in Peiper 1920b, 18). This statement evidences that the German colonial administration de facto did persecute those East Africans who provided assistance with abortions.

In addition to such strict regulation and control, social policies and interventions aimed at changing belief systems were proposed in order to increase population numbers. As already mentioned in chapter 5, the suggested measures included – on the one hand – increasing the number of German doctors and midwives in German health facilities, training East Africans in nursing and midwifery and building health facilities and – on the other – propagating Christianity and education on hygiene, maternity and infant care. It was also deemed necessary to develop institutions to gather data on births, deaths and diseases; set up epidemic institutes; and even pay premiums for having children (Feldmann 1923).

As mentioned earlier, policies tended to aim towards a change in women's social position. A transformation of female (and male) roles was expected to improve the health of women, to yield higher birth rates and to allow women to better look after their children. Christianity was perceived as particularly appropriate for transforming relations between men and women. Mission physician Ittameier expressed the all-embracing curative effect of proselytisation as follows:

[C]onveying Christianity to the natives should bear fruit. It should manifest itself in the moral uplifting of the people. The woman should be uplifted from her low position, in which the man only appreciated her as workforce or effectively as a slave. She would become a companion to the man, who shares the work fairly with her. Attention and care of the children would become more thorough. Practically, the value of an influence through Christianity has to manifest itself in a decline of abortions or miscarriages, in reduced child mortality and an increase in births. (1923, 56)

Monogamy and certain gender roles were, above all, introduced and propagated by missions. The aim was for women to 'receive the position accorded to her by nature's order: the concern for the upbringing and care of the children as well as keeping house' (Peiper 1920a, 457). European notions of what constituted femininity and masculinity were thus introduced and propagated, with a subsequent transformation of gender relations to the disadvantage of women (cf. Oyèwùmí 2005; Lugones 2008). According to Colwell (2001), advocacy of monogamy – in combination with the spread of male wage labour and thus the absence of men from homesteads – meant that women had less support and had to shoulder field work and other tasks on their own, which had not been the case when they had co-wives. The gender roles promoted were highly patriarchal, reflecting the hetero-normative capitalist-bourgeois gender relations in Germany at the time (Usborne 1994).

POPULATION GROWTH, THE NEED FOR AN 'UNMET NEED' AND GENDER RELATIONS

Having ascertained the prevalence of racialised, gendered discourses and practices during colonial rule, I now examine how population size and reproduction are understood in the context of contemporary German development 'cooperation'. Present-day German development policy considers the 'high population growth in Tanzania of 2.9%' excessive (GTZ 2010). While German development agents commonly mention Africa as a whole as cause for concern due to high fertility rates (DSW 2010), the Tanzanian rate of approximately 5.5 children per woman is considered particularly alarming (evaplan 2009). References to gender relations and women's social position are omnipresent in contemporary policy on population and reproductive health, and one of the three 'guiding principles for a comprehensive approach' in this field is termed a 'gender-sensitive approach' (BMZ 2008, 6–7). This emphasis on women and gender is particularly attributable to feminist struggles prior to, during and following the 1994 Cairo Conference.

German development policy documents do not explicitly link gender relations to population growth. The connection is rather indirectly invoked through discussion of women's oppression and SRHR. 'Gender-based violence' and oppressive gender relations are associated with women's lack of 'decision-making' ability in issues of sexuality:

> Widespread gender-based discrimination against women, deficits in legal certainty and a lack of true gender equality are structural factors which contribute to violence and abuse against women and girls and to their being unable to make their own decisions or protect themselves. . . . In many societies, women are not in a position to make decisions about whether sexual contacts take place in a safe or unsafe, forced or voluntary way. (BMZ 2008, 7)

Whether women's and girls' oppression has influence on fertility or population growth is not spelled out in this key German policy document. Yet, as discussed in detail later, German development agents are convinced that if women were to decide freely, they would opt for fewer children.

Interviews with development professionals point more explicitly to a connection between gender and population growth. German professionals see women in Tanzania as having no say in sexual and reproductive matters, as oppressed by their male partners and as reduced to child-bearing. In the words of a former senior manager of the German health programme in Tanzania, Tanzanian men do not 'give a shit' about whether their female partners feel like having sex or want more children (Interview 10, 21 April 2010). According to my interviewees, women in Tanzania have little control over their sexual and reproductive lives due to societal oppression and discrimination, and this leads them to have more children than they desire and can care for (Interviews 08, 31 and 37). It is this reasoning that establishes causality between gender relations and population growth. Societal structures and norms pertaining to gender are thus held responsible for high fertility and population growth.

High birth rates of Tanzanian women are generally interpreted as signs of backwardness by German development actors. This is exemplified by the following statement by a desk officer at the headquarters of the German Development Bank (KfW): 'And one sees as well that the fertility rates are still high, that, I would say, the whole context in Tanzania is still very conservative with regard to women, with regard to the societal stance of women. But also, I would say, one looks within the family and so on, it still is very classical and goes hand in hand with a certain oppression' (Interview 14, 18 March 2010). The adjective 'conservative' and the adverb 'still' point to the assumption of linear societal progress. It is taken for granted that 'there is just a huge demand for fewer births', 'because the people are also more informed, more urban, incomes improve, these usual, normal processes' (Interview 11, 19 March 2010). Another interviewee also stated that once Tanzanians became wealthier, they would naturally want fewer children; this occurred elsewhere, so 'why shouldn't it happen in Africa' (Interview 29, 8

June 2010). Thus, a low fertility rate is not only seen characteristic of 'modernity', but 'modernity' is also understood as leading to the desire for fewer children. High population growth and fertility rates as well as associated oppressive gender relations serve as indicators for ascertaining Tanzania's lack of 'modernity'. In line with the idea of a 'demographic transition', which every society is supposedly bound to undergo on its way to 'modernity' (Halfon 1997), Tanzania is thus homogenously constructed as 'traditional', as 'culturally' different from, and inferior to, 'modern' societies.

According to German development 'cooperation', its involvement in reproductive health is in accordance with the principles of the Cairo Conference, as it has supposedly moved 'from a mainly demographically-oriented to a people-centred and human-rights-based approach' (BMZ 2008, 4). In combination with the goal of lowering population growth, this is a contradictory objective which has been referred to as 'ideological schizophrenia' by the Committee on Women, Population, and the Environment in 1999. Voicing that a population reduction policy in Tanzania was not necessary because people had a 'natural' desire for family planning (Interview 11, 19 March 2010) implies that the dissemination of 'modern' contraceptives can be presented as a response to demands by Tanzanians. Assumptions that there is a high 'unmet need' for contraceptives in Tanzania and that women desire to have fewer children than they actually have (evaplan 2009; GTZ 2009) are, however, called into question by reports suggesting that the desired family size was 5.4 children for married women and 5.9 for married men at the time of my research, and thus about as high as the actual fertility rate (Leahy and Druce 2009).

When faced with the situation of no explicit 'unmet need', German development professionals formulate the exigency to create a need for 'modern' contraceptives. This is spelled out in the following quote from my interview with a manager of the TGPSH reproductive health area:

> Before I came here, Tanzania was a country for me . . . in which the topic population growth was extremely prominent. . . . In contrast to that, surprisingly, the interest or the demand for contraceptives, which one can survey through the unmet need, is not that high. This means that the acceptance of family planning is not yet as high as we would hope. . . . Well, I think, that is a special case in this country here, where we . . . want to better understand why this is not yet demanded that much. And what can we as German development cooperation do . . . well, to support the ministry and the civil society in generating this demand. (Interview 24, 2 June 2010)

This strategic employment of the concept 'unmet need' is consistent with its origin. After demographic target and quotas for contraceptive distribution had been delegitimised at the Cairo Conference, the new main conceptual reference was statistical measures of an 'unmet need' of contraceptives. Providing 'modern' contraceptives could thus be promoted as answering people's needs. The BMZ policies (similar to that of other international population programmes) use the indicator 'contraceptive prevalence rate' as a self-explanatory benchmark for development success.

In line with such a position, the various German development 'aid' institutions and organisations active in Tanzania work towards increasing the 'need', acceptance, availability and use of contraceptives. TGPSH is involved in the social marketing of contraceptives (via the NGO PSI [Population Services International])[1] and in the provision of contraceptives via 'community-based distributors' (CBDs) – the idea of CBDs was introduced by German development policy, and such distributors are now part of the official Tanzanian health system. TGPSH has also trained health personnel in family planning and contraception in health facilities. The German Foundation for World Population (DSW) as well as TGPSH educate young people to make use of 'modern' contraceptives (DSW 2012; TGPSH 2012). KfW (2005), furthermore, made possible the supply of three-month contraceptive injections to Tanzanian health facilities between 1996 and 2001. More generally, Germany finances the Basket Fund for Health, from which contraceptives are purchased.

German development actors consider transformation of gender relations crucial for lowering fertility rates and population growth. Access to, availability and use of 'modern' contraceptives is seen as one means to empower women, as an 'instrument for the self-confident behaviour of women in society' (Interview 10, 12 March 2010). Contraceptives would allow women to freely decide on the number of children they have. As shown earlier, the expectation behind this is that free choice would mean fewer children. Proposals to improve women's situation focus on education in order to change 'attitudes and behaviours' (BMZ 2008, 8). The desire to influence gender relations was evident in several of my interviews, such as in the one with a physician working for DED in a Tanzanian hospital: 'I always tried to . . . have them think of the fact that they can decide how many children they want. Basically, because it's also the husband who decides, and the family. . . . Most of the time, this is not a decision a woman makes herself' (Interview 08, 14 February 2010).

Free, individual decisions are associated with women's desire for having fewer children. It is implied that men are impediments to the women's free and more 'modern' choice. This desire is seen as linked to 'education', since, allegedly, 'educated women have children later and have fewer children' (DSW 2005, 3). That German development policy does not trust women's natural or education-induced desire for fewer children became evident in a study of the foreign policy think tank German Institute for International and

Security Affairs (SWP). The authors state that the problem in many African countries was not necessarily an unmet need for contraceptives but that people – across social classes – wished to have too many children (Angenendt and Popp 2014). Sophisticated family planning programmes as well as 'political appreciation' of smaller families are presented as central, and it was 'advisable to support the governments of partner countries more vehemently in their quest for balanced population dynamics' (Angenendt and Popp 2014, 27).

While formal education plays a particularly central role in government and NGO policies, the idea of Christianisation as an antidote to hierarchical gender relations – markedly present in colonial-era debates – is discernible among German professionals working for faith-based NGOs. This is expressed in the following excerpt from a conversation with a German couple – the husband working as a physician in a mission hospital and both involved in the church life of the German mission running the hospital: 'Through the congregation the women get rights, the chaos changes, a whole new social structure develops. Where heart and mind change, and are converted, things become more positive. Then you also see men who affectionately have children sitting on their lap' (Interview 32, 20 June 2010). The idea that values claimed to be Christian, such as love and partnership, lead to more equal gender relations is also vividly expressed in figure 6.1, a drawing from a pamphlet written by a German missionary doctor and circulated in Tanzania (Interview 34, 21 June 2010). These pictures are intended to demonstrate the change in gender relations towards equality generated by the workshops on 'natural family planning'[2] which this doctor provides for Tanzanian couples as part of her

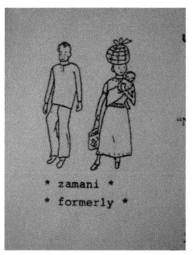

Figure 6.1. Pictures of drawings from a pamphlet published by a German missionary doctor, taken on 21 June 2010, by Daniel Bendix.

proselytising efforts. Evident in these pictures is the temporal, linear, progressive view of change. In the past ('formerly') women were oppressed and had to shoulder child-rearing as well as all other work; with the help of the missionary doctor's workshop, an unburdening of women – a sign of 'progress' and 'modernity' – is supposedly achievable.

RELATING THE PRESENT TO THE PAST

German commentators in colonial times attributed 'population decline', on the one hand, to colonial intrusion and subsequent transformation of people's living conditions and, on the other hand, to East African 'customs' and 'culture'. These ideas were grounded in the racialised distinction between a static, 'primitive', 'traditional' situation in East Africa and a complex, flexible, moving German 'modernity'. Even though the concept of gender as referring to women's and men's social roles was not yet in hand, German physicians, missionaries and administrators assumed social relations between men and women as well as women's oppression to be causes of 'population decline'. These diagnoses served to justify comprehensive intervention by German administrators, physicians and missionaries. All in all, understandings of, and interventions to prevent, 'population decline' were marked by racialised, gendered discourses that were based on an assumed dichotomy between German 'modernity' and East African 'tradition'.

In contemporary German development policy, issues of reproductive health and population are understood by associating high fertility with backwardness and 'tradition'. Reference to gender relations plays a central role as high population growth and fertility rates are seen as related to general oppression of women. In stark contrast to colonial times, the excessive number of children serves as an indicator of women's oppression today. These ways of explaining population growth are evidence of the establishment of racialised difference between Tanzania and the West, since high fertility and gender oppression are seen as linked to Tanzanian 'culture' and society. While propagating the principle of 'free choice', Germans deem it irrational and a sign of the backwardness of Tanzanian society when Tanzanians do not restrict their number of children. When a desire and demand for lower fertility does not exist, German development 'cooperation' rationalises it as lack of information, or 'education', and sees the need to create such desire. German colonial-era policy and practice as well as current development policy and practice thus subordinate East African people's choices to the overall objective of controlling population. Current German interventions in Tanzania not only present the European experience of a movement towards a small nuclear family as universally desirable but also push for this on the material level by spreading 'modern' contraceptives and 'education', as well as by transforming gender relations.

SELF-INTEREST AND THE EXPLOITATION OF EAST AFRICANS AS LABOUR FORCE

Having ascertained colonial legacies in the way population development in East Africa is understood and intervened into by German development policy, the remainder of the chapter examines how this is related to the way interventions are justified as well as to potential material interests by Germany. German professionals during colonial times generally put forward self-interested legitimisations for intervention into population and reproductive health, as they understood East Africans as endangered resources on which the success of the colonisation depended. Recruiting workers for various colonial economic endeavours – porter services, plantations, construction and so on – was a primary concern for the colonial administration in 'German East Africa' (Koponen 1994). Thus, the issue of labour supply or the so-called labour question became a central policy concern. Reformists regarded a 'healthy, numerous native population [as] the prerequisite for an effective and continuous exploitation of the tropical territories' (Deutsche Gesellschaft für Eingebornenschutz 1914b, 3). Given the need for labour, policies emerged which began to represent African inhabitants of the colony as an 'important resource' (Dernburg 1907, 7). Colonial reformists formed associations such as the previously mentioned German Society for the Protection of the Natives and advocated for recognition of the problem of 'population decline' on grounds of economic rationality.

Such a dehumanising understanding of people was based on the idea that people were 'capital' (Dernburg 1907, 7). After the turn of the twentieth century, German scientific and political thinking on the commodification of people had changed from an 'unreflected usage of human resources to ideas giving precedence to the biological reproduction of colonial subjects' (Grosse 2000, 143). The 'consumption of humans' or the 'predatory exploitation' of 'human material' was bemoaned by German commentators (Peiper 1920a, 435; Löbner 1914, 269). Inner-German debates had switched from a fear of 'overpopulation' (of the working class) to that of a 'birth decline', and people became defined as 'biological capital' analogous to other means of production of a national economy (Halling, Schäfer, and Vögele 2005, 388). Micro-economic commodification of people went hand in hand with the dominant neo-mercantilist macroeconomic paradigm which bound national wealth to the population size of a nation (Grosse 2000). Whereas the German colonies were seen as foreign territories at the beginning of colonisation in the 1880s and 1890s, turn of the century colonial reformists regarded colonial subjects as economically belonging to the German nation (Grosse 2000).

Although the discussion on population during German colonialism mainly referred to Germany's self-interest, humanist-philanthropic legitimisations for intervention also held sway. For example, the Medical Department of 'German East Africa' referred to the interests of East Africans to 'preserve their race or family' in the face 'of the looming danger for their land or tribe due to low procreation' (Medizinalreferat in Daressalam 1914, 443). Such positions on colonisation, and in particular on issues of health and population, highlighted a humanist, altruistic imperative to improve the living conditions of the colonised. This is also explicitly invoked in statements such as that 'from a medical-humane, from a moral-religious . . . standpoint, a comprehensive care for the natives is necessary' (Feldmann 1923, 119–20). Actors with philanthropic self-conceptions such as missionaries and some physicians saw the colonial reform debates as an opportunity to implement their ideas and policies. Pastor G. Paul, for instance, mentioned that he hoped the 'philanthropic and economic perspectives' would be united and expressed his conviction that their integration would lead to improved health care provision for the colonised people (1908, 98).

PHILANTHROPY, 'FUNCTIONING SOCIETIES' AND CONTRACEPTIVE MARKETS

Intervention in population and reproductive health in contemporary German development policy abroad is primarily conveyed as an altruistic endeavour to support Tanzanian economic and social 'development'. In interviews with German professionals working in this realm, I inquired as to what they saw as the reasons for Germany's involvement. Interviewees regularly brought up Germany's commitment to reaching the Millennium Development Goals and highlighted a 'humanitarian interest' in the well-being of Tanzanian women (Interview 28, June 5, 2010). A desk officer at the BMZ emphasised that development work in the field of 'sexual and reproductive health and rights' primarily followed an 'ethical-moral' imperative: 'We are doing so well here, we cannot accept that people, I mean, that ridiculous amounts are lacking, to save children, to save women's lives' (Interview 06b, 15 January 2010).

When I asked whether he thought that there were any self-interested motivations for Germany's involvement in development policy in SRHR, he replied the following: 'I would . . . resist saying that we have any interest to support our German pharmaceutical industry. . . . I think it just becomes clear that it [reproductive health and population policy, DB] is one building block to create functioning, long-term functioning societies' (Interview 06b, 15 January 2010). This reference to 'functioning societies' is in line with other interviews and also with documents on German development policy which primarily connect the need for reproductive health measures and population control to the improvement of social, economic and ecological conditions in Tanzania. Here, population growth in Tanzania is regarded as detrimental to poverty reduction (see also GTZ 2010; BMZ 2012). This understanding of population and reproductive health is based on the idea of Tanzanians as consumers of limited resources. German development agents relate population growth to negative impacts on the provision of health care, education and food as well as on natural resources such as water and forests (DSW 2008).

While the 'carrying capacity' model that allows for solutions other than population control (Hummel 2007) is evoked in such reasoning, German development policy tends to reduce the concept to a problem of the number of children per family: 'If women have access to family planning and can plan their births, the whole family profits: In a smaller family, more gets invested into the well-being of each individual child – into food, health, and education. Important prerequisites for breaking the cycle of poverty' (DSW 2005, 2). Thus, Tanzanian adults are asked to adjust the number of their offspring to their material resources. Notwithstanding, German development 'cooperation' evidences concern for improving SRHR as well as curbing population growth in Tanzania for the sake of individual Tanzanians and Tanzania's 'development' as a whole. Interventions are thus principally legitimised as altruistic and philanthropically motivated.

In stark contrast to colonial-era policies, at first glance self-interested motivations appear to be non-existent in narratives which legitimise intervention into population and reproductive health. Yet, these do surface at times. For example, the German government understands population growth not only to be related to resources in countries of the global South but also to be a 'tremendous challenge to sustainable development, at . . . the global level' (BMZ 2008, 5). The concept of 'sustainable development' emerged in the 1980s in international debates in the United Nations and other international organisations and suggests that the global South and North have a common destiny – and, therefore, a common interest. Thus, in the face of limited natural resources and climate change, population growth in Tanzania can be construed as being related to and harming the global community, and therefore also Germany.[3] Albeit indirectly, German development policy abroad also invokes self-interest with regard to intervention in population and reproductive health in the global South. This mirrors the way population growth is brought up as a problem for sustainability in German development education (chapter 3).

While the BMZ officer emphasised 'ethical-moral' reasons, he also hesitantly connected SRHR policies and their consequences to German economic
profitability:

> I would argue that it is difficult to directly deduce an economic interest from this
> SRHR area. Well, the causal links are much more complex, you see. . . . So, here
> it is the case, we have an interest in stable countries, in stable partners, yes. . . .
> I mean the countries that function, where the people then also have purchasing
> power, that will in the long term . . . also be of benefit to the former . . . still
> export world champion. (Interview 06b, 15 January 2010)

In this quote, the logic becomes evident that curbing population growth in Tanzania would mean that more resources are available for Tanzanians, that this
would lead to the 'development' of Tanzania and that 'development' means an
increase in purchasing power from which the German economy would profit.
Such a position aligns with tendencies in the last conservative-liberal coalition government to explicitly voice Germany's self-interest in development
'cooperation', and – as pointed out in chapter 4 – has just been confirmed by
the 'Marshall Plan with Africa' and the G20 Compact with Africa Initiative
launched in the context of Germany's G20 presidency. Germany's desire for
'stability' (Handelsblatt Global 2017) is reminiscent of Cold War anxieties
'about the possibility that oppressed majorities would succeed in carrying out
radical redistributions of power and resources' (Wilson 2012, 96).

The statement by the BMZ officer also references the concept of 'demographic dividend' that suggests that countries with a decreasing birth rate
can almost automatically benefit in terms of economic growth (Hendrixson
2007). Accordingly, countries with high fertility rates should be brought
towards 'demographic transition' as quickly as possible to make use of the
'demographic dividend'. Transition countries in turn should invest in youth
education and youth employment as the adequate means for a policy that takes
account of population dynamics (BMZ 2014a, 11). The reverse argument is
equally crude: If countries do not move towards a demographic transition,
economic development will not occur. The characterisation of young people
in countries categorised as 'in demographic transition' remains ambivalent:
If their 'human potential' is not fostered and economised sufficiently, they
might primarily pose a danger to a country's stability. The 'youth bulge'
concept sees young men as potential perpetrators of violence, with a 'high
percentage of young people' being a 'threat to peace and security' (BMZ
2014a, 4). Here, the SWP study talks of 'inner-state conflicts induced by
youth bulges' (Angenendt and Popp 2014, 27). Such a demographic perspective tends to overlook the crisis-laden nature of capitalism, global struggles
for resources, dependency on global markets, increasing precarisation and
social inequality (cf. Bernhold 2014).

While the previous statement by the BMZ staff member points to the global political-economic structures in which population control in Tanzania is embedded and by which German capitalist interests are served, more direct German economic interests also exist in the area of reproductive health in Tanzania. Whereas interviewees commonly stated that they did not believe that German interests were pursued through activities in SRHR in Tanzania, contraceptives produced by German firms are widely used in Tanzanian health facilities. Even fairly poor countries such as Tanzania appear to be attractive markets for German pharmaceutical companies. A large portion of government- and donor-funded oral contraceptives in Tanzania are provided by Bayer HealthCare (e-mail communication with John Snow, Inc. [JSI]). In 2010, this company won the bid to supply the USAID, the largest donor, with the oral contraceptive Microgynon. In addition, Bayer provides the contraceptive pill Microlut, the three-month injectable Noristerat and the hormonal implant Jadelle. German companies' profits are also served by distributing the three-month injectable Petogen-Fresenius via the Medical Stores Department (MSD) which is an autonomous department of Tanzania's Ministry of Health and Social Welfare responsible for furnishing drugs and medical equipment to Tanzanian institutions. Petogen-Fresenius is manufactured by the German pharmaceutical firm Fresenius and marketed by the German company HELM. MSD has also purchased condoms from HELM. Contraceptive injections obtained by PSI, which spearheads 'social marketing' of family planning in Tanzania, are also manufactured by Fresenius and marketed by HELM. From my research, it became clear that German pharmaceutical companies have a great investment in the two main pharmaceutical contraceptives promoted and distributed in Tanzania, as injections and oral contraceptives made up approximately two-thirds of all 'modern' contraceptives used.

According to a desk officer at the headquarters of Bayer HealthCare, the company gives 'preferential treatment' to poor countries such as Tanzania, which means that their selling price is the cost of production (Interview 55, 21 April 2011). This appears to be a purely charitable endeavour. However, it is still quite profitable for Bayer HealthCare to sell at production cost due to economies of scale: Production costs are thus decreased, and products sold on the regular market yield a higher margin and are more competitive. However, it is perhaps more significant that increased distribution of pharmaceutical companies' products establishes these as known brands. Countries of the global South are considered as markets, especially as they are projected to greatly increase their demand for contraceptives in the future (Global Industry Analysts, Inc. 2014). JSI, responsible for the implementation of USAID's project on health commodity supply chains in Tanzania, estimated that expenses for pharmaceutical contraceptives would more than double within five years (e-mail communication with JSI).

In addition to the supply to the Tanzanian government and donors at production cost, Bayer HealthCare sells the oral contraceptive Microgynon Fe via the Contraceptive Security Initiative (CSI) since 2014 and thus further strengthens its brands in the Tanzanian private market (Bayer HealthCare 2011; BUKO Pharma-Kampagne 2014, 39). Bayer HealthCare had launched this initiative in cooperation with USAID as public-private partnership in 2000. The aim is to establish private markets for oral contraceptives in African countries for the growing middle class. According to Bayer (2011), CSI is 'a new strategic approach and an innovative way to tap into markets in developing countries'. It is understood as an '[a]ssisted market interventions to move customers up the value chain' (Brill and von Gilardi 2011). The BUKO Pharma-Kampagne, a German NGO critical of pharmaceutical companies' activities, considers the CSI 'a marketing tool to defend Bayer's position as global market leader for oral contraceptives and its market position in the field of women's health' (2014, 40). The recent Jadelle Access Program, in which Bayer cooperates with the Bill & Melinda Gates Foundation to sell 27 million implants at a reduced price, will also see the hormonal implant Jadelle penetrating the Tanzanian contraceptive market (Bendix and Schultz 2018). Implant use quadrupled in Tanzania between 2004 and 2011 (Jacobstein and Stanley 2013). Thus, the economic interests of German pharmaceutical companies in the area of population and reproductive health in Tanzania are obvious.

RELATING THE PRESENT TO THE PAST

To discern colonial power in German development abroad today, policy and practice in the past needs, once again, to be related to the present. German colonisers were in need of workers to exploit the colony and regarded East Africans as a resource to be made use of. They regarded population numbers in 'German East Africa' as too low for optimal economic exploitation of the colony. This was based on the idea of the economic value of individual human beings as a workforce and on the conviction that the wealth of Germany depended on the number of its economically productive people, which included the colonised people in 'German East Africa'. Legitimisation for intervention into population numbers was thus primarily marked by German self-interest. To a lesser degree, some colonial stakeholders, particularly missionaries, voiced philanthropic rationales for engaging in population and health policy in 'German East Africa'. Whether legitimising strategies referred to self-interest or altruism, population control was clearly embedded in political-economic structures of exploiting the East African workforce.

Germany today regards Tanzania's population growth as being too high for the country's 'development' and evokes the self-interest of Tanzanians in order to curb fertility rates. In the light of allegedly limited resources with regard to Tanzania's environment and social services as well as families' funds, population growth and high fertility are seen as problematic. Tanzanians are no longer perceived as the resources they appeared to be during colonial rule but as resource consumers. Development policy is primarily legitimised through philanthropic rationales in which Tanzania's interests take centre stage. However, the rationale that intervention in population and reproductive health serves Germany's economic interests in the long term was also discernible in German development policy. It is, furthermore, evident that German pharmaceutical companies are heavily invested in procuring contraceptives for the Tanzanian public and private markets.

CONCLUSION

Regardless of the fact that German policies during colonial rule highlighted 'underpopulation' while contemporary German development policy stresses population growth to be the problem, German agents in both periods have associated what they considered problematic population size and fertility rates with a general backwardness of East Africans, particularly with regard to gender relations. Such racialised, gendered discourses were in both periods accompanied by actual interventions to change East African population, fertility rates and gender relations. While forceful measures, 'schooling' and Christianisation dominated during formal colonisation, today the promotion of 'modern' contraceptives takes centre stage. German colonial intervention to increase population was explicitly legitimised with reference to economic interests; contemporary German policies in the field of population and reproductive health are primarily presented as philanthropic, altruistic endeavours. Yet, long-term German interests to transform Tanzania into a 'stable', 'functioning' society with which Germany could engage in profitable economic exchange seem to also warrant interventions into reproductive health and reducing population growth in Tanzania. This resonates with M. Bahati Kuumba's argument that population policies in the global South serve countries of the global North through the 'containment of a superfluous or redundant labour force, the maintenance of political stability, and the perpetuation of dependent social relations' (1999, 455). Attention to contraceptive procurement furthermore evidences immediate German stakes in population control in Tanzania.

This chapter has focused on continuities and divergences between colonial-era interventions and contemporary interventions in order to discern the articulation of colonial power in German development policy abroad. Whether pro-natalist and argued for economically as during colonial rule or anti-natalist and argued for altruistically as today, German intervention into population and reproductive health is in line with profitability for Germany's economy. Colonial power in current German development policy on population and reproductive health is thus evident in the interconnectedness among racialised, gendered discourses and the political economy of population control. Notwithstanding the valuable contribution of bringing to the fore the persistence of discourses from the colonial era in contemporary development 'cooperation', research needs to take into account 'the racialised patterns of global accumulation which both underpin and are sustained by these discursive representations' (Wilson 2012, 208). This chapter highlights that colonial power in development abroad can only be fully comprehended by tracing the continuity of colonial discourses to material practices as well as economic interests of the global North.

NOTES

1. During the 2010 visit of the German BMZ and foreign minister to Tanzania, Germany pledged an additional €8.5 million for purchase and marketing of contraceptives via PSI.

2. This term refers to the Billings ovulation method developed by Australian physicians Evelyn and John Billings in the 1950s to determine fertile and infertile periods through changes in cervical mucus. This method was introduced in Tanzania in the 1980s by missionary health professionals working in the St. Benedict's Hospital in Ndanda, in the Mtwara Region. It has since been mainly propagated by Catholic health facilities and is commonly used by those Catholics in Tanzania who do not accept hormonal, 'modern' contraceptives or condoms (Interview 34, 21 June 2010).

3. Gayatri Chakravorty Spivak has criticised that such reasoning disregards the 'fact that one Euro-American child consumes 183 times what one Third World child consumes' (2007, 195).

Conclusion

Colonial Power Transnationally, the German Case and Postcolonial Future

In this final chapter, I first bring together the empirical insights gained from the investigation of four policy areas in order to highlight the book's contribution to the general debate on colonialism and development. I then reflect on the instructiveness of the German case and discuss the relevance of my research for settings beyond Germany. In a further step, I draw on my study to deduce some methodological insights for the research on colonial power in development. The chapter ends with some thoughts on how challenges to and transformations of colonial power may help pave the way towards a postcolonial future.

THE TRANSNATIONAL WORKINGS OF COLONIAL POWER IN GLOBAL DEVELOPMENT

A synthesis of the empirical analyses of German development policy at home and abroad reveals that colonial power is marked by (1) the transnational construction of hierarchical difference and disregard of non-Western knowledge, (2) developmentalist ideology and the practice of trusteeship and (3) the furthering of political-economic interests of the 'developers'.

First, this book's investigation of various policy fields demonstrates the persistence of transnational workings to maintain white or Western superiority. Billboard advertising transports racialised, gendered discourses to ascertain the need for German interventions in the South, and development education (DE) as well as reproductive health policy serve to justify interventions into population growth in the South. Chapter 6 also shows how discourses that declare backward social conditions and gender relations in the global South responsible for allegedly problematic fertility rates persist in German policy and practice today. Furthermore, the analysis of German narratives and practices related to obstetric care indicates that they continue to be based on racialised difference between East Africans and Germans or Westerners in the realms of knowledge, planning capacities and attitudes. Billboard advertising invokes the idea that African children are neglected and need white mothering. This stance is mirrored by narratives in German obstetric care interventions that diagnose a lack of care orientation in Tanzanian hospital staff. The development perspective of the global South as deficient connects development imagery at home with interventions abroad. Alternatives to the hegemonic notion of Western, capitalist development are invoked only sporadically – as in the case of Buen Vivir in the new edition of the curriculum framework (chapter 3). Colonial power is evident not only in the construction of racialised difference but also in the non-recognition of other knowledge systems – that is, non-capitalist, non-developmental, non-expert ways of organising society.

Second, in combination with the omnipresence of colonial-racist representations and the obliteration of agency of people in poorer countries in billboard advertising, the global South continues to be constructed as in need of intervention in the sense of help or guidance. At home, DE socialises young Germans into development discourse, issues of global inequality and questions of agency in such a manner that colonial continuities become invisible. In development policy abroad, interventions are put into practice, in which Germans – convinced of their superiority – enact trusteeship through interventions, for example, into reproductive health. However, while development policy at home serves to affirm the superiority of the 'European mind' (chapter 3), this sense of authority is sometimes challenged in development contexts abroad. The manner in which German development professionals dealt with their frustrations regarding teaching the partograph to Tanzanian health professionals (chapter 5) serves as an example. While uncertain about the value of their work and whether or not the epistemology they adhered to was suitable for the Tanzanian context, German professionals ultimately located the problem in Tanzania. Trapped in their comfortable identity as helpers in need, they were unable to imagine other ways of pursuing or teaching midwifery and ultimately had no doubts whatsoever about the need for intervention as such or the comprehensive superiority of their knowledge and skills. Even when criticism of development intervention was expressed, it did not touch on the need for Germans to contribute to the 'development' of Tanzania and its health care system. This echoes James Ferguson's (1994) argument that international development serves to construct the 'recipients' as objects of intervention while not touching on macro-structural, political issues such as the division of the world into 'developers' and 'those to be developed'. While some billboard advertising criticises structural levels and DE at times sees the North as at least part of the problem, on the whole it does not go so far as to unsettle development policy's colonial tendency to 'reproduce end-lessly the separation between reformers and those to be reformed by keeping alive the premise of the Third World as different and inferior, as having a limited humanity in relation to the accomplished European' (Escobar 1994, 54–55).

This book, thirdly, demonstrates that, in order to understand the role of colonial power in current development policy, we need to go beyond discourse and address actual practices and the global political economy in which development interventions are embedded. Chapter 6 highlights the fact that racialised discourses are interconnected with the political economy of population control and the interests of private capital. This connection is in line with the German government's interest in biopolitically ensuring the 'stability' of countries for foreign investment (chapter 6) as well as with the neocolonial and neoliberal approach to development policy towards Africa analysed in the discussion of 'The Big Five!' campaign (chapter 4). This macro-economic perspective guiding German development policy has become even more evident with the latest policy declarations in the context of the G20 presidency. Development professionals' ignorance regarding Ger-man economic interests (chapter 6) is in line with the ways billboard advertis-ing as well as DE fail to reveal the links between development and economic interests. In development policy at home, the relevance of German political and economic interests in development abroad is hardly laid open. And, there is a limited recognition of the social and historical forces that connect the global North and South.

In sum, the book confirms the connectedness of educational and public relations work in Germany intranationally with Germany's international global South policy. In contrast to its altruistic self-image as an improver of the lives of people in the global South, contemporary German development policy at home and abroad turns out to be 'a neo-colonial . . . [endeavour] in which particular gendered and racial formations constructed through colonial processes are re-presented and re-articulated' (Kothari 1996, 3). This research suggests that colonial power in contemporary global develop-ment remains firmly in place due to its transnational embeddedness in, and interplay between, policies towards the South and activities within so-called donor countries. By disregarding this complex framework, 'donors' create or perpetuate the inequalities and injustices that their development policy claims to battle against.

THE INSTRUCTIVENESS OF THE GERMAN CASE

The empirical contribution of this book consists in its focus on the largely under-researched case of German development policy. Although a relative wealth of information exists on the connection between colonialism and development, postcolonial development studies to date focus on the case of British colonial rule and development intervention. Contributing to individual postcolonial studies of Danish and Swedish (Eriksson Baaz 2005), Canadian (Heron 2007), Portuguese (Power 2006) and Slovak (Profant 2015) development endeavours, this book zooms in on Germany and its interventions at home and abroad. The implications are both an affirmation of the similarities between (post-)colonial undertakings and a challenge to an assumed uniformity of colonialism and its legacy. The analysis provides an insight into the resemblance of colonial power in German development policy to that of other European nations' endeavours. For example, after the turn of the twentieth century, various European states began to perceive the regulation of population size, birthing and women's health as essential for their colonising endeavours (Jolly 1998) and today intervene in the global South to curb population growth (Wilson 2017). Development policy at home in the form of DE is also faced with the problem of colonial legacies in European countries other than Germany (Andreotti 2011; Mikander 2016). And colonial iconography as well as the de-politicising effect of development advertising also play a role in the context of other countries' development communication at home (Manzo 2008; Rideout 2011). The implications of moving beyond the Anglocentric bias of postcolonial development studies are thus, first of all, an affirmation of the pan-European nature of (post-)colonial undertakings – even for cases hitherto not considered important, such as Germany.

At the same time, and more importantly, this book challenges the idea of the uniformity of colonisation and its legacy as it highlights the fact that different colonial projects cannot be subsumed under one single understanding of colonialism. Since colonial rule was characterised by a 'dispersed space of power and a disseminated apparatus, wielded by diverse agents and effecting multiple situations and relations' (Parry 2004, 14), differences between colonial legacies need to be acknowledged. While colonialism was undoubtedly a pan-European project, one cannot assume that Germans held the same convictions, followed the same policies and carried out the same practices as other European colonisers in other territories. This means that contemporary development interventions by different countries from the global North draw on different cultural experiences and backgrounds and are embedded in different socio-economic and political conditions. David Theo Goldberg's argument regarding the specificity of racisms can be well transferred to the realm of colonial power:

> There are differences having to do with national and local specificities; with differing colonial, neocolonial, and postcolonial histories as well as with different experiences of empire; with weightier or lighter legacies of colonizing and

scientific racisms; with distinct population presence or absence as a result of migration and refugee crises; with uneven modes of situatedness in relation to postindustrialization and globalization, different experiences of economic decline and reinvention, and contrasting standpoints in relation to World War II and postcolonial decadence and melancholia, resurgence and euphoria. (2006, 350)

For example, the specific German colonial disremembering – acknowledgement of the fact that Germany has a colonial past but denial of a colonial guilt – means that its colonial history is not taken into account as particularly relevant, which prompts the German government to produce billboards such as 'The Big Five!'. More generally, the differences in the histories of anti-racist struggles (when compared to the USA and the UK, for example) can help explain the relative unself-consciousness with which German development non-governmental organisations (NGOs) regularly decorate the streets of Germany with colonial-racist imagery (without receiving much protest). The absence of substantial migration from former German colonies to Germany has contributed to the fact that discussions on the impact of colonialism in the present are negligible. That 'the empire is striking back' in DE and that activists demand postcolonial justice in terms of content and equality in terms of representation in institutions is a fairly recent phenomenon. The fact that a decidedly postcolonial critique of development policy which includes a focus on racism in North-South relations has remained marginal in Germany until very recently can also be explained by the general tendency in German society to equal racism with the German fascist experience and to disregard the links between (German) colonialism, the Holocaust and the pervasiveness of racism today.

Germany's particular economic global position needs to be taken into account, as well. Pushing for private investment and building economically strong societies in the global South is of specific interest for a powerful trading nation such as Germany. The simultaneity of German development professionals' philanthropic arguments to legitimise interventions and their ignorance of German economic stakes in reproductive health in Tanzania can be explained with reference to this context (chapter 6).

As stated before, this book's insights challenge an assumed uniformity of colonialism and its legacy. While the findings of the four empirical chapters give evidence to the fact that contemporary development policy is part of a general racialised and neoliberal agenda, they also show that it draws on cultural-historical experiences, backgrounds and political-economic conditions specific to the respective colonising nation, thus constituting a particularly German colonial power formation. As colonialism was both a trans-European and a multi-faceted endeavour, postcolonial development studies must account for the similarities and divergences in colonial power in contemporary international development. To take the empirical investigation of colonial power in development further would imply comparing British, French, Dutch, Belgian or Portuguese development policy with the German case and also taking into consideration countries without a history as colonial occupiers, such as Switzerland, or the 'new donors' (for example, Brazil, South Korea or Poland) in a comparative study. Such a comparative study could also include the interesting question whether colonial power in development abroad and at home persists where former colonised countries now act as 'donors'.

RESEARCHING COLONIAL POWER IN DEVELOPMENT

Since postcolonial development studies have thus far primarily focused on general policy orientations and developers' subjectivities (for exceptions, see Chimhowu and Woodhouse 2005; Wainwright 2008), an analysis of specific areas of intervention substantiates the value of a postcolonial approach to development. The focus on policy and practice in the particular fields under scrutiny in this book adds to the understanding of the interrelatedness of discourses with practices, institutions and political-economic conditions. Chapter 6, for example, highlights German pharmaceutical companies' stakes in 'modern' contraception in Tanzania, and chapter 5 deals with the practices following from particular perceptions of what some German professionals considered appropriate obstetric care. It also describes how obstetric practices such as the supine birth position, introduced by Germans during colonial rule, now serve as evidence of Tanzanian 'backwardness'. Chapter 3 describes the way anti-racist critique and struggles in Germany affect the field of DE at the level of government policy. The comprehensive take of the study on selected policy fields makes it possible to trace ideas and practices from programmatic top-level policy statements to particular educational materials, concrete projects in Tanzania and German professionals' accounts of their day-to-day work in reproductive health.

Such a multi-level and multi-faceted examination can yield a nuanced picture and highlight specificities and contradictions. The concrete scrutiny of interventions means that an examination of colonial power in present-day development does not remain abstract. Instead of merely finding that policy papers construct people in the global South as backward, the study identifies colonial discourses of African inability to think rationally in concrete instances such as German development professionals' accounts of their attempts to teach Tanzanian nurses to use the partograph. Rather than criticising development for generally taking Western 'modernity' as a benchmark, the analysis casts a light on how such an approach plays out in particular ways of depicting the global South (e.g., infantilisation in billboard advertising), the promotion of specific practices (e.g., 'modern' contraceptives) and manners of thinking (rational 'if, then' reasoning in obstetric care) and feeling or acting (work ethics in healthcare).

This book also hopes to refine existing approaches in postcolonial development studies that focus on the analysis of discourse. It does so by addressing the complexity and multidimensionality of power and thus highlights the need to expand upon discourse analysis in order to understand power: The connectedness of discourses to actual practices and political-economic conditions and also the actors' capacity to move within and beyond dominant discourses are taken into account. Accordingly, this book does not only show how German colonial-era professionals presented East African childbirth-related practices as backward but also that they effectively replaced East African with Western health care practices and institutions (chapter 5). Dispositif analysis has also helped to identify shifts in power: A good decade ago, DE had not yet been sensitised to postcolonial issues of epistemic violence or diversity of target groups; an analysis of key policy documents and observation of the field shows how these were introduced by specific actors who pushed that agenda and have gained momentum. And while Germany's economic stakes in enhancing population growth were evident in the discursive as well as in the material sense during the colonial period, economic rationales for intervention are seldom expressed explicitly in contemporary development policy, despite German pharmaceutical companies' heavy involvement in the procurement of contraceptives for Tanzania (chapter 6).

This book makes use of a variety of sources, ranging from archives, publications and observations to interviews with professionals. It hopes to provide broad, differentiated insights into the respective dimensions of global development at home and abroad. Until now, most of the empirical work on postcolonial development has relied on analyses of contemporary documents (e.g., Slater and Bell 2002; Biccum 2005). Some scholars used interviews to tease out nuances and contradictions in interviewees' accounts of their life and work in development (e.g., Heron 2007; Kothari 2006b). Research that incorporates data such as historical sources, observation and statistics helps to unearth the variety and complexity of narratives, practices and political-economic conditions. For the focus of chapters 5 and 6 on the connections between the period of formal colonial rule and contemporary development, it was indispensable to consult original historical sources in such a specific manner that the past could indeed be compared with the present. Attention to what is not expressed in writing is also crucial: Had I not been involved in the debate on DE in Germany and spoken to other stakeholders, I would not have been aware of the struggles and changes taking place in this field; had I not observed billboard advertising over the period of a decade, I would have noticed neither the changes in representation nor the occurrences of adbusting and subvertising; and had I not visited hospitals and spoken with staff at the Tanzanian Medical Stores Department, I would not have realised that German pharmaceutical companies had stakes in population and reproductive health politics. By developing and applying the methodology of dispositif analysis, this book thus emphasises the need to draw upon a variety of sources in order to do justice to the complexity and specificity of colonial power in a specific national case as well as in distinct policy fields of development and their transnational interrelationship.

CHALLENGING AND TRANSFORMING COLONIAL POWER

The purpose of an investigation into colonial power in development is to confront and alter such power in order to render imaginable and possible 'de-colonized, de-whitened, post-colonial' transnational solidarity (Crush 1994, 334). Here, challenges to, and transformations of, colonial power that became evident in the different empirical studies discussed in this book point towards a postcolonial future and may be instructive for politicians and practitioners involved in development policy, development educators or anti-colonial or international solidarity activists. The postcolonial perspective implemented in this book 'provides directions that point to a move beyond ethnocentrism and its claims of cultural supremacy, towards "planetary citizenship" . . . based on a deep understanding of interdependence (in "material" and cultural terms) and causal responsibility towards the South' (Andreotti 2006, 11).

For the example of DE, further reflection on colonial power is crucial, but a truly postcolonial agenda depends on the transformation of the whole field and demands changes of institutional and political frameworks. Change would need a broad questioning of power structures in DE: at the pedagogical level (e.g., materials and didactics), in structures of governmental and non-governmental institutions (e.g., recruitment) and on the ideological level of organisations. In addition, more exchange and networking between organisations, facilitators, consultants and funders that are devoted to decolonising DE is necessary. People of Color networks' and anti-racist initiatives' interventions have played a crucial role to date. These would need to be seriously acknowledged by institutionalised actors and given more space to influence educational agendas and structures.

The chapter on billboard advertising lists some positive examples of moving beyond colonial difference while criticising global material inequality. Here, NGOs committed to anti-racism and global solidarity can find inspiration from activists' adbusting and subvertising. While these strategies have not yet made use of billboards, the Christliche Initiative Romero ('Christian

Initiative Romero'), which lobbies for human and labour rights in Central America, has produced a booklet employing subvertising. It pretends to advertise for the discount shop KiK but changes the messages in order to inform readers about KiK's conduct. It also connects the issue of labour conditions in the factories in the South to those of workers in the KiK shops in Germany. In addition to the campaign by medico international discussed in chapter 4, this campaign shows that a(i)dvertising cannot only highlight the potential of solidarity with social movements in the South but may also address the interconnectedness of struggles in the North and South head-on.

As far as obstetric care interventions go, colonial power does not seem to be fundamentally challenged by the doubts and criticism of German professionals. Critique of development interventions by Tanzanian professionals may point to fruitful directions. It points out the problem that German professionals allegedly behave as if they were going to the 'jungle' and interacting with ignorant people. Thus, anti-racist, postcolonial education and supervision for development professionals in their training and during their stay abroad seem necessary. This might also lead to development professionals' acknowledgement of the much broader role played by health care workers as well as TBAs in society (Langwick 2011).

Regarding international population policy, the access to good contraceptive methods – free of charge and with few adverse drug reactions – must be a key element of comprehensive health care. That, with significant German involvement, the dissemination of long-acting reversible contraception with considerable negative adverse drug reactions has heavily increased within a few years in certain African countries (including Tanzania) does not point to respect for reproductive health and rights but to an interest in effective population control in combination with marketing strategies. The danger that reproductive needs, demands and rights are pushed to the margin continues if the focus remains on population numbers. If the principle of sexual and reproductive health and rights is taken seriously and extended to that of 'reproductive justice' (SisterSong 2017), women and men in the South should have access to health care as well as to the social and economic support that allows them to have the number of children they – and not national or international population policies – deem right.

While the impulses for transforming colonial power, mentioned thus far, tend to remain within the framework of development policy, a fundamentally anti-colonial agenda needs to look beyond the horizon of the development gaze. Initiatives that critically observe the dissemination of contraceptives and changes in population policy need to be integrated into a broader leftist, feminist and anti-imperialist or postcolonial political debate on development paradigms and policies and protest against philanthro-capitalist alliances within development and population policies. An anti-colonial agenda needs to concern itself with 'externalization societies' such as the German one (Lessenich 2016) and the 'imperial mode of living' (Brand and Wissen 2013). The former are highly problematic, as they live off the resources, labour and life chances of other societies (mainly in the global South), and the latter – also found in former colonised countries – is based on continued exploitation of people and nature in the context of postcolonial inequalities. Thus, 'the priority should not be Third World development . . . but First World 'de-development'' (Bennett 2012, 983).

In this perspective, the instruments of domination of capitalist elites that are principally still located in the West and of the respective nations need to be reduced (Spehr 1996); this includes inhibiting the capacity for military interventions in the South, pushing back the global economic sector (i.e., reducing the capacity for economic intervention in the South), re-appropriating living spaces and contexts and implementing strategies for enabling autonomous food and resource provision in the North. Such structural changes amount to a 'decolonisation of the North', by which I refer to both a reduction of exploitation of the South and a creation of emancipatory perspectives for marginalised people in the North. A reconsideration of ecofeminist thought seems fruitful (Werlhof, Mies, and Bennholdt-Thomsen 1988), particularly in light of increasing ecological crises, and could be complemented by more recent postcolonial perspectives on human-nature hierarchies in development (Casas 2014). This indicates the necessity to counter the continuing reluctance in development thought to value different ways of knowing and to thus work towards pluriversity (Dussel 2010, 167). Reparations for European colonialism need to manifest themselves materially – for instance, in monetary form, in return of stolen land and artefacts, in support for global freedom of movement – but need to entail measures against the continued epistemic violence that differentiates between holders of knowledge and targets of intervention along racial, gender and class lines.

Appendix

List of Cited Interviews

01: Former media officer of a German NGO working on reproductive health in Tanzania. Tape recording, Germany, 11 November 2009.

02: Consultant and former manager of the reproductive health area of the German-Tanzanian health programme. Tape recording, Germany, 6 January 2010.

03: Consultant for BMZ and GTZ; researcher on reproductive health in Tanzania. Tape recording, Germany, 14 January 2010.

04: Former manager of the district health and quality management area of TGPSH. Tape recording, Germany, 14 January 2010.

06b: Desk officer at the BMZ, responsible for sexual and reproductive health and rights. Tape recording, Germany, 15 January 2010.

08: Former DED doctor in a Tanzanian district hospital. Tape recording, the Netherlands, 14 February 2010.

10: Former senior manager of the German health programme in Tanzania. Tape recording, Germany, 12 March 2010.

11: Former manager of the reproductive health area of TGPSH. Tape recording, Germany, 19 March 2010.

14: Desk officer at KfW, responsible for the Tanzanian health sector. Tape recording, Germany, 18 March 2010.

15: Nurse and midwife who worked for a German faith-based NGO in a Tanzanian mission hospital. Tape recording, Germany, 21 April 2010.

18: Advisor to the Tanzanian government working for TGPSH. Tape recording, Tanzania, 20 and 25 May 2010.

19: Advisor to Tanzanian faith-based organisations, working for TGPSH. Tape recording, Tanzania, 26 May 2010.

24: Manager of the TGPSH reproductive health area. Tape recording, Tanzania, 2 June 2010.

28: Consultant advising the Tanzanian government in a KfW-financed project. Tape recording, Tanzania, 5 June 2010.

29: German nurse working in a Tanzanian training centre for midwifery. Tape recording, Tanzania, 8 June 2010.

30: Missionary and nurse who runs her own NGO in Tanzania. Tape recording, Tanzania, 8 June 2010.

31: Physician working for a German faith-based NGO in a Christian hospital in Tanzania. Tape recording, Tanzania, 8 June 2010.

32: Physician and missionary who headed a mission hospital in Tanzania. Tape recording, Tanzania, 20 June 2010.

34: German missionary doctor working in a Tanzanian hospital. Tape recording, Tanzania, 21 June 2010.

35: German physician working in a Tanzanian hospital via CIM. Tape recording, Tanzania, 22 June 2010.

37: Physician working for DED in a Tanzanian district hospital. Tape recording, Tanzania, 25 June 2010.

38: Advisor to a Tanzanian regional hospital, working for DED. Personal interview, Tanzania, 29 June 2010.

39: Instructor in a Tanzanian nursing school. Personal interview, Tanzania, 3–7 July 2010.

43: Physician working for DED in a Tanzanian district hospital. Tape recording, Tanzania, 9 July 2010.

52: Tanzanian former manager of a regional hospital who worked for German development 'cooperation'. Personal interview, Tanzania, 30 July 2010.

53: CIM physician working in a regional hospital in Tanzania. Tape recording, Tanzania, 31 July 2010.

54: Retired physician working as a volunteer in a Tanzanian mission hospital. Personal interview, Tanzania, 22 June 2010.

55: Desk officer at the headquarters of Bayer HealthCare. Tape recording, Germany, 21 April 2011.

Bibliography

Adams, Maurianne, Lee Bell, and Pat Griffin, eds. 1997. *Teaching for Diversity and Social Justice. A Sourcebook*. New York and London: Routledge.

Adams, William M., and Martin Mulligan. 2003. *Decolonizing Nature: Strategies for Conservation in a Post-Colonial Era*. London: Earthscan.

Adichie, Chimananda Ngozi. 2007. 'Presentation at the Christopher Okigbo Conference'. Barker Center, Harvard University. Accessed 24 July 2014. http://www.youtube.com/watch?v=NlelreqrfQ4.

———. 2011. 'Narratives of Europe. Stories That Matter'. SPUI25, Amsterdam. Accessed 24 July 2014. http://www.youtube.com/watch?v=-YEWg1vIOyw.

AfricAvenir International, Berlin Postkolonial, and Tanzania-Network. 2013. 'Afrika ist keine Wildnis! "The Big Five!"-Kampagne des BMZ reproduziert kolonialrassistisches Afrikabild' [Africa Is Not Wilderness! 'The Big Five!' Campaign by BMZ Reproduces Colonial-Racist Image of Africa]. Accessed 15 June 2017. http://www.africavenir.org/nc/news-details/article/pm-afrika-ist-keine-wildnis-the-big-five-kampagne-des-bmz-reproduziert-kolonialrassistisc/print.html.

Afrika-Rat. 2013. 'Afrika ist keine Wildnis'. [Africa Is Not Wilderness]. Accessed 15 June 2017. http://www.berlin-postkolonial.de/cms/index.php/9-news/kurzmeldungen/93-2013-05-27-11-30-04.

AFRODAD, and Africa Development Interchange Network. 2017. 'The G20 Compact with Africa and the Germany Proposed Marshall Plan for Africa. Welcoming the Initiatives with Caution'. Accessed 15 June 2017. https://info.brot-fuer-die-welt.de/sites/default/files/blog-downloads/africa_voice_g20_compact.pdf.

Ahmad, Aijaz. 1995. 'Postcolonialism: What's in a Name?' In *Late Imperial Culture*, edited by Román de la Campa, E. Ann Kaplan, and Michael Sprinker, 11–32. London: Verso.

Ahrendt, Cordula. 2012. 'Hebammenrolle, Kommunikation und pädagogische Hebammenaufgaben' [Role of Midwives, Communication, and Pedagogical Tasks of Midwives]. In *Hebammenkunde: Lehrbuch für Schwangerschaft, Geburt, Wochenbett und Beruf* [Midwifery: Textbook on Pregnancy, Childbirth, Childbed and Profession], edited by Andrea Stiefel, Christine Geist, and Ulrike Harder, 5th ed., 33–61. Stuttgart: Georg Thieme.

Akakpo-Numado, Sena Yawo. 2007. *Mädchen- und Frauenbildung in den deutschen Kolonien (1884–1914)* [Education of Girls and Women in the German Colonies (1884–1914)]. Frankfurt am Main: IKO.

Albrecht-Heide, Astrid. 2005. 'Weißsein und Erziehungswissenschaft' [Whiteness and Educational Science]. In *Mythen, Masken und Subjekte. Kritische Weißseinsforschung in Deutschland*, edited by Maureen Maisha Eggers, Grada Kilomba, Peggy Piesche, and Susan Arndt, 444–59. Münster: Unrast.

Allen, Denise Roth. 2002. *Managing Motherhood, Managing Risk. Fertility and Danger in West Central Tanzania*. Ann Arbor: University of Michigan Press.

Anderson, Warwick. 2000. 'The Third-World Body'. In *Medicine in the Twentieth Century*, edited by Roger Cooter and John Pickstone, 235–45. Amsterdam: Harwood Academic Publishers.

Andreotti, Vanessa. 2006. 'The Contributions of Postcolonial Theory to Development Education'. DEA Thinkpiece: 1–12. https://think-global.org.uk/wp-content/uploads/dea/documents/dea_thinkpiece_andreotti.pdf.

———. 2011. *Actionable Postcolonial Theory in Education*. New York: Palgrave Macmillan.

———. 2012. 'HEADS UP Checklist'. Global What? http://globalwh.at/heads-up-checklist-by-vanessa-de-oliveira-andreotti/.

Andreotti, Vanessa, and Lynn T.M. de Souza. 2012. *Postcolonial Perspectives on Global Citizenship Education*. London: Routledge.

Angenendt, Steffen, and Silvia Popp. 2014. 'Bevölkerungswachstum, Fertilität und Kinderwunsch. Herausforderungen für die Entwicklungszusammenarbeit am Beispiel Subsahara-Afrikas' [Population Growth, Fertility, and the Desire to Have Children. Challenges for Development Cooperation, the Example of Sub-Saharan Africa]. SWP-Studien 20.

Arndt, Susan, and Nadja Ofuatey-Alazard, eds. 2011. *Wie Rassismus aus Wörtern spricht: (K)Erben des Kolonialismus im Wissensarchiv deutsche Sprache – ein kritisches Nachschlagewerk* [How Racism Speaks from Words: Scars/Heritage of Colonialism in the Knowledge Archive of the German Language – A Critical Work of Reference]. Münster: Unrast.

Asbrand, Barbara, and Annette Scheunpflug. 2014. 'Globales Lernen' [Global Learning]. In *Handbuch politische Bildung*, edited by Wolfgang Sander, 4th ed., 401–12. Schwalbach am Taunus: Wochenschau Verlag.

Autor*innenkollektiv. 2016. 'Rassismuskritik unter prekären Bedingungen – ehrenamtliche Erfahrungen mit rassismuskritischer Organisationsentwicklung' [Racism Critique under Precarious Conditions – Experiences with Honorary Work in Racism-Critical Organisational Development]. In *Bon Voyage! Rassismuskritische Wege in der entwicklungspolitischen Bildungs- und Projektarbeit*, edited by Berliner Entwicklungspolitischer Ratschlag, 52–56. Berlin: Berliner Entwicklungspolitischer Ratschlag e.V.

Autor*innenKollektiv Rassismuskritischer Leitfaden. 2015. *Rassismuskritischer Leitfaden zur Reflexion bestehender und Erstellung neuer didaktischer Lehr- und*

Lernmaterialien für die schulische und außerschulische Bildungsarbeit zu Schwarzsein, Afrika und afrikanischer Diaspora [Racism-Critical Guide for Reflection on Existing and To-Be-Developed Didactic Teaching and Learning Materials for Educational Work in Schools and Out-of-School on Blackness, Africa, and the African Diaspora]. Berlin: Projekt Lern- und Erinnerungsort Afrikanisches Viertel beim Amt für Weiterbildung und Kultur des Bezirksamts.

Axenfeld, Karl. 1907. 'Gesellschaft zur Beförderung der evangelischen Missionen unter den Heiden: Schreiben von Lic. Theol. Axenfeld, Missionsinspektor' [Society for the Advancement of the Protestant Mission amongst the Heathens: Letter by Lic. Theol. Axenfeld, Mission Superintendent]. Berlin, 2 December 1907; Federal German Archives: R1001/5673.

———. 1913. 'Vom Arbeitsfelde der ärztlichen Mission' [On the Field of Work for the Medical Mission]. *Mitteilungen des Berliner Vereins für ärztliche Mission* 6 (5): 1–24; Federal German Archives: R1001/6038.

Ayeko-Kümmeth, Jane. 2017. 'Tanzania to Press Germany for Damages for Colonial Era "Atrocities"'. dw.com. Accessed 15 June 2017. http://www.dw.com/en/tanzania-to-press-germany-for-damages-for-colonial-era-atrocities/a-37479775.

Bandarage, Asoka. 1997. *Women, Population and Global Crisis. A Political-Economic Analysis*. London: Zed Books.

Barley, Alexander. 2001. 'Battle of the Image'. *New Statesman*, 21 May. Accessed 15 June 2017. http://www.newstatesman.com/node/153475.

Barlösius, Eva. 2007. 'Die Demographisierung des Gesellschaftlichen. Zur Bedeutung der Repräsentationspraxis' [The Demographization of the Social. On the Significance of Representational Practice]. In *Demographisierung des Gesellschaftlichen. Analysen und Debatten zur demographischen Zukunft Deutschlands*, edited by Eva Barlösius and Daniela Schiek, 9–32. Wiesbaden: VS – Verlag für Sozialwissenschaften.

Bauer, George Kibala. 2017. 'Germany's Marshall Plan for Africa'. Africasacountry. 15 March. Accessed 15 June 2017. http://africasacountry.com/2017/03/germanys-marshall-plan-for-africa/.

Baughan, Emily. 2015. 'A Short History of Helping Far-Off Peoples'. Africasacountry. 12 November. Accessed 15 June 2017. http://africasacountry.com/2015/11/a-short-history-of-helping-far-off-peoples/.

Bauhardt, Christine. 2011. 'Gesellschaftliche Naturverhältnisse und globale Umweltpolitik – Ökofeminismus, Queer Ecologies, (Re)Produktivität und das Konzept "Ressourcenpolitik"' [Societal Relationship to Nature and Global Environmental Policy – Ecofeminism, Queer Ecologies, (Re)Productivity and the Concept 'Resource Policy']. In *Geschlechterforschung. Theorien, Thesen, Themen zur Einführung*, edited by Barbara Rendtorff, Claudia Mahs, and Verena Wecker, 44–58. Stuttgart: W. Kohlhammer Verlag.

Bayer HealthCare. 2011. 'Wir kooperieren mit USAID, um einen nachhaltigen Markt für Verhütungsmittel in Afrika zu schaffen' [We Cooperate with USAID to Create a Sustainable Market for Contraceptives in Africa]. Accessed 15 June 2017. http://www.bayerhealthcarepharmaceuticals.com/de/presse/im_fokus/contraceptive_security_initiative.php.

Bayly, Christopher, Vijayendra Rao, Simon Szreter, and Michael Woolcock, eds. 2011. *History, Historians and Development Policy. A Necessary Dialogue*. Manchester and New York: Manchester University Press.

Bebel, August. 1889. 'August Bebel's Reichstag Speech against Colonial Policy in German East Africa'. http://germanhistorydocs.ghi-dc.org/sub_document. cfm?document_id=1870.

Bechtum, Alexandra, and Bernd Overwien. 2017. 'Kann postkoloniale Kritik Schule machen? Über ihre Grenzen und Potenziale für (entwicklungs-)politische Bildungsarbeit' [Can Postcolonial Critique Work? On the Limits and Potentials for (Development-)Political Education]. In *Entwicklungstheorie von heute – Entwicklungspolitik von morgen*, edited by Hans-Jürgen Burchardt, Stefan Peters, and Nico Weinmann, 59–84. Baden-Baden: Nomos.

Beck, Ann. 1977. 'Medicine and Society in Tanganyika, 1890–1930: A Historical Inquiry'. *Transactions of the American Philosophical Society, New Series*, 67 (3): 1–59. doi: 10.2307/1006330.

Becker, Gabriele, Silvia Bovenschen, and Helmut Brackert. 1977. *Aus der Zeit der Verzweiflung. Zur Genese und Aktualität des Hexenbildes* [From the Times of Despair. On the Genesis and Topicality of the Image of the Witch]. Frankfurt am Main: Suhrkamp.

Becker, Jörg, and Rosmarie Rauter, eds. 1978. *Die Dritte Welt im Kinderbuch. Theorie und soziale Praxis* [The Third World in Children's Books. Theory and Social Practice]. Wiesbaden: Akademische Verlagsgesellschaft.

Behrend, Hanna, ed. 1995. *German Unification: The Destruction of an Economy*. London: Pluto.

Bendix, Daniel. 2013a. 'Auf den Spuren kolonialer Macht. Eine genealogische Dispositivanalyse von Entwicklungspolitik' [Tracing Colonial Power. A Genealogical Dispositif Analysis of Development Policy]. In *Rekonstruktive Methoden der Weltpolitikforschung. Anwendungsbeispiele und Entwicklungstendenzen*, edited by Ulrich Franke and Ulrich Roos, 181–218. Baden-Baden: Nomos.

———. 2013b. 'The Big Five as Dangerous as Ever – German Development Cooperation, Colonial-Racist Imagery, and Civil Society's Response'. *Critical Literacy: Theories and Practices* 7 (2): 48–57. http://criticalliteracy.freehostia.com/index. php?journal=criticalliteracy&page=article&op=view&path%5B%5D=142&path% 5B%5D=113.

———. 2016a. 'The Colonial Present in International Development: The Case of German Interventions in Obstetric Care in Tanzania'. *Progress in Development Studies* 16 (3): 229–43. doi: 10.1177/1464993416641579?rss=1.

———. 2016b. 'From Fighting Underpopulation to Curbing Population Growth: Tracing Colonial Power in German Development Interventions in Tanzania'. *Postcolonial Studies* 18 (4): 53–70. doi: 10.1080/13688790.2016.1228137.

Bendix, Daniel, Chandra-Milena Danielzik, and Timo Kiesel. 2015. 'Education for Sustainable Inequality? A Postcolonial Analysis of Materials for Development Education in Germany'. *Critical Literacy: Theories and Practices* 9 (2): 47–63. http://criticalliteracy.freehostia.com/index.php?journal=criticalliteracy&page=arti cle&op=view&path%5B%5D=159&path%5B%5D=140.

Bendix, Daniel, Chandra-Milena Danielzik, Timo Kiesel, and Kristina Kontzi. 2016. 'Sustaining Inequality – The Neocolonial Politics of Development Education, North-South Volunteering and Fair Trade in Germany'. Darkmatter. In the Ruins of Imperial Culture 13. http://www.darkmatter101.org/site/2016/04/02/sustain ing-inequality-%E2%80%93-the-neocolonial-politics-of-development-education-north-south-volunteering-and-fair-trade-in-germany/.

Bendix, Daniel, and Susanne Schultz. 2018. 'The Political Economy of Family Planning: Population Dynamics and Contraceptive Markets'. *Development and Change* 49 (2). doi: 10.1111/dech.12363.

Bennett, Cary. 2012. 'Supporting the Posts in Development Discourse: Under-Development, Over-Development, Post-Development'. *Sociology Compass* 6 (12): 974–86. doi: 10.1111/soc4.12005.

Berliner Entwicklungspolitischer Ratschlag, ed. 2007. *Von Trommlern und Helfern. Beiträge zu einer nicht-rassistischen entwicklungspolitischen Bildungs- und Projektarbeit* [On Drummers and Helpers. Contributions to Non-Racist Development Education and Project Work]. Berlin: Berliner Entwicklungspolitischer Ratschlag e.V.

———. ed. 2010. *Checkliste zur Vermeidung von Rassismus in der entwicklungspolitischen Öffentlichkeitsarbeit. Anhang zur Broschüre 'Von Trommlern und Helfern'* [Checklist to Prevent Racism in PR for Development Policy. Annex to the Booklet 'On Drummers and Helpers']. Berlin: Berliner Entwicklungspolitischer Ratschlag e.V. Accessed 15 June 2017. http://eineweltstadt.berlin/wie-wir-arbeiten/ rassismuskritik/checklisten-zur-vermeidung-von-rassismen/.

———. ed. 2013. *Develop-Mental Turn. Neue Beiträge zu einer rassismuskritischen entwicklungspolitischen Bildungs- und Projektarbeit* [Develop-Mental Turn. New Contributions to Non-Racist Development Education and Project Work]. Berlin: BER.

———. ed. 2016. *Bon Voyage! Rassismuskritische Wege in der entwicklungspolitischen Bildungs- und Projektarbeit* [Bon Voyage! Racism-Critical Paths in Development Education and Project Work]. Berlin: BER.

Bernal, Martin. 1987. *Black Athena: The Afroasiatic Roots of Classical Civilization.* New Brunswick: Rutgers University Press.

Bernau, Olaf. 2017. 'Anlageobjekt Afrika. Die deutsche G20-Präsidentschaft propagiert "Investitionspartnerschaften" im Kampf gegen Armut und Hunger' [Investment Object Africa. The German G20 Presidency Propagates 'Investment Partnerships' to Fight Poverty and Hunger]. *ak – Zeitung für linke Debatte und Praxis* 628: 14.

Bernhold, Christin. 2014. 'Die "neue" Afrika-Politik der BRD: "Chancenkontinent" der deutschen Wirtschafts- und Machtpolitik' [The 'New' German Africa Policy: The 'Continent of Opportunities' of German Economic and Power Politics]. *Informationsstelle Militarisierung* 3: 9–14.

Bernstein, Henry. 2006. 'Studying Development/Development Studies'. *African Studies* 65 (1): 45–62. doi: 10.1080/00020180600771733.

Bhabha, Homi K. 1990. 'The Other Question: Difference, Discrimination and the Discourse of Colonialism'. In *Out There: Marginalization and Contemporary Cultures,* edited by Russell Ferguson, Martha Gever, Trinh T. Minh-ha, and Cornel West, 71–88. London: MIT Press.

————. 1994. *The Location of Culture*. London and New York: Routledge.

Biccum, April. 2002. 'Interrupting the Discourse of Development: On a Collision Course with Postcolonial Theory'. *Culture, Theory and Critique* 43: 33–50. doi: 10.1080/14735780210162094.

————. 2005. 'Development and the "New" Imperialism: A Reinvention of Colonial Discourse in DFID Promotional Literature'. *Third World Quarterly* 26 (6): 1005–20. doi: 10.1080/01436590500139656.

Blystad, Astrid. 1999. ' "Dealing with Men's Spears". Datooga Pastoralists Combating Male Intrusion on Female Fertility'. In *Those Who Play with Fire. Gender, Fertility and Transformation in East and Southern Africa*, edited by Henrietta L. Moore, Todd Sanders, and Bwire Kaare, 187–223. London and New Brunswick: The Athlone Press.

BMZ. 2008. 'Sexual and Reproductive Health and Rights, and Population Dynamics'. BMZ Policy Paper 149. Bonn-Berlin: BMZ. Accessed 15 April 2012. https://health. bmz.de/what_we_do/Reproductive-maternal-and-child-health/policies_and_con cepts/Sexual_and_Reproductive_Health_and_Rights_and_Population_Dynamics/ Sexual_and_Reproductive_Health_and_Rights_and_Population_Dynamics.pdf.

————. 2011a. 'BMZ Initiative on Rights-Based Family Planning and Maternal Health'. Accessed 15 June 2012. http://www.bmz.de/en/zentrales_downloadar chiv/themen_und_schwerpunkte/gesundheit/bmz_initiative_familienplanung_ en_1107.pdf.

————. 2011b. 'The German Contribution to Promoting Sexual and Reproductive Health'. Accessed 15 June 2012. http://www.bmz.de/en/what_we_do/issues/ Health/reproduktive_gesundheit/deutscher_beitrag/index.html.

————. 2011c. 'Umsetzung der deutschen G8-Zusage 2010 ist auf gutem Wege' [The Implementation of the German G8 Commitment 2010 Is Well on Its Way]. Accessed 15 June 2017. http://www.bmz.de/mobil/aktuelles/ meldungen/20110526_pm_83_g8.html.

————. 2011d. 'Press Release: Gudrun Kopp Salutes 50 Years of Development Cooperation with Tanzania'. 8 December. Accessed 15 June 2012. http://www. bmz.de/en/press/aktuelleMeldungen/2011/December/20111208_pm_231_tansa nia/index.html.

————. 2012. 'Länderbeitrag Tansania' [Country Contribution Tanzania]. Accessed 15 June 2013. http://www.bmz.de/de/was_wir_machen/laender_regionen/subsa hara/tansania/zusammenarbeit.html.

————. 2014a. 'Population Dynamics in German Development Cooperation. Position Paper'. BMZ Strategy Paper 10. www.bmz.de/en/publications/type_of_publi cation/strategies/Strategiepapier339_10_2013.pdf.

————. 2014b. 'The BMZ's New Africa Policy. From a Continent of Crises to One of Opportunities'. BMZ Paper 6. Bonn-Berlin: BMZ. Accessed 15 June 2016. https://www.bmz.de/en/publications/type_of_publication/strategies/Strategiepa pier344_06_2014.pdf.

————. 2016. 'Leistungen von Nichtregierungsorganisationen aus Eigenmitteln an Entwicklungsländern 2011–2015' [Contributions of Non-Governmental Organisations to Developing Countries from Own Resources 2011–2015]. Accessed 15 June 2017. http://www.bmz.de/de/ministerium/zahlen_fakten/oda/ngo/index.html.

———. 2017a. 'Africa and Europe – A New Partnership for Development, Peace, and a Better Future. Cornerstones of a Marshall Plan with Africa'. Bonn and Berlin: BMZ. Accessed 15 June 2017. https://www.bmz.de/en/publications/type_of_publication/information_flyer/information_brochures/Materialie270_africa_marshall-plan.pdf.

———. 2017b. 'Table of Cooperation Countries'. Accessed 15 June 2017. http://www.bmz.de/en/countries_regions/laenderkonzentration/index.html.

———. 2017c. 'Tanzania. Situation and Cooperation'. Accessed 18 May 2017. http://www.bmz.de/en/countries_regions/subsahara/tansania/zusammenarbeit/index.html.

———. 2017d. 'Development Information and Education Work'. Federal Ministry for Economic Cooperation and Development. Accessed 27 June 2017. http://www.bmz.de/en/ministry/approaches/inlandsarbeit/index.html.

Boahen, Adu. 1996. 'Africa: Colonialism and Independence'. In *Africa Today*, edited by Ralph Uwechue, 137–50. London: Africa Books.

Bohnet, Michael. 2000. 'Development Policy in Sub-Saharan Africa and the Case of Tanzania'. In *Tanzania Revisited: Political Stability, Aid Dependency and Development Constraints*, edited by Ulf Engel, Gero Erdmann, and Andreas Mehler, 4–20. Hamburg: Institut für Afrikakunde.

Brand, Ulrich, and Markus Wissen. 2013. 'Crisis and Continuity of Capitalist Society-Nature Relationships: The Imperial Mode of Living and the Limits to Environmental Governance'. *Review of International Political Economy* 20 (4): 687–711. doi: 10.1080/09692290.2012.691077.

Brigg, Morgan. 2001. 'Empowering NGOs: The Microcredit Movement through Foucault's Notion of Dispositif'. *Alternatives: Global, Local, Political* 26 (3): 233–58. doi: 10.1177/030437540102600301.

Briggs, John, and Joanne Sharp. 2004. 'Indigenous Knowledges and Development: A Postcolonial Caution'. *Third World Quarterly* 25 (4): 661–76. doi: 10.1080/01436590410001678915.

Brill, Klaus, and Ulrike von Gilardi. 2011. '2nd Tier Marketing Project: Ethiopia (Bayer-USAID Contraceptive Security Initiative)'. Presented at the Annual Membership Meeting Reproductive Health Supplies Coalition, Addis Ababa, 24 June. Accessed 15 June 2017. https://www.rhsupplies.org.

Brot für die Welt. 2008. 'Weniger ist leer' [Less Is Empty]. Accessed 15 June 2017. http://www.weniger-ist-leer.de/.

———. 2013a. 'Lebensmittelspekulation: ein mörderisches Spiel'. Accessed 15 June 2017. http://weyandt.de/wp-content/uploads/2013/12/plakat_banane-300x212.jpg.

———. 2013b. 'Verspielen Sie nicht das Leben von Menschen' [Don't Gamble Away the Lives of Human Beings]. Accessed 15 June 2017. http://www.billy-board.de/verspielen-sie-nicht-das-leben-von-menschen/leben-verspielen/.

Bruchhausen, Walter. 2006. *Medizin zwischen den Welten. Geschichte und Gegenwart des medizinischen Pluralismus im südöstlichen Tansania* [Medicine between the Worlds. History and Present of Medical Pluralism in South-Eastern Tanzania]. Göttingen: V&R unipress.

Bryan, Audrey, and Meliosa Bracken. 2011. 'Learning to Read the World? Teaching and Learning about Global Citizenship and International Development in

Post-Primary Schools'. Irish Aid. Accessed 15 February 2017. http://www.ubuntu.
ie/media/bryan-learning-to-read-the-world.pdf.

Bührmann, Andrea, and Werner Schneider. 2008. *Vom Diskurs zum Dispositiv. Eine Einführung in die Dispositivanalyse* [From Discourse to Dispositif. An Introduction to Dispositif Analysis]. Bielefeld: trancript.

BUKO. 2013. 'BUKO – Wer wir sind' [BUKO – Who We Are]. Accessed 10 January 2012. www.buko.info/wer-wir-sind/buko-positionen/nachhaltigkeitskritik.

BUKO Pharma-Kampagne. 2014. 'Arm und vergessen. Untersuchung des Geschäftsverhaltens von Boehringer Ingelheim, Bayer und Baxter in Uganda' [Poor and Forgotten. Examination of the Commercial Behaviour of Boehringer Ingelheim, Bayer und Baxter in Uganda]. *Pharma-Brief Spezial* 1.

Bundesinstitut für Bevölkerungsforschung. 2014. 'Müttersterblichkeit in Deutschland, 1892 Bis 2012' [Maternal Mortality in Germany, 1892 until 2012]. Accessed 15 January 2017. http://www.bib-demografie.de/DE/ZahlenundFak ten/08/Abbildungen/a_08_32_muettersterblichkeit_d_ab1892.html;jsessionid=897 B9A5E46A10C9BC8B79527A204DA18.2_cid321?nn=3071458.

Bundeszentrale für politische Bildung. 2007. *Afrika verstehen lernen. 12 Bausteine für Unterricht und Projekttage* [Learning to Understand Africa. 12 Modules for Teaching and Project Days]. Bonn: Bundeszentrale für politische Bildung.

———. 2014. 'About'. 20 May. Accessed 15 June 2017. http://www.bpb.de/ die-bpb/138852/the-federal-agency-for-civic-education.

Büschel, Hubertus. 2010. 'Geschichte der Entwicklungspolitik' [History of Development Policy]. Docupedia-Zeitgeschichte. 11 February. Accessed 15 June 2013. https://docupedia.de/zg/Geschichte_der_Entwicklungspolitik?oldid=84614.

Campt, Tina, Pascal Grosse, and Yara-Colette Lemke-Muniz de Faria. 1998. 'Blacks, Germans, and the Politics of Imperial Imagination, 1920–60'. In *The Imperialist Imagination. German Colonialism and Its Legacy*, edited by Sara Friedrichsmeyer, Sara Lennox, and Susanne Zantop, 205–30. Michigan: University of Michigan Press.

Casas, T. 2014. 'Transcending the Coloniality of Development: Moving Beyond Human/Nature Hierarchies'. *American Behavioral Scientist* 58 (1): 30–52. doi: 10.1177/0002764213495030.

Castro Varela, María do Mar, and Alisha M.B. Heinemann. 2016. 'Globale Bildungsbewegungen – Wissensproduktionen verändern' [Global Educational Movements – Changing Knowledge Productions]. *ZEP – Zeitschrift für internationale Bildungsforschung und Entwicklungspädagogik* 39 (2): 17–22. https://www.wax mann.com/index.php?eID=download&id_artikel=ART101991&uid=frei.

Césaire, Aimé. 1953. *Discours sur le Colonialisme*. Paris: Présence Africaine.

Chachage, Chachage S.L. 2006. 'A Patriot's Response to Hon. Wolfgang Ringe, German Ambassador to Tanzania'. 22 March. Accessed 15 June 2010. http:// www.tanzania-network.de/upload/PDF/MajiMaji/Songea/2006_03_20_Cha- chage_response.pdf.

Chachage, Chachage S.L., and Marjorie Mbilinyi, eds. 2003. *Against Neoliberalism. Gender Democracy and Development*. Dar es Salaam: E and D.

Chimhowu, Admos, and Philip Woodhouse. 2005. 'Development Studies, Nature and Natural Resources: Changing Narratives and Discursive Practices'. In *A Radical*

History of Development Studies: Individuals, Institutions and Ideologies, edited by Uma Kothari, 180–99. London: Zed Books.

Chouliaraki, Lilie. 2010. 'Post-Humanitarianism: Humanitarian Communication beyond a Politics of Pity'. *International Journal of Cultural Studies* 13 (2): 107–26. doi: 10.1177/1367877909356720.

CIA World Factbook. 2014. 'Country Comparison: Maternal Mortality Rate'. Accessed 15 June 2016. https://www.cia.gov/library/publications/the-world-fact book/rankorder/2223rank.html.

Cole, Teju. 2012. '5 – The White Savior Industrial Complex Is Not about Justice. It Is about Having a Big Emotional Experience That Validates Privilege'. Microblog. @tejucole. 8 March. Accessed 11 April 2017. https://twitter.com/tejucole/status/1 77810262223626241?lang=en.

Colwell, Anne Stacie. 2001. 'Vision and Revision: Demography, Maternal and Child Health Development, and the Representation of Native Women in Colonial Tanzania'. PhD diss., University of Illinois.

CONCORD. 2012. 'Aid We Can – Invest More in Global Development'. AidWatch Report. Brussels: CONCORD.

———. 2016. 'AidWatch Report 2016'. Brussels: CONCORD.

Conrad, Sebastian. 2004. ' "Eingeborenenpolitik" in Kolonie und Metropole. "Erziehung zur Arbeit" in Ostafrika und Ostwestfalen' ['Native Policy' in Colony and Metropolis. 'Educating for Work' in East Africa and East Westphalia]. In *Das Kaiserreich transnational. Deutschland in der Welt 1871–1914*, edited by Sebastian Conrad and Jürgen Osterhammel, 107–28. Göttingen: Vandenhoeck & Ruprecht.

———. 2008. *Deutsche Kolonialgeschichte* [German Colonial History]. München: C.H. Beck.

Cooke, Bill. 2001. 'From Colonial Administration to Development Management'. IDPM Discussion Paper Series 63.

Cowen, Michael, and Robert Shenton. 1996. *Doctrines of Development*. London: Routledge.

Crewe, Emma, and Elizabeth Harrison. 1998. *Whose Development? An Ethnography of Aid*. London and New York: Zed Books.

Crush, Jonathan. 1994. 'Post-Colonialism, De-Colonization and Geography'. In *Geography and Empire*, edited by Anne Godlewska and Neil Smith, 333–50. Oxford: Blackwell.

———. 1995a. 'Introduction. Imagining Development'. In *Power of Development*, edited by Jonathan Crush, 1–23. London: Routledge.

———. ed. 1995b. *Power of Development*. London: Routledge.

Danielzik, Chandra-Milena. 2013. 'Überlegenheitsdenken fällt nicht vom Himmel. Postkoloniale Perspektiven auf Globales Lernen und Bildung für Nachhaltige Entwicklung' [Superiority Thinking Does Not Fall from the Sky. Postcolonial Perspectives on Global Learning and Education for Sustainable Development]. *ZEP – Zeitschrift für internationale Bildungsforschung und Entwicklungspädagogik* 13 (1): 26–33. https://www.waxmann.com/index. php?eID=download&id_artikel=ART101266&uid=frei.

Danielzik, Chandra-Milena, and Daniel Bendix. 2010. 'Exotismus. "Get into the Mystery . . ."' [Exoticism. 'Get into the Mystery . . .']. *ROSA – Die Zeitschrift für Geschlechterforschung* 40: 4–7.

———. 2013a. 'Bacardi-Feeling und Entwicklungsauftrag – zum Zusammenhang von Exotismus und Entwicklungszusammenarbeit' [Bacardi Feeling and the Development Mission – On the Relationship between Exoticism and Development Cooperation]. In *Develop-Mental Turn. Neue Beiträge zu einer rassismuskritischen entwicklungspolitischen Bildungs- und Projektarbeit*, edited by Berliner Entwicklungspolitischer Ratschlag e.V., 36–37. Berlin: BER.

———. 2013b. '(In)Security in Postcolonial Development Education in Germany'. *Critical Studies on Security* 1 (3): 352–54. doi: 10.1080/21624887.2013.850223.

———. 2016. 'Mit dem postkolonialen Pflug über entwicklungspolitische Felder – die Beispiele Tourismus- und reproduktive Gesundheitspolitik' [With the Postcolonial Plough across Fields of Development Policy – The Examples of Tourism and Reproductive Health Policy]. In *Postkoloniale Politikwissenschaft: Theoretische und Empirische Zugänge*, edited by Aram Ziai, 273–91. Bielefeld: trancript.

Danielzik, Chandra-Milena, and Beate Flechtker. 2012. 'Wer mit zweitens anfängt. Bildung für nachhaltige Entwicklung kann Machtwissen tradieren' [To Start with Secondly. Education for Sustainable Development Can Transmit Power-Knowledge]. *iz3w* 329: D8–10.

Danielzik, Chandra-Milena, Timo Kiesel, and Daniel Bendix. 2013. 'Bildung für nachhaltige Ungleichheit? Eine postkoloniale Analyse von Materialien der entwicklungspolitischen Bildungsarbeit in Deutschland' [Education for Sustainable Inequality? A Postcolonial Analysis of Materials for Development Education in Germany]. Berlin: glokal e.V. http://www.glokal.org/publikationen/bildung-fuer-nachhaltige-ungleichheit/.

Darnton, Andrew, and Martin Kirk. 2011. *Finding Frames. New Ways to Engage the UK Public in Global Poverty.* http://valuesandframes.org/.

decolonize orientierungsrahmen! 2014. 'Decolonize Orientierungsrahmen!' https://decolonizeorientierungsrahmen.wordpress.com.

Delegates to the I. Transnational Congress on the Ovaherero and Nama Genocides. 2016. 'Berlin Resolution 2016. Restorative Justice after Genocide'. Accessed 11 April 2017. http://genocide-namibia.net/2016/10/berlin-resolution-2016/.

Der Professorenrat des Hamburgischen Kolonialinstituts. 1913. 'Koloniale Preisaufgabe' [Colonial Contest Task]. *Archiv für Schiffs- und Tropenhygiene* 17 (16): 567.

Dernburg, Bernhard. 1907. *Zielpunkte des deutschen Kolonialwesens* [Goals for German Colonial Matters]. Berlin: Ernst Siegfried Mittler und Sohn.

Deuser, Patricia. 2010. 'Genderspezifische Entwicklungspolitiken und Bevölkerungsdiskurse. Das Konzept der "Sexuellen und Reproduktiven Gesundheit und Rechte" aus postkolonialer Perspektive' [Gender-Specific Development Policies and Population Discourses. The Concept of 'Sexual and Reproductive Health and Rights' from a Postcolonial Perspective]. *Peripherie. Zeitschrift für Politik und Ökonomie in der Dritten Welt* 120: 427–51.

Deutsche Gesellschaft für Eingebornenschutz. 1914a. 'Eingabe der deutschen Gesellschaft für Eingebornenschutz an den Reichstag und das Reichs-Kolonialamt'

[Petition by the Society for the Protection of the Natives to the Reichstag and the Imperial Colonial Office]. *Koloniale Rundschau – Monatsschrift für die Interessen unserer Schutzgebiete und ihrer Bewohner* 3: 129–32.

———. 1914b. 'Eingebornenschutz' [Protection of the Natives]. *Koloniale Rundschau – Monatsschrift für die Interessen unserer Schutzgebiete und ihrer Bewohner* 1: 1–5.

Deutsche Welle. 2012. 'Seven Billion and Climbing, But Not Everywhere'. dw.com, 11 July. Accessed 11 April 2017. http://dw.com/p/15V5w.

Deutscher Entwicklungsdienst. 2006. *Globales Lernen. Arbeitsblätter für die entwicklungspolitische Bildungsarbeit* [Global Learning. Worksheets for Development Education]. 2. Revised edition. Bonn: DED. Accessed 11 April 2017. http://www.epn-hessen.de/wp-content/uploads/DED_Globales_Lernen_Arbeitsblaetter.pdf.

Deutscher Frauenverein für Krankenpflege in den Kolonien. 1909. 'Schreiben an den Staatssekretär des Reichskolonialamtes' [Letter to the State Secretary of the Imperial Colonial Office]. 13 August 1909; Federal German Archives: R1001/6032/13.

DIANOKIE. 2016. 'Adbusting zu humanitärer Spendenwerbung – es reicht mit rassistischer Werbung' [Adbusting of Humanitarian Billboard Advertising – It's Enough Racist Advertising]. Accessed 11 April 2017. http://maqui.blogsport.eu/2016/12/26/b-adbusting-zu-humanitaerer-spendenwerbung-es-reicht-mit-rassistischer-werbung/.

Dietze, Gabriele. 2016. 'Ethnosexismus. Sex-Mob-Narrative um die Kölner Sylvesternacht' [Ethnosexism. Sex-Mob-Narratives in the Context of New Year's in Cologne]. *Movements. Journal für kritische Migrations- und Grenzregimeforschung* 2 (1). http://movements-journal.org/issues/03.rassismus/10.dietze--ethnosexismus.html.

Dirlik, Arif. 1997. *The Postcolonial Aura. Third World Criticism in the Age of Global Capitalism*. Oxford: Westview Press.

Dogra, Nandita. 2011. 'The Mixed Metaphor of "Third World Woman": Gendered Representations by International Development NGOs'. *Third World Quarterly* 32 (2): 333–48. doi: 10.1080/01436597.2011.560472.

DSW. 2005. 'Reproduktive Gesundheit fördern – Armut bekämpfen' [Promoting Reproductive Health – Fighting Poverty]. Hannover: Deutsche Stiftung Weltbevölkerung. Accessed 11 April 2011. http://www.weltbevoelkerung.de.

———. 2008. 'Wie viele Menschen (er)trägt die Erde?' [How Many People Can the Earth Carry/Endure?]. Hannover: Deutsche Stiftung Weltbevölkerung. Accessed 11 April 2012. http://www.weltbevoelkerung.de/pdf/fs_ressourcen.pdf.

———. 2010. 'DSW-Datenreport 2010. Soziale und demographische Daten zu Weltbevölkerung' [DSW Data Report 2010. Social and Demographic Data on Global Population]. Hannover: Deutsche Stiftung Weltbevölkerung. Accessed 11 April 2016. http://www.weltbevoelkerung.de/pdf/dsw_datenreport_10.pdf.

———. 2012. 'DSW Tanzania'. Accessed 11 April 2016. http://www.dsw-online.org/dsw-worldwide/east-africa/tanzania/news.html.

———. 2015. 'Jahresbericht 2014/2015' [Annual Report 2014/2015]. Accessed 6 June 2016. http://www.weltbevoelkerung.de/uploads/tx_aedswpublication/JB_2015_web.pdf.

Duden, Barbara. 1997. 'Population'. In *The Development Dictionary. A Guide to Knowledge as Power*, edited by Wolfgang Sachs, 146–57. Johannesburg: Witwatersrand University Press.

Duffield, Mark. 2006. 'Racism, Migration and Development'. *Progress in Development Studies* 6 (1): 68–79. doi: 10.1191/1464993406ps128oa.

Dussel, Enrique. 1995. *The Invention of the Americas. Eclipse of 'the Other' and the Myth of Modernity*. New York: Continuum. http://bibliotecavirtual.clacso.org.ar/ar/libros/dussel/1492in/1492in.html.

———. 2010. *Der Gegendiskurs der Moderne – Kölner Vorlesungen*. Wien-Berlin: Turia + Kant.

Dyer, Richard. 1997. *White: Essays on Race and Culture*. London and New York: Routledge.

Dziedzic, Daniela, and Ute Renköwitz. 1999. 'Zur Kulturgeschichte der Gebärhaltung' [On the Cultural History of Birth Positions]. In *Hebammenkunst gestern und heute. Zur Kultur des Gebärens durch drei Jahrhunderte*, edited by Marita Metz-Becker, 57–69. Marburg: Jonas.

Eckart, Wolfgang. 1997. *Medizin und Kolonialimperialismus: Deutschland 1884–1945* [Medicine and Colonial Imperialism: Germany 1884–1945]. Paderborn; München; Wien; and Zürich: Ferdinand Schöningh.

Eckert, Andreas, and Albert Wirz. 2002. 'Wir nicht, die anderen auch. Deutschland und der Kolonialismus' [Not Us, the Others as Well. Germany and Colonialism]. In *Jenseits des Eurozentrismus. Postkoloniale Perspektiven in den Geschichts- und Kulturwissenschaften*, edited by Sebastian Conrad and Shalini Randeria, 373–93. Frankfurt am Main: Campus.

El-Tayeb, Fatima. 2011. *European Others. Queering Ethnicity in Postnational Europe*. Minneapolis: Minnesota University Press.

———. 2016. *Undeutsch. Die Konstruktion des Anderen in der postmigrantischen Gesellschaft* [Ungerman. The Construction of the Other in the Postmigrant Society]. Bielefeld: transcript.

Entwicklungspolitisches Bildungs- und Informationszentrum Berlin. 2011. *Schöne Ferien für Tourismuskaufleute* [Nice Holidays for Tourism Entrepreneurs]. Accessed 11 April 2017. http://www.epiz-berlin.de/wp-content/uploads/2011-AH-Schoene-Ferien.pdf.

EPIZ et al. 2013. 'Plakatkampagne "The Big Five"' [Billboard Campaign 'The Big Five']. Accessed 11 April 2017. https://www.inkota.de/fileadmin/user_upload/Aktuelles/Kampagnen/Offener_Brief_EPIZ_Plakat_Big_Five.pdf.

Eriksson Baaz, Maria. 2005. *The Paternalism of Partnership. A Postcolonial Reading of Development Politics*. London and New York: Zed Books.

Escobar, Arturo. 1994. *Encountering Development. The Making and Unmaking of the Third World*. Princeton: Princeton University Press.

evaplan. 2009. 'Tanzania Progress Review Report'. GTZ. Accessed 18 May 2011. http://www.tgpsh.or.tz/index.php?eID=tx_nawsecuredl&u=0&file=uploads/media/Pfk-Final_aproved.pdf&t=1249058046&hash=a5a5a33ea78d342ecf74f1989a06b708.

FairBindung, and Konzeptwerk Neue Ökonomie. 2013. *Endlich Wachstum! Wirtschaftswachstum – Grenzen – Alternativen* [Finally/Finite Growth! Economic Growth – Limits – Alternatives]. Berlin: FairBindung.

Fanon, Frantz. 1965. *The Wretched of the Earth*. New York: Grove Press.
———. 2008. *Black Skin, White Masks*. New York: Grove Press.
Farr, Arnold. 2005. 'Wie Weißsein sichtbar wird. Aufklärungsrassismus und die Struktur eines rassifizierten Bewusstseins' [How Whiteness Becomes Visible. Enlightenment Racism and the Structure of a Racialised Consciousness]. In *Mythen, Masken und Subjekte. Kritische Weißseinsforschung in Deutschland*, edited by Maureen Maisha Eggers, Grada Kilomba, Peggy Piesche, and Susan Arndt, 40–55. Münster: Unrast.
Faust, Jörg, and Sebastian Ziaja. 2012. 'German Aid Allocation and Partner Country Selection. Development-Orientation, Self-Interests and Path Dependency'. Discussion Paper 7. Bonn: Deutsches Institut für Entwicklungspolitik. Accessed 11 April 2017. http://www.die-gdi.de/CMS-Homepage/openwebcms3. nsf/%28ynDK_contentByKey%29/ANES-8V8A59/$FILE/DP%207.2012.pdf.
Federal Ministry of Finance. 2017. 'Bundeshaushaltsplan 2017. Einzelplan 23: Bundesministerium für wirtschaftliche Zusammenarbeit und Entwicklung' Federal Budget 2017. Section 23. Federal Ministry for Economic Cooperation and Development. Accessed 11 July 2017. https://www.bundeshaushalt-info.de/fileadmin/ de.bundeshaushalt/content_de/dokumente/2017/soll/epl23.pdf#page=23.
Feldmann, Hermann. 1923. 'Die Erhaltung und Vermehrung der Eingeborenen-Bevölkerung' [Preservation and Reproduction of the Native Population]. In *Abhandlungen aus dem Gebiet der Auslandskunde. Wissenschaftliche Beiträge zur Frage der Erhaltung und Vermehrung der Eingeborenen-Bevölkerung. Ergebnisse der Eduard-Woermann-Preisaufgabe* 13: 83–148. Hamburg: L. Friederichsen & Co.
Ferdinand, Ursula. 1999. *Das Malthusische Erbe. Entwicklungssträge der Bevölkerungstheorie im 19. Jahrhundert und deren Einfluß auf die radikale Frauenbewegung in Deutschland* [The Malthusian Legacy. Development Strands of Population Theory in the 19th Century and Its Influence on the Radical Women's Movement in Germany]. Münster: LIT.
Ferguson, James. 1994. *The Anti-Politics Machine. 'Development', Depolitization, and Bureaucratic Power in Lesotho*. Minneapolis: University of Minnesota Press.
Ferzacca, Steve. 2003. 'Post-Colonial Development and Health'. In *Encyclopedia of Medical Anthropology. Health and Illness in the World's Cultures*, edited by Carol R. Ember and Melvin Ember, 184–91. New York: Springer.
Fiske, John. 1987. *Television Culture*. London: Routledge.
Flechtker, Beate, Alice Stein, and Urmila Goel. 2013. 'Eine unmögliche Verbindung? Rassismuskritische Bildung und entwicklungspolitische Spendenwerbung' [An Impossible Connection? Racism-Critical Education and Development Fundraising]. In *Develop-Mental Turn. Neue Beiträge zu einer rassismuskritschen entwicklungspolitischen Bildungs- und Projektarbeit*, 68–72. Berlin: BER.
Foucault, Michel. 1972. *The Archaeology of Knowledge*. London: Tavostock.
———. 1977. 'Nietzsche, Genealogy, History'. In *Language, Counter-Memory, Practice. Selected Essays and Interviews*, edited by Donald F. Bouchard, 139–64. Ithaca: Cornell University Press.
———. 1979. *The History of Sexuality Volume 1: An Introduction*. London: Allen Lane.
———. 1980. *Power/Knowledge. Selected Interviews and Other Writings, 1972–1977*, edited by Colin Gordon. New York: Pantheon Book.

FP2020. 2016. 'Government of Germany Announces New FP2020 Commitment'. Accessed 11 April 2017. http://www.familyplanning2020.org/articles/14458.

Frey, Marc. 2007. 'Experten, Stiftungen und Politik. Zur Genese des globalen Diskurses über Bevölkerung seit 1945' [Experts, Foundations, and Politics. On the Genesis of the Global Discourse on Population since 1945]. Zeithistorische Forschungen/Studies in Contemporary History 4. http://www.zeithistorische-forschungen.de/16126041-Frey-2-2007.

Friedrichsmeyer, Sara, Sara Lennox, and Susanne Zantop. 1998. 'Introduction'. In *The Imperialist Imagination. German Colonialism and Its Legacy*, edited by Sara Friedrichsmeyer, Sara Lennox, and Susanne Zantop, 1–29. Michigan: University of Michigan Press.

Gann, Lewis H. 1987. 'Marginal Colonialism: The German Case'. In *Germans in the Tropics. Essays in German Colonial History*, edited by Arthur J. Knoll and Lewis H. Gann, 1–17. New York: Greenwood.

Gemeinsam für Afrika. 2009. 'Ein anderes Bild von Afrika. Anregungen für den Unterricht in den Sekundarstufen I und II' [A Different Image of Africa. Suggestions for Teaching in Secondary Levels I and II]. Accessed 11 April 2017. http://www.gemeinsam-fuer-afrika.de/wp-content/uploads/2012/04/UM-Sek-I+II_Ein-anderes-Bild-von-Afrika-2006.pdf.

———. 2011. 'Mädchen und Frauen bewegen Afrika. Unterrichtsmaterialien für die Grundschule' [Girls and Women Move Africa. Materials for Teaching for Primary School]. Accessed 11 April 2017. http://www.gemeinsam-fuer-afrika.de/wp-content/uploads/2012/04/UM-GS_Maedchen-und-Frauen-1.pdf.

German Embassy Dar es Salaam. 2012. 'Tanzanian-German Development Cooperation'. Dar es Salaam: German Embassy Dar es Salaam. Accessed 11 April 2013. http://www.daressalam.diplo.de/contentblob/1594010/Daten/89281/brochure.pdf.

German Federal Foreign Office. 2011. *Germany and Africa: A Strategy Paper by the German Government*. Berlin: German Federal Foreign Office.

———. 2012. 'Tanzania'. Accessed 14 April 2014. http://www.auswaertiges-amt.de/EN/Aussenpolitik/Laender/Laenderinfos/01-Nodes/Tanzania_node.html.

German-African Business Association. 2015. *Made in Germany*. Accessed 11 April 2017. http://www.afrikaverein.de/uploads/media/Afrika-Verein_Made-in-Germany_A4_final.pdf.

Global Industry Analysts, Inc. 2014. *Contraceptives – A Global Strategic Business Report*. San Jose: GIA.

Goel, Urmila. 2011. 'Rassismus- und privilegienkritische Bildungsarbeit' [Racism- and Privilege-Critical Educational Work]. In *weltwärts pädagogisch begleiten*, edited by Diana Grundmann and Bernd Overwien, 24–31. Kassel: Kassel University Press.

Goldberg, David Theo. 2006. 'Racial Europeanization'. *Ethnic and Racial Studies* 29 (2): 331–64. doi: 10.1080/01419870500465611.

Goldman, Michael. 2005. *Imperial Nature. The World Bank and Struggles for Social Justice in the Age of Globalization*. New Haven and London: Yale University Press.

Gouverneur von Deutsch-Ostafrika. 1909. 'Anregung des Frauen-Vereins, ein Wöchnerinnenheim für farbige Frauen in Dar zu errichten' [Suggestion by the Women's

Association to Construct a Maternity Home for Coloured Women in Dar]. 11 October 1909; Federal German Archives: R1001/6032/13.

———. 1913. 'Verordnung des Gouverneurs von Deutsch-Ostafrika, betr. Die Bildung von Gesundheitskommissionen' [Decree of the Governor of German East Africa, Regarding the Creation of Health Commissions]. *Deutsches Kolonialblatt. Amtsblatt für die Schutzgebiete in Afrika und in der Südsee* 24 (10): 436–37.

Green, Maia. 1999. 'Women Work Is Weeping. Constructions of Gender in a Catholic Community'. In *Those Who Play with Fire. Gender, Fertility and Transformation in East and Souther Africa*, edited by Henrietta L. Moore, Todd Sanders, and Bwire Kaare, 255–80. London and New Brunswick: The Athlone Press.

Grosse, Pascal. 2000. *Kolonialismus, Eugenik und bürgerliche Gesellschaft in Deutschland 1850–1918* [Colonialism, Eugenics, and Bourgeois Society in German 1850–1918]. Frankfurt am Main and New York: Campus.

Gründer, Horst, ed. 1999. '. . . da und dort ein junges Deutschland gründen'. Rassismus, Kolonien und kolonialer Gedanke vom 16. bis 20. Jahrhundert [' . . . to Establish a Young Germany Here and There'. Racism, Colonialism, and the Colonial Idea from the 16th to the 20th Century]. München: dtv.

GTZ. 2009. 'TGPSH Programme Progress Review'. Accessed 11 April 2011. http://www.tgpsh.or.tz/index.php?eID=tx_nawsecuredl&u=0&file=uploads/media/Pfk-Final_aproved.pdf&t=1249058046&hash=a5a5a33ea78d342ecf74f1989a06b708.

———. 2010. 'Press Release: German Development Cooperation with Tanzania on a Glance'. Accessed through German Development Professional.

Gupta, Akhil, and James Ferguson. 1997. 'Discipline and Practice. "The Field" as Site, Method, and Location in Anthropology'. In *Anthropological Locations. Boundaries and Grounds of a Field Science*, edited by Akhil Gupta and James Ferguson, 1–46. Berkeley; Los Angeles; and London: University of California Press.

Gutiérrez Rodríguez, Encarnación. 2010. *Migration, Domestic Work and Affect. A Decolonial Approach on Value and the Feminization of Labour*. London and New York: Routledge.

Ha, Kien Nghi. 2005. 'Macht(t)Raum(a) Berlin – Deutschland als Kolonialgesellschaft' [Power Space/Trauma Berlin – Germany as Colonial Society]. In *Mythen, Masken und Subjekte. Kritische Weißseinsforschung in Deutschland*, edited by Maureen Maisha Eggers, Grada Kilomba, Peggy Piesche, and Susan Arndt, 105–17. Münster: Unrast.

Hachfeld, David, Christine Pohl, and Marita Wiggerthale. 2012. 'Mit Essen spielt man nicht! Die deutsche Finanzbranche und das Geschäft mit dem Hunger' ['Don't Play with Food! The German Financial Sector and the Business with Hunger]. Berlin: Oxfam Germany. Accessed 11 April 2017. https://www.oxfam.de/system/files/o_nms_2013_mb_web.pdf.

Halfon, Saul. 1997. 'Over-Populating the World: Notes toward a Discursive Reading'. In *Changing Life: Genomes, Ecologies, Bodies, Commodities*, edited by Peter Taylor, Saul Halfon, and Paul Edwards, 121–48. Minneapolis: University of Minnesota Press.

Hall, Stuart. 1980. 'Encoding/Decoding'. In *Culture – Media – Language*, edited by Stuart Hall, Dorothy Hobson, Andrew Lowe, and Paul Willis, 128–38. London: Hutchinson.

————. 1996. 'When Was "the Post-Colonial"? Thinking at the Limit'. In *The Post-Colonial Question. Common Skies, Divided Horizons*, edited by Iain Chambers and Lidia Curti, 242–60. London: Routledge.

————. 2011. 'The Neo-Liberal Revolution'. *Cultural Studies* 25 (6): 705–28. doi: 10.1080/09502386.2011.619886.

Halling, Thorsten, Julia Schäfer, and Jörg Vögele. 2005. 'Volk, Volkskörper, Volkswirtschaft – Bevölkerungsfragen in Forschung und Lehre von Nationalökonomie und Medizin' [Nation, National Body, National Economy – Population Questions in Research and Teaching of National Economy and Medicine]. In *Das Konstrukt 'Bevölkerung' vor, im und nach dem 'Dritten Reich'*, edited by Rainer Mackensen and Jürgen Reulecke, 388–428. Wiesbaden: VS Verlag für Sozialwissenschaften.

Handelsblatt Global. 2017. 'Helping Africa to Help Germany'. 5 May. Accessed 11 April 2017. https://global.handelsblatt.com/politics/helping-africa-to-help-germany-760232.

Hansen, Peo, and Stefan Jonsson. 2014. *Eurafrica. The Untold History of European Integration and Colonialism*. London: Bloomsbury Academic.

Hartmann, Betsy. 1997a. 'Population Control I: Birth of an Ideology'. *International Journal of Health Services* 27 (3): 523–40. doi: 10.2190/bl3n-xajx-0yqb-vqbx.

————. 1997b. 'Population Control II: The Population Establishment Today'. *International Journal of Health Services* 27 (3): 541–57. doi: 10.2190/hkgj-1ymy-q3jw-96lu.

Hauck, Gerhard. 2003. *Die Gesellschaftstheorie und ihr Anderes. Wider den Eurozentrismus der Sozialwissenschaften* [Social Theory and Its Other. Against the Eurocentrism in the Social Sciences]. Münster: Westfälisches Dampfboot.

Hegel, G. W. F. 1822. *Vorlesungen, ausgewählte Nachschriften und Manuskripte. Bd. 12. Vorlesungen über die Philosophie der Weltgeschichte* [Lectures, Selected Postscripts and Manuscripts. Vol. 12. Lectures on the Philosophy of World History], edited by Karl Bremer. Hamburg: Meiner.

Hendrixson, Anne. 2007. 'What's Wrong with the "Demographic Dividend" Concept?' *DifferenTakes* 44. https://dspace.hampshire.edu/handle/10009/898.

Heron, Barbara. 2007. *Desire for Development. Whiteness, Gender, and the Helping Imperative*. Waterloo: Wilfrid Laurier University Press.

Hesselink, Lisbeth. 2011. *Healers on the Colonial Market: Native Doctors and Midwives in the Dutch East Indies*. Leiden: KITLV Press. http://www.oapen.org/download?type=document&docid=400271.

Hodge, John M. 2007. *Triumph of the Expert. Agrarian Doctrines of Development and the Legacies of British Colonialism*. Athens: Ohio University Press.

hooks, bell. 1994. *Teaching to Transgress. Education as the Practice of Freedom*. New York: Routledge.

Howell, Jude. 1994. 'The End of an Era: The Rise and Fall of G.D.R. Aid'. *The Journal of Modern African Studies* 32 (2): 305–28. doi: 10.2307/161772.

Hummel, Diana. 2006. 'Demographisierung gesellschaftlicher Probleme?' [Demographization of Social Problems]. In *Der demographische Wandel*, edited by Peter Berger and Heike Kahlert, 27–52. Frankfurt am Main: Campus.

————. 2007. 'Bevölkerungsentwicklung und gesellschaftliche Naturverhältnisse – Eine sozial-ökologische Perspektive' [Population Development and Societal

Relationship to Nature – A Social-Ecological Perspective]. In *Grenzen der Bevölkerungspolitik. Strategien und Diskurse demographischer Steuerung*, edited by Diana Auth and Barbara Holland-Cunz, 181–94. Opladen and Farmington Hills: Budrich.

Hunt, Nancy Rose. 1999. *A Colonial Lexicon. Of Birth Ritual, Medicalization, and Mobility in the Congo*. Durham and London: Duke University Press.

Iliffe, John. 1969. *Tanganyika under German Rule 1905–1912*. Cambridge: Cambridge University Press.

Informationsbüro Nicaragua. 2011a. *Fokuscafé Lateinamerika – von der Kolonialzeit zur Unabhängigkeit in die Gegenwart – Werkheft zum Modul Geschichte und Klischees* [Focus Café Latin America – From Colonial Times to Independence in the Present – Booklet to the Module History and Clichés]. Wuppertal: Informationsbüro Lateinamerika.

———. ed. 2011b. *Fokuscafé Lateinamerika – Wenn der Lohn zum Überleben nicht reicht – Werkheft zum Modul Ökonomie* [Focus Café Latin America – When Wages Are Not Enough to Survive – Booklet to the Module Economy]. Wuppertal: Informationsbüro Lateinamerika.

InWEnt, and BMZ. 2007. *Förderprogramme Entwicklungspolitische Bildungsarbeit* [Funding Programmes for Development Education Work]. www.ewik.de/coreme dia/generator/ewik/de/Externe_20Links/Referenten_2C_20Finanzierung/F_C3_ B6rderprogramme_20ep_20Bildung.pdf.

ISD et al. 2013. 'Offene Brief an Venro – von einem Zusammenschluss deutscher Nicht-Regierungsorganisationen in der Entwicklungszusammenarbeit' [Open Letter to Venro – by a Network of German Non-Governmental Organisations in Development Cooperation]. 21 March. Accessed 11 April 2017. http://isdon-line.de/offene-brief-an-venro-von-einem-zusammenschluss-deutscher-nicht-regier ungsorganisationen-in-der-entwicklungszusammenarbeit/.

Ittameier, Carl. 1923. 'Die Erhaltung und Vermehrung der Eingeborenen-Bevölkerung' [Preservation and Reproduction of the Native Population]. In *Abhandlungen aus dem Gebiet der Auslandskunde. Wissenschaftliche Beiträge zur Frage der Erhaltung und Vermehrung der Eingeborenen-Bevölkerung. Ergebnisse der Eduard-Woermann-Preisaufgabe* 13: 1–82. Hamburg: L. Friederichsen & Co.

Jacobstein, Roy, and Harriet Stanley. 2013. 'Contraceptive Implants: Providing Better Choice to Meet Growing Family Planning Demand'. *Global Health: Science and Practice* 1 (1): 11–17. doi: 10.9745/GHSP-D-12–00003.

Jensen, Robert. 2005. *The Heart of Whiteness. Confronting Race, Racism, and White Privilege*. San Francisco: City Lights.

Jentzsch, Corinna. 2013. 'Germany's African "Big Five"'. Africasacountry. Accessed 11 April 2014. http://africasacountry.com/germanys-african-big-five/.

Jolly, Margret. 1998. 'Introduction. Colonial and Postcolonial Plots in Histories of Maternities and Modernities'. In *Maternities and Modernities: Colonial and Postcolonial Experiences in Asia and the Pacific*, edited by Kalpana Ram and Margret Jolly, 1–25. Cambridge: Cambridge University Press.

Jouhy, Ernest. 1985. *Bleiche Herrschaft – Dunkle Kulturen. Essais zur Bildung in Nord und Süd* [Pale Domination – Dark Cultures. Essays on Education in North and South]. Frankfurt am Main: IKO.

Kahlon, Rajkamal, Lena Ziyal, Isaiah Lopez, and Aïcha Diallo. 2016. 'We Never Need to Have Our Hands Out'. In *Die Spitze des Eisbergs. Spendenwerbung der Internationalen Hilfsorganisationen – Kritik und Alternativen*, edited by glokal and ISD, 18–24. Berlin: glokal and ISD. Accessed 11 April 2017. http://www.glokal. org/wp-content/uploads/2017/02/Die-Spitze-des-Eisbergs_e-pub_final.pdf.

Kapoor, Ilan. 2004. 'Hyper-Self-Reflexive Development? Spivak on Representing the Third World "Other"'. *Third World Quarterly* 25 (4): 627–47. doi: 10.1080/01436590410001678898.

———. 2008. *The Postcolonial Politics of Development*. Oxon: Routledge.

Kebede, Messay. 2004. 'African Development and the Primacy of Mental Decolonization'. *African Development* 19 (1): 107–29. doi: 10.4314/ad.v29i1.22188.

Kerchner, Brigitte. 2006. 'Genealogie und Performanz. Überlegungen zu einer kritischen Analyse des Regierens' [Genealogy and Performance. Thoughts on a Critical Analysis of Governance]. In *Politisierung und Ent-Politisierung als performative Praxis*, edited by Detlef Georgia Schulze, Sabine Berghan, and Frieder Otto Wolf, 58–81. Münster: Westfälisches Dampfboot.

KfW. 2005. 'Tanzania: Sector Programme Family Planning I and II. Ex-Post Evaluation'. Frankfurt am Main: Kreditanstalt für Wiederaufbau. Accessed 23 November 2017. https://www.kfw-entwicklungsbank.de/migration/Entwicklungs bank-Startseite/Development-Finance/Evaluation/Results-and-Publications/PDF-Dokumente-R-Z/Tanzania_Family_Planning_2004.pdf.

Kiesel, Timo, and Daniel Bendix. 2010. 'White Charity: Eine postkoloniale, rassismuskritische Analyse der entwicklungspolitischen Plakatwerbung in Deutschland' [White Charity: A Postcolonial, Race-Critical Analysis of Billboard Advertising by Development Aid Organisations in Germany]. *Peripherie. Zeitschrift für Politik und Ökonomie in der Dritten Welt* 120: 482–95. http://www.budrich-journals.de/ index.php/peripherie/article/view/24068/21030.

Kiesel, Timo, and Tahir Della. 2014. ' "Wir befreien weltweit!" Rassismuskritik und entwicklungspolitische Spendenwerbung, aktuelle Herausforderungen' ['We Liberate Worldwide!' Critique of Racism and Charity Advertising]. Accessed 13 September 2017. http://www.whitecharity.de/wp-content/uploads/Della_Kiesel_Wir-befreien-Weltweit.pdf.

Kindernothilfe. 2017a. 'Das Leben in der Stadt ist kein Kinderspiel' [Life in the City Is No Child's Game]. Accessed 11 April 2017. https://www.kindernothilfe.de/ keinkinderspiel.html.

———. 2017b. 'Wir schließen Bildungslücken' [We Close Gaps in Education]. Accessed 11 April 2017. http://bernhard-koppenhoefer.de/texter-arbeiten-plakate/ texter-plakat-kindernothilfe0/.

Kjekshus, Helge. 1996. *Ecology Control and Economic Development in East African History: The Case of Tanganyika 1850–1950*. London: James Currey.

Kleinschmidt, Malte, Sebastian Fischer, Florian Fischer, and Dirk Lange. 2015. 'Globalisierung, globale Ungleichheit und Entwicklung in den Vorstellungen von Schüler/Inne/n. Die empirische Untersuchung von Lernvoraussetzungen als Ausgangspunkt für die Gestaltung Globalen Lernens' [Globalization, Global Inequality and Development in the Perceptions of Students.

The Empirical Analysis of Learning Conditions as Precondition for the Design of Global Learning]. *ZEP – Zeitschrift für internationale Bildungsforschung und Entwicklungspädagogik* 38 (3): 26–30. https://www.waxmann.com/index. php?eID=download&id_artikel=ART101799&uid=frei.

KMK, and BMZ. 2007. *Orientierungsrahmen für den Lernbereich Globale Entwicklung im Rahmen einer Bildung für nachhaltige Entwicklung* [Curriculum Framework for Global Development Education in the Context of Education for Sustainable Development]. Bonn and Berlin: BMZ and KMK. Accessed 28 March 2017. http://www.kmk.org/fileadmin/Dateien/veroeffentlichungen_ beschluesse/2007/2007_06_00_Orientierungsrahmen_Globale_Entwicklung.pdf.

———. 2009. *A Cross-Curricular Framework for Global Development Education in the Context of Education for Sustainable Development – Condensed Version*. Bonn and Berlin: KMK and BMZ.

———. 2014. *Orientierungsrahmen für den Lernbereich Globale Entwicklung im Rahmen einer Bildung für nachhaltige Entwicklung (Arbeitsdokument – Zur Anhörung und Kommentierung freigegeben)* [Curricular Framework for Global Development Education in the Context of Education for Sustainable Development (Working Document – Released for Consultation and Commenting)]. 2nd updated and extended edition. Berlin: H. Heenemann.

———. 2015. *Curriculum Framework Education for Sustainable Development*. 2nd updated and extended edition. Bonn and Berlin: KMK and BMZ.

Koepsell, Philipp Khabo. 2010. 'Dein Afrika und Albtraum (ein besseres Spendengesuch)' [Your Africa and Nightmare (A Better Request for Donations)]. In *Die Akte Jim Knopf: Afrodeutsche Wort- und Streitkunst*, edited by Philipp Khabo Koepsell, 18–20. Münster: Unrast.

Köhler, Volkmar. 2000. 'Zum Stellenwert Tanzanias in der deutschen Entwicklungszusammenarbeit' [On the Significance of Tanzania in German Development Cooperation]. In *Tanzania Revisited: Political Stability, Aid Dependency and Development Constraints*, edited by Ulf Engel, Gero Erdmann, and Andreas Mehler, 21–30. Hamburg: Institut für Afrikakunde.

Kontzi, Kristina. 2015. *Postkoloniale Perspektiven auf 'weltwärts'. Ein Freiwilligendienst in weltbürgerlicher Absicht* [Postcolonial Perspectives on 'weltwärts'. A Volunteer Service with Cosmopolitan Intent]. Baden-Baden: Nomos.

Koponen, Juhani. 1994. *Development for Exploitation. German Colonial Policies in Mainland Tanzania, 1884–1914*. Hamburg: LIT.

Kößler, Reinhart. 2015. *Namibia and Germany. Negotiating the Past*. Münster: Westfälisches Dampfboot.

Kößler, Reinhart, and Henning Melber. 2004. 'Deutscher Kolonialismus. Vergangenes in der Gegenwart. Kontinuitäten des deutschen Kolonialismus' [German Colonialism. The Past in the Present. Continuities of German Colonialism]. iz3w 275. Accessed 28 March 2017. http://www.sopos.org/aufsaetze/40324b941504c/1.phtml.

Kothari, Uma. 1996. 'Development Studies and Post-Colonial Theory'. IDPM Discussion Paper Series. 46.

———. 2006a. 'An Agenda for Thinking about "Race" in Development'. *Progress in Development Studies* 6 (1): 9–23. doi: 10.1191/1464993406ps124oa.

————. 2006b. 'From Colonialism to Development: Reflections of Former Colonial Officers'. *Commonwealth & Comparative Politics* 44 (1): 118–36. doi: 10.1080/14662040600624502.

————. 2011. 'Commentary: History, Time and Temporality in Development Discourse'. In *History, Historians and Development Policy. A Necessary Dialogue*, edited by Christopher Bayly, Vijayendra Rao, Simon Szreter, and Michael Woolcock, 65–70. Manchester and New York: Manchester University Press.

Krämer, Georg. 2013. 'Augen zu vor der Schuld der Anderen. Für radikale Antirassisten sind die Bösen immer weiß' [Closing One's Eyes to the Liability of the Others. For Radical Anti-Racists the Bad Guys Are Always White]. *Welt-Sichten* 9. https://www.welt-sichten.org/brennpunkte/17572/augen-zu-vor-der-schuld-der-anderen.

Kuhn, Berthold. 2011. 'Deutsche Entwicklungspolitik im Kontext des Regierungswechsels' [German Development Policy in the Context of the Change of Government]. *Zeitschrift für Politikberatung* 3 (3): 509–18. doi: 10.1007/s12392-011-0262-3.

Külz, Ludwig. 1913. 'Die seuchenhaften Krankheiten des Kindesalters der Eingeborenen und ihre Bedeutung für die koloniale Bevölkerungsfrage' [Plague-Like Diseases during Childhood amongst the Natives and Its Significance for the Colonial Population Question]. *Koloniale Rundschau – Monatsschrift für die Interessen unserer Schutzgebiete und ihrer Bewohner* 6: 321–30.

Kuumba, M. Bahati. 1999. 'A Cross-Cultural Race/Class/Gender Critique of Contemporary Population Policy. The Impact of Globalization'. *Sociological Forum* 14 (3): 447–63. http://www.jstor.org/stable/684874.

Lambert, David, and Alan Lester, eds. 2006. *Colonial Lives across the British Empire: Imperial Careering in the Long Nineteenth Century*. Cambridge and New York: Cambridge University Press.

Landeszentrale für politische Bildung Baden-Württemberg. 2003. 'Globalisierung. Aspekte einer Welt ohne Grenzen' [Globalization. Aspects of a World without Borders]. *Politik & Unterricht* 29 (4). http://www.politikundunterricht.de/4_03/globalisierung.pdf.

————, ed. 2011. 'Weltweite Ernährungskrisen. Ursachen und Konsequenzen' [Food Crises Worldwide. Causes and Consequences]. *Politik & Unterricht* 37 (1). http://www.politikundunterricht.de/1_11/ernaehrungskrisen.pdf.

Langwick, Stacey. 2011. *Bodies, Politics, and African Healing. The Matter of Maladies in Tanzania*. Bloomington: Indiana University Press.

Larch, Mario, Jutta Albrecht, Stephan Klasen, Rigmar Osterkamp, Immaculada Martínez-Zarzoso, Bernd Meyer, and D. Felicitas Nowak-Lehmann. 2007. 'Bilaterale Entwicklungszusammenarbeit und Export- und Arbeitsplatzeffekte im Geberland – Das Beispiel Deutschland' [Bilateral Development Cooperation and the Effects on Exports and Employment in the Donor Country – The Example of Germany]. Bonn: BMZ. Accessed 28 March 2017. http://www.cesifo-group.de/de/w/4Gu5TxRHH.

Leahy, Elizabeth, and Nel Druce. 2009. 'A Case Study of Reproductive Health Supplies in Tanzania'. Washington: Population Action International. Accessed 28 March 2012. http://www.populationaction.org/Publications/Reports/Reproductive_Health_Supplies_in_Six_Countries/Tanzania.pdf.

Lemke, Thomas. 1997. *Eine Kritik der politischen Vernunft. Foucaults Analyse der modernen Gouvernementalität* [A Critique of Political Common Sense. Foucault's Analysis of Modern Governmentality]. Hamburg: Argument.

Lensing, Mechthild. 2006. 'Deine Handflächen sind ja ganz weiß! Menschen aus anderen Kontinenten als Referenten in der Schule' [But the Palms of Your Hands Are All White! People from Other Continents as Instructors in School]. In *Bildung trifft Entwicklung. Rückkehrer in der Entwicklungspolitischen Bildung*, edited by Deutscher Entwicklungsdienst, 8–9. Bonn: DED. Accessed 28 March 2017. http://www.entwicklungsdienst.de/fileadmin/Redaktion/ENGAGEMENT_WELTWEIT/Publik_/Bildung/DEDforum_Bildung_trifft_Entwicklung.pdf.

Lentin, Alana, and Juliane Karakayali. 2016. 'Bringing Race Back In. Racism in "Post-Racial" Times'. *Movements. Journal für Kritische Migrations- und Grenzregimeforschung* 2 (1). http://movements-journal.org/issues/03.rassismus/07.lentin,karakayali--bringing.race.back.in.html.

Lessenich, Stephan. 2016. *Neben uns die Sintflut. Die Externalisierungsgesellschaft und ihr Preis* [Next to Us Comes the Flood. The Externalization Society and Its Cost]. Berlin: Hanser.

Lingelbach, Gabriele. 2007. 'Das Bild des Bedürftigen und die Darstellung von Wohltätigkeit in den Werbemaßnahmen bundesrepublikanischer Wohltätigkeitsorganisationen' [The Image of the Needy and the Representation of Charity in Advertising Measures of German Charity Organisations]. *Archiv für Kulturgeschichte* 89: 345–65.

Löbner, M.H. 1914. 'Zur Entvölkerungsfrage Unyamwezis' [On the Question of Depopulation of Unyamwezi]. *Koloniale Rundschau – Monatsschrift für die Interessen unserer Schutzgebiete und ihrer Bewohner* 11: 267–70.

Loomba, Ania. 2005. *Colonialism/Postcolonialism*. 2nd ed. New York: Routledge.

Lugalla, Joe L.P. 1995. 'The Impact of Structural Adjustment Policies on Women's and Children's Health in Tanzania'. *Review of African Political Economy* 22 (63): 43–53. doi: 10.1080/03056249508704099.

Lugard, Frederick John Dealtry. 1923. *The Dual Mandate in British Tropical Africa*. 2nd ed. Edinburgh and London: William Blackwood and Sons.

Lugones, Mara. 2008. 'The Coloniality of Gender'. *The Worlds & Knowledges Otherwise Project* 2 (2). https://globalstudies.trinity.duke.edu/wp-content/themes/cgsh/materials/WKO/v2d2_Lugones.pdf.

Major, Sabine. 2003. 'Zur Geschichte der außerklinischen Geburtshilfe in der DDR' [On the History of Out-of-Hospital Midwifery in the GDR]. PhD diss., Humboldt-Universität zu Berlin. http://edoc.hu-berlin.de/dissertationen/major-sabine-2003-02-14/HTML/.

Malter, Bettina, and Ali Hotait, eds. 2012. *Was bildet ihr uns ein? Eine Generation fordert die Bildungsrevolution* [What Do You Educate into Us? A Generation Demands the Education Revolution]. Berlin: Vergangenheitsverlag.

Manzo, Kate. 2008. 'Imaging Humanitarianism: NGO Identity and the Iconography of Childhood'. *Antipode* 40 (4): 632–57. doi: 10.1111/j.1467–8330.2008.00627.x.

Marmer, Elina, Dalia Marmer, Leona Hitomi, and Papa Sow. 2010. 'Racism and the Image of Africa in German Schools and Textbooks'. *International Journal of Diversity in Organizations, Communities and Nations* 10 (5): 1–12.

Marmer, Elina, and Aram Ziai. 2015. 'Racism in the Teaching of "Development" in German Secondary School Textbooks'. *Critical Literacy: Theories and Practices* 9 (2): 64–84. http://criticalliteracy.freehostia.com/index.php?journal=criticalliterac y&page=article&op=view&path%5B%5D=165&path%5B%5D=141.

Marx, Christoph. 2004. 'Siedlerkolonien in Afrika' [Settler Colonies in Africa]. In *Rassenmischehen – Mischlinge. Zur Politik der Rasse im Deutschen Kolonialreich*, edited by Frank Becker, 82–96. Stuttgart: Franz Steiner Verlag.

Masebo, Oswald. 2010. 'Society, State, and Infant Welfare: Negotiating Medical Interventions in Colonial Tanzania, 1920–1950'. PhD diss., University of Minnesota.

Mbembe, Achille. 2001. *On the Postcolony*. Berkeley: University of California Press.

———. 2003. 'Necropolitics'. *Public Culture* 15 (1): 11–40. doi: 10.1057/9780 230584334_9.

McClintock, Anne. 1992. 'The Angel of Progress: Pitfalls of the Term "Post-Colonialism"'. *Social Text* 31/32: 84–98. doi: 10.2307/466219.

McEwan, Cheryl. 2009. *Postcolonialism and Development*. New York: Routledge.

McKinnon, Katharine. 2008. 'Taking Post-Development Theory to the Field: Issues in Development Research, Northern Thailand'. *Asia Pacific Viewpoint* 49 (3): 281–93. doi: 10.1111/j.1467-8373.2008.00377.x.

Mecheril, Paul, Maria do Mar Castro Varela, Inci Dirim, Annita Kalpaka, and Claus Melter. 2010. *Bachelor | Master: Migrationspädagogik* [Bachelor | Master: Pedagogy of Migration]. Weinheim: Beltz.

medico international. 2015. 'Textilfabriken in Südasien. Arbeiten wie die Sklaven' [Textile Factories in South Asia. Working like Slaves]. Accessed 28 March 2017. https://www.medico.de/toedliche-textilfabriken-16030/.

Medizinalreferat in Daressalam. 1914. 'Familien-Nachwuchsstatistik über die Eingeborenen von Deutsch-Ostafrika' [Statistics of Family Offspring of Natives in German East Africa]. *Deutsches Kolonialblatt. Amtsblatt für die Schutzgebiete in Afrika und in der Südsee* 25 (10): 440–57.

Meixner, Hugo. 1914. 'Säuglings- und Kinderernährung in Deutsch-Ostafrika' [Infant and Child Feeding in German East Africa]. *Deutsches Kolonialblatt. Amtsblatt für die Schutzgebiete in Afrika und in der Südsee* 25 (8): 354–65.

Melber, Henning. 1992. *Der Weißheit letzter Schluß. Rassismus und kolonialer Blick* [Whiteness the Answer to Everything. Racism and Colonial Gaze]. Frankfurt am Main: Brandes & Apsel.

Memmi, Albert. 2000. *Racism*. Minneapolis: University of Minnesota Press.

Michailof, Serge. 2016. 'Vorprogrammierte Explosion? Welche Folgen das rasante Bevölkerungswachstum in Afrika südlich der Sahara haben könnte' [Inevitable Explosion? The Potential Consequences of the Rapid Population Growth in Sub-Saharan Africa]. *Auslandsinformationen* 32 (4): 43–56. Accessed 28 March 2017. http://www.kas.de/wf/doc/kas_47597-544-1-30.pdf?170614162832.

Mignolo, Walter. 2002. 'The Geopolitics of Knowledge and the Colonial Difference'. *South Atlantic Quarterly* 101 (1): 57–96. doi: 10.1215/00382876-101-1-57.

Mikander, Pia. 2016. 'Globalization as Continuing Colonialism – Critical Global Citizenship Education in an Unequal World'. *Journal of Social Science Education* 15 (2): 70–79. doi: 10.4119/UNIBI/jsse-v15-i2-1475.

Misereor. 2011. 'Mut ist' [Courage Is]. Accessed 28 March 2017. https://www.kolle-rebbe.de/arbeiten/mut-ist/.

———. 2015a. 'Helping Others to Help Themselves'. Accessed 28 March 2017. https://www.kolle-rebbe.de/en/work/hilfe-zur-selbsthilfe/.

———. 2015b. 'Hilfe zur Selbsthilfe in Vietnam'. Accessed 28 March 2017. https://www.misereor.de/informieren/hilfe-zur-selbsthilfe/vietnam/.

missio. 2011. 'Große Flächen für gute Werbung' [Big Surfaces for Good Advertising]. Accessed 25 March 2017. https://www.missio-hilft.de/de/angebote/publikation/kontinente/ausgabe-5-2011/plakate.html.

Mohanty, Chandra Talpade. 1991. 'Under Western Eyes. Feminist Scholarship and Colonial Discourses'. In *Third World Women and the Politics of Feminism*, edited by Chandra Talpade Mohanty, Ann Russo, and Lourdes Torres, 51–80. Bloomington: Indiana University Press.

———. 2002. '"Under Western Eyes" Revisited: Feminist Solidarity through Anti-capitalist Struggles'. *Signs: Journal of Women in Culture and Society* 28 (2): 499–535. doi: doi.org/10.1086/342914.

Mohio. 2011. '"Das Boot ist voll" und 10 weitere Dialoge zu Ethik und Globalisierung mit Kaiser und König, Einleitung' ['The Boat Is Full' and 10 Further Dialogues on Ethics and Globalization with Kaiser and King, Introduction]. Accessed 28 March 2016. http://boot.kaiser-und-koenig.de.

Moraña, Mabel, Enrique Dussel, and Carlos A. Jauregui, eds. 2008. *Coloniality at Large: Latin America and the Postcolonial Debate*. Durham: Duke University Press.

Mudimbe, Valentin Y. 1988. *The Invention of Africa. Gnosis, Philosophy, and the Order of Knowledge*. Bloomington: Indiana University Press.

———. 1994. *The Idea of Africa*. Bloomington: Indiana University Press.

Müller, Rolf-Dieter, Nicole Schönherr, and Thomas Widera, eds. 2010. *Die Zerstörung Dresdens am 13./15. Februar 1945: Gutachten und Ergebnisse der Dresdner Historikerkommission zur Ermittlung der Opferzahlen (Berichte und Studien)* [The Destruction of Dresden on February 13/15, 1945: Survey and Results of the Commission of Historians of Dresden to Determine the Number of Casualties (Reports and Studies)]. Göttingen: Vandenhoeck & Ruprecht.

Murrell, Nathaniel Samuel, William David Spencer, and Adrian Anthony McFarlane. 1998. *Chanting Down Babylon: The Rastafari Reader*. Philadelphia: Temple University Press.

Nandy, Ashis. 1983. *The Intimate Enemy. Loss and Recovery of Self under Colonialism*. New Delhi: Oxford University Press.

National Bureau of Statistics, and ICF Macro. 2010. 'Tanzania Demographic and Health Survey 2009–2010'. Calverton: ICF Macro. Accessed 28 March 2012. http://hdptz.esealtd.com/fileadmin/documents/DPGH_Meeeting_Documents_2010/TDHS_Prelim_Report_16_Sept_2010_Final_DocumentPrinter.pdf.

Nchimbi, B. R. 1977. *The Black-Eaters*. 2nd ed. Dar es Salaam: Ruvu.

Ndumbe III, Kum'a. 1993. *Was wollte Hitler in Afrika? NS-Planungen für eine faschistische Neugestaltung Afrikas* [What Did Hitler Want in Africa? National Socialist Planning for a Fascist Reshaping of Africa]. Frankfurt am Main: IKO.

———. 2006. 'Wie ich mich in ihren Augen sah. Afrika im Spiegel der Medien – Bilder eines Kontinents und was sie bewirken' [How I Saw Myself in Their Eyes.

Africa in Media Coverage – Images of a Continent and Their Impact]. In *Wettkampf um die Globalisierung Afrikas*, edited by Kum'a Ndumbe III, 29–40. Berlin: Exchange & Dialogue.

Nederveen Pieterse, Jan. 1992. *White on Black: Images of Africa and Blacks in Western Popular Culture*. New Haven: Yale University Press.

Nestel, Sheryl. 1998. '(Ad)Ministering Angels: Colonial Nursing and the Extension of Empire in Africa'. *Journal of Medical Humanities* 19 (4): 257–77. doi: 10.1023/A:1024908110021.

Niebel, Dirk. 2013. 'Ich hole Entwicklungspolitik aus der Schlabberpulli-Ecke'. bild. de. Accessed 20 May 2017. http://www.bild.de/politik/inland/dirk-niebel/bild-interview-mit-entwicklungsminister-29354560.bild.html.

No Amnesty on Genocide! 2017. 'Our Colonial Present: Germany's Herero and Nama Genocide'. Accessed 28 July 2017. http://genocide-namibia.net/.

Noxolo, Patricia. 2006. 'Claims: A Postcolonial Geographical Critique of "Partnership" in Britain's Development Discourse'. *Singapore Journal of Tropical Geography* 27 (3): 254–69. doi: 10.1111/j.1467–9493.2006.00261.x.

Nuscheler, Franz. 2006. 'Deutsche Entwicklungspolitik. Interessengeleitete Kontinuitäten und Veränderungen [German Development Policy. Interest-Based Continuities and Transformations]. In *Entwicklungszusammenarbeit. Akteure, Handlungsmuster und Interessen*, edited by Bea de Abreu Fialho Gomes, Irmi Maral-Hanak, and Walter Schicho, 189–205. Wien: Mandelbaum.

OECD. 2016. 'Query Wizard for International Development Statistics'. Accessed 20 May 2017. http://stats.oecd.org/qwids/.

———. 2017a. 'Development Aid Rises again in 2016'. Accessed 20 May 2017. https://www.oecd.org/dac/financing-sustainable-development/development-finance-data/ODA-2016-detailed-summary.pdf.

———. 2017b. 'Development Aid Rises again in 2016 but Flows to Poorest Countries Dip'. Accessed 20 May 2017. http://www.oecd.org/dac/development-aid-rises-again-in-2016-but-flows-to-poorest-countries-dip.htm.

Open Aid Data. 2017. 'Offene Entwicklungshilfe | Empfängerland: Tansania' [Open Development Aid | Recipient Country: Tanzania]. Accessed 20 May 2017. http://www.offene-entwicklungshilfe.de/land/282/2011/.

Open School 21. 2017. 'Decolonize Globales Lernen! Warum wir als Open School 21 den Offenen Brief "Decolonize Orientierungsrahmen" unterstützen' [Decolonize Global Learning! Why We as Open School 21 Support the Open Letter 'Decolonize Curriculum Framework']. Accessed 9 April 2017. http://www.ven-nds.de/images/ven/projekte/globales_lernen/Decolonize_Globales_Lernen-_open_school21.pdf.

Overwien, Bernd. 2013. 'Critical Whiteness I: Falsche Polarisierung – Die Critical Whiteness-Kritik am Globalen Lernen wird ihrem Gegenstand nicht Gerecht'. *iz3w* 338: 38–41.

Oyèwùmí, Oyèrónké. 2005. 'Colonizing Bodies and Minds. Gender and Colonialism' In *Postcolonialisms. An Anthology of Cultural Theory and Criticism*, edited by Gaurav Desai and Supriya Nair, 339–61. New Brunswick: Rutgers University Press.

Packard, Randall M. 2000. 'Post-Colonial Medicine'. In *Medicine in the Twentieth Century*, edited by Roger Cooter and John Pickstone, 97–112. Amsterdam: Harwood Academic Publishers.

Parry, Benita. 2004. *Postcolonial Studies. A Materialist Critique*. London: Routledge.
Paschke, Susanne. 2011. 'Globales Lernen in Theorie und Praxis. Ein Pädagogisches Konzept in Begründungsnot' [Global Learning in Theory and Practice. A Pedagogical Concept with Difficulties of Justification]. Master's thesis, University of Vienna. http://othes.univie.ac.at/13574/.
Paul, G. 1908. 'Die ärztliche Mission in den deutschen Kolonien' [The Medical Mission in the German Colonies]. *Das Kirchliche Jahrbuch*, 97–104; Federal German Archives: R1001/6037–6038.
Peiper, Otto. 1910. 'Schwangerschaft, Geburt und Wochenbett bei den Suaheli von Kilwa' [Pregnancy, Birth and Childbed of the Swahili of Kilwa]. *Archiv für Schiffs- und Tropenhygiene* 14 (15): 461–69.
———. 1912. 'Sozial-medizinische Bilder aus Deutsch-Ostafrika' [Social-Medical Impressions from German East Africa]. *Zeitschrift für Säuglingsschutz*, 244–59.
———. 1920a. 'Der Bevölkerungsrückgang in den tropischen Kolonien Afrikas und der Südsee, – Seine Ursachen und seine Bekämpfung' [The Population Decline in the Tropical Colonies of Africa and the South Sea, – Its Causes and Fighting It]. In *Veröffentlichungen aus dem Gebiete der Medizinalverwaltung. Im Auftrage des Ministeriums für Volkswohlfahrt XI/7*, edited by Abteilung I des Ministeriums, 417–508. Berlin: Richard Schoetz.
———. 1920b. 'Geburtenhäufigkeit, Säuglings- und Kinder-Sterblichkeit und Säuglingsernährung im früheren Deutsch-Ostafrika' [Birth Rates, Infant and Child Mortality, and Infant Feeding in Former German East Africa]. In *Veröffentlichungen aus dem Gebiete der Medizinalverwaltung. Im Auftrage des Ministeriums für Volkswohlfahrt, XI/6*, edited by Abteilung I des Ministeriums, 371–412. Berlin: Richard Schoetz.
PERIPHERIE, ed. 2008. *Klima – Politik und Profit* [Climate – Politics and Profits]. Münster: Westfälisches Dampfboot.
Philipp, Carolin, and Timo Kiesel. 2011. *White Charity*. Documentary. http://www.whitecharity.de/.
Plumelle-Uribe, Rosa Amelia. 2007. 'Von der kolonialen Barbarei zur Vernichtungspolitik des Nationalsozialismus'. In *African Reflections*, edited by AfricAvenir International, 4–11. Berlin: AfricAvenir.
Poenicke, Anke. 2001. 'Afrika in deutschen Medien und Schulbüchern' [Africa in German Media and School Books]. 29. Zukunftsforum Politik. Konrad-Adenauer-Stiftung. Accessed 20 May 2009. http://www.kas.de/wf/doc/kas_177-544-1-30.pdf?040415180721.
Pogge von Strandmann, Hartmut. 2009. *Imperialismus vom grünen Tisch. Deutsche Kolonialpolitiker zwischen wirtschaftlicher Ausbeutung und 'zivilisatorischen' Bemühen* [Imperialism on a Drawing Board. German Colonial Politicians between Economic Exploitation and 'Civilizational' Efforts]. Berlin: Ch. Links Verlag.
Policy Forum. 2012. 'Health Spending in Tanzania Is Still Far Less Than What Is Recommended by the World Health Organisation'. Accessed 23 November 2017. http://www.policyforum-tz.org/health-spending-tanzania-still-far-less-what-recommended-world-health-organisation.
Power, Marcus. 2006. 'Anti-Racism, Deconstruction and "Overdevelopment"'. *Progress in Development Studies* 6 (1): 25–39. doi: 10.1191/1464993406ps125oa.

Profant, Tomáš. 2015. 'The Pontis Foundation: Partly Disrupting the Development Discourse through Partnership'. *Forum for Development Studies* 42: 265–87. doi: 10.1080/08039410.2015.1018312.

Promoe. 2006. 'White Man's Burden'. In *White Man's Burden*. David vs Goliath Records.

Quijano, Anibal. 2000. 'Coloniality of Power, Eurocentrism, and Latin America'. *Nepantla: Views from South* 1 (3): 533–80. https://muse.jhu.edu/article/23906.

Raghuram, Parvati, Clare Madge, and Patricia Noxolo. 2009. 'Rethinking Responsibility and Care for a Postcolonial World'. *Geoforum* 40 (1): 5–13. doi: 10.1016/j.geoforum.2008.07.007.

Ram, Kalpana, and Margret Jolly, eds. 1998. *Maternities and Modernities: Colonial and Postcolonial Experiences in Asia and the Pacific*. Cambridge: Cambridge University Press.

Rao, Mohan, and Sarah Sexton, eds. 2010. *Markets and Malthus: Population, Gender and Health in Neo-Liberal Times*. New Delhi: Sage.

Reichs-Kolonialamt, ed. 1913. *Medizinal-Berichte über die Deutschen Schutzgebiete für das Jahr 1910/11* [Medical Reports on the German Protectorates for the Year 1910/11]. Berlin: Ernst Siegfried Mittler und Sohn.

———, ed. 1914. *Die Deutschen Schutzgebiete in Afrika und der Südsee 1912/13* [The German Protectorates in Africa and the South Sea 1912/13]. Berlin: Ernst Siegfried Mittler und Sohn.

———, ed. 1915. *Medizinal-Berichte über die Deutschen Schutzgebiete für das Jahr 1911/12* [Medical Reports on the German Protectorates for the Year 1911/12]. Berlin: Ernst Siegfried Mittler und Sohn.

Richey, Lisa Ann. 2008. *Population Politics and Development. From the Policies to the Clinics*. New York: Palgrave Macmillan.

Rideout, Lisa. 2011. 'Representations of the "Third World" in NGO Advertising: Practicalities, Colonial Discourse and Western Understandings of Development'. *Journal of African Media Studies* 3 (1): 25–41. doi: 10.1386/jams.3.1.25_1.

Robinson, Jennifer. 2006. *Ordinary Cities. Between Modernity and Development*. London and New York: Routledge.

Rodenwaldt, Ernst. 1912. 'Eingeborene Hebammen in Anecho, Togo, Westafrika' [Native Midwives in Anecho, Togo, West Africa]. *Deutsche Medizinische Wochenschrift* 38 (6): 273–75.

Rodney, Walter. 2012. *How Europe Underdeveloped Africa*. Cape Town: Pambazuka.

Sachs, Wolfgang. 1992. *The Development Dictionary. A Guide to Knowledge as Power*. London: Zed Books.

Said, Edward. 1978. *Orientalism*. New York: Vintage Books.

SAIH. 2014. 'New Reality TV Spoof Mocks Westerners' Stereotypes of Africa'. Accessed 20 May 2017. https://saih.no/artikkel/2014/11/new-reality-tv-spoof-mocks-westerners-stereotypes-of-africa.

Santos, Boaventura de Sousa. 2010. 'From the Postmodern to the Postcolonial – and beyond Both'. In *Decolonizing European Sociology. Transdisciplinary Approaches*, edited by Encarnación Gutiérrez Rodríguez, Manuela Boatcă, and Sérgio Costa, 225–42. London: Ashgate.

————. 2012. 'The World Is Changing in a More Progressive Way, and It's Taking Place Here'. Democracy Now! Accessed 13 May 2016. http://www.democracynow. org/2010/4/21/the_world_is_changing_in_a.

Sauerteig, Lutz D. H. 2001. ' "The Fatherland Is in Danger, Save the Fatherland!" Venereal Disease, Sexuality and Gender in Imperial and Weimar Germany'. In *Sex, Sin and Suffering. Venereal Disease and European Society since 1870*, edited by Roger Davidson and Lesley A. Hall, 76–92. London and New York: Routledge.

Schäfer, Julia. 2007. ' "Organisches Kapital" – Deutsche Kolonialärzte in Afrika zwischen Labor und praktischer Bevölkerungspolitik' ['Organic Capital' – German Colonial Doctors in Africa between Laboratory and Practical Population Policy]. In *Bevölkerungsfragen. Prozesse des Wissenstransfers in Deutschland und Frankreich (1870–1939)*, 232–54. Köln; Weimar; and Wien: Böhlau.

Scheunpflug, Annette. 2012. 'Globales Lernen – Geschichte' [Global Learning – History]. In *Handlexikon Globales Lernen*, edited by Gregor Lang-Wojtasik and Ulrich Klemm, 89–93. Münster and Ulm: Klemm & Oelschläger.

————. 2014. 'Globales Lernen und die Debatte um Postkolonialität' [Global Learning and the Debate around Postcoloniality]. *ZEP – Zeitschrift für internationale Bildungsforschung und Entwicklungspädagogik* 37 (4): 31–32.

Scheunpflug, Annette, and Klaus Seitz. 1995. *Die Geschichte der entwicklungspolitischen Bildung. Zur pädagogischen Konstruktion der 'Dritten Welt'* [The History of Development Education. On the Pedagogical Construction of the 'Third World']. Band I: Entwicklungspolitische Unterrichtsmaterialien. Frankfurt am Main: IKO.

Schilling, Britta. 2014. *Postcolonial Germany: Memories of Empire in a Decolonized Nation*. Oxford: Oxford University Press.

————. 2015. 'German Postcolonialism in Four Dimensions: A Historical Perspective'. *Postcolonial Studies* 18 (4): 427–39. doi: 10.1080/13688790.2015.1191988.

Schlebusch, Cornelia. 1994. *Bevölkerungspolitik als Entwicklungsstrategie – Historisches und Aktuelles zu einem fragwürdigen Argument* [Population Policy as Development Strategy – Historical and Contemporary Perspectives on a Questionable Argument]. Frankfurt am Main: IKO.

Schneider, Leander. 2006. 'Colonial Legacies and Postcolonial Authoritarianism in Tanzania: Connects and Disconnects'. *African Studies Review* 49 (1): 93–118. doi: 10.1353/arw.2006.0091.

Schultz, Susanne. 2006. *Hegemonie – Gouvernementalität – Biomacht. Reproduktive Risiken und die Transformation internationaler Bevölkerungspolitik* [Hegemony – Governmentality – Biopower. Reproductive Risks and the Transformation of International Population Policy]. Münster: Westfälisches Dampfboot.

————. 2010. 'Redefining and Medicalizing Population Policies: NGOs and Their Innovative Contributions to the Post-Cairo Agenda'. In *Markets and Malthus. Population, Gender, and Health in Neo-Liberal Times*, edited by Mohan Rao and Sarah Sexton, 173–214. New Delhi: Sage.

————. 2015. 'Reproducing the Nation: The New German Population Policy and the Concept of Demographization'. *Distinktion: Scandinavian Journal of Social Theory* 16: 337–61. doi: 10.1080/1600910X.2015.1080744.

Schultz, Susanne, and Daniel Bendix. 2015. 'A Revival of Explicit Population Policy in Development Cooperation: The German Government, Bayer, and the Gates Foundation'. *DifferenTakes 89* https://dspace.hampshire.edu/handle/10009/851.

Scott, James C. 1990. *Domination and the Arts of Resistance: Hidden Transcripts.* New Haven and London: Yale University Press.

Seidler, Eduard. 1993. 'Das 19. Jahrhundert. Zur Vorgeschichte des Paragraphen 218' [The 19th Century. On the Prehistory of Paragraph 218]. In *Geschichte der Abtreibung: Von der Antike bis zur Gegenwart*, edited by Robert Jütte, 120–39. München: C.H. Beck.

Sexton, Sarah, and Sumati Nair. 2010. 'A Decade and More after Cairo: Women's Health in a Free Market Economy'. In *Markets and Malthus. Population, Gender, and Health in Neo-Liberal Times*, edited by Mohan Rao and Sarah Sexton, 31–52. New Delhi: Sage.

Shilliam, Robbie. 2014. 'Race and Development'. In *The Politics of Development: A Survey*, edited by Heloise Weber, 31–48. Abingdon: Routledge.

———. 2015. *The Black Pacific. Anti-Colonial Struggles and Oceanic Connections.* London: Bloomsbury Academic.

SisterSong. 2017. 'Reproductive Justice'. SisterSong – Women of Color Reproductive Justice Collective. Accessed 20 May 2017. http://sistersong.net/reproductive-justice/.

Slater, David. 2005. *Geopolitics and the Post-Colonial: Rethinking North-South Relations.* Oxford: Blackwell.

Slater, David, and Morag Bell. 2002. 'Aid and the Geopolitics of the Post-Colonial: Critical Reflections on New Labour's Overseas Development Strategy'. *Development and Change* 33 (2): 335–60. doi: 10.1111/1467–7660.00257.

Smith, Woodruff D. 2011. *The German Colonial Empire.* Chapel Hill: University of North Carolina Press.

Spehr, Christoph. 1996. *Die Ökofalle. Nachhaltigkeit und Krise* [The Eco-Trap. Sustainability and Crisis]. Wien: Promedia.

Speitkamp, Winfried. 2005. *Deutsche Kolonialgeschichte* [German Colonial History]. Stuttgart: Reclam.

Spivak, Gayatri Chakravorty. 2003. 'Can the Subaltern Speak?' *Die Philosophin. Forum für Feministische Theorie und Philosophie* 14 (27): 42–58.

———. 2007. 'Feminism and Human Rights'. In *The Present as History: Critical Perspectives on Global Power*, edited by Nermeen Shaikh, 172–201. New York: Columbia University Press.

Steinbrink, Christoph. 2014. 'Die Komplexität der Stärkung mündiger Subjekte' [The Complexity of Strengthening Responsible Subjects]. *ZEP – Zeitschrift für internationale Bildungsforschung und Entwicklungspädagogik* 37 (4): 33.

Steinwachs, Luise. 2012. ' "Arm, aber glücklich". Persönliche Begegnungen in Schulpartnerschaften' ['Poor, but Happy'. Personal Encounters in School Partnerships]. Berlin: Berlin Postkolonial. Accessed 20 May 2014. http://berlin-postkolonial.de/cms/images/dokumente/partnerschaftentwickleln/steinwachs_2012_zitat_arm_aber_gluecklich_schuelerbegegnungen.pdf.

Stelzer, Hans Georg. 1984. *'Mit herrlichen Häfen versehen'. Brandenburgisch-Preußische Seefahrt vor dreihundert Jahren* ['Provided with Wonderful Ports'. Brandenburg-Prussian Seafaring Three Hundred Years Ago]. Berlin: Ullstein.

Steyerl, Hito. 2003. 'Postkolonialismus und Biopolitik' [Postcolonialism and Bio-politics]. In *Spricht die Subalterne Deutsch? Migration und postkoloniale Kritik*, edited by Encarnación Gutiérrez Rodríguez and Hito Steyerl, 38–55. Münster: Unrast.

Stielike, Laura. 2013. 'Wo die wilden Tiere wohnen. Die neue Plakatkampagne "The Big Five!" reproduziert kolonial-rassistische Bilder' [Where the Wild Animals Are. The New Billboard Campaign 'The Big Five!' Reproduces Colonial-Racist Images]. ak – Zeitung für linke Debatte und Praxis 583. Accessed 20 December 2013. http://www.akweb.de/ak_s/ak583/14.htm.

Stockholm International Peace Research Institute. 2015. '10. International Arms Transfers and Arms Production. Oxford: Oxford University Press'. Accessed 20 May 2016. https://www.sipri.org/yearbook/2015/10.

Stockmann, Reinhard, Ulrich Menzel, and Franz Nuscheler. 2010. *Entwicklungspolitik: Theorien – Probleme – Strategien* [Development Policy: Theories – Problems – Strategies]. München: Oldenbourg Wissenschaftsverlag.

Stoecker, Helmuth. 1991. *Drang nach Afrika. Die deutsche koloniale Expansionspolitik und Herrschaft in Afrika von den Anfängen bis zum Verlust der Kolonien* [The Drive for Africa. The German Colonial Policy of Expansion and Domination in Africa from the Beginnings to the Loss of the Colonies]. Berlin: Akademie.

Szász, Nora, Andrea Stiefel, and Monika Tschernko. 2012. 'Geschichte des Hebammenberufs' [History of the Midwifery Profession]. In *Hebammenkunde: Lehrbuch für Schwangerschaft, Geburt, Wochenbett und Beruf*, 5th ed., 2–15. Stuttgart: Georg Thieme.

TGPSH. 2008. 'History of the German Technical Cooperation in the Health Sector – Tanzania'. Accessed 20 December 2008. http://www.tgpsh.or.tz/about-tgpsh/history-german-technical-cooperation-in-tanzania-health-sector.html.

———. 2009a. 'Reproductive Health'. Accessed 12 May 2010. http://www.tgpsh.or.tz/reproductive-health.html.

———. 2009b. 'Safer Motherhood'. Accessed 12 May 2010. http://www.tgpsh.or.tz/reproductive-health/safer-motherhood.html.

———. 2009c. 'Tanzanian German Programme to Support Health – Background'. Accessed 12 May 2010. http://www.tgpsh.or.tz/about-tgpsh.html.

———. 2012. 'Prevention and Awareness in Schools of HIV & AIDS (PASHA)'. Accessed 12 September 2013. http://www.tgpsh.or.tz/our-focus/sexual-reproductive-health-and-rights-hivaids/pasha/.

Thiong'o, Ngũgĩ wa. 1986. *Decolonising the Mind. The Politics of Language in African Literature*. New Hampshire: Heinemann.

Tomic, Manuela. 2013. 'Deutscher Entwicklungstag in Berlin: Schwarze Künstler, weiße Experten'. *Der Tagesspiegel*, 26 May. Accessed 12 May 2017. http://www.tagesspiegel.de/berlin/deutscher-entwicklungstag-in-berlin-schwarze-kuenstler-weisse-experten/8256044.html.

UNFPA. 2012. 'Procurement Statistics'. UNFPA. Accessed 12 May 2016. http://
www.unfpa.org/resources/procurement-statistics-2012.
————. 2013a. 'Contraceptives and Condoms for Family Planning and STI & HIV
Prevention. External Procurement Support Report 2012'. UNFPA. Accessed
12 May 2016. http://www.unfpa.org/sites/default/files/pub-pdf/UNFPA%20
donor%20support%20report%202013%20web_4_5.pdf.
————. 2013b. 'Procurement Statistics 2013'. UNFPA. Accessed 12 May 2016.
http://www.unfpa.org/resources/procurement-statistics-2013.
————. 2014. 'Contraceptives and Condoms for Family Planning and STI & HIV
Prevention. External Procurement Support Report 2013'. UNFPA. Accessed 12
May 2016. http://www.unfpa.org/publications/contraceptives-and-condoms-family-
planning-and-stihiv-prevention-external-procurement-0#sthash.uBnoIzKX.dpuf.
United Nations' Working Group of Experts on People of African Descent. 2017.
'Statement to the Media by the United Nations' Working Group of Experts on Peo-
ple of African Descent, on the Conclusion of Its Official Visit to Germany, 20–27
February 2017'. Accessed 12 May 2017. http://www.ohchr.org/EN/NewsEvents/
Pages/DisplayNews.aspx?NewsID=21233&amp%3BLangID=E.
Usborne, Cornelie. 1994. *Frauenkörper – Volkskörper: Geburtenkontrolle und Bev-
ölkerungspolitik in der Weimarer Republik* [Female Body – National Body: Birth
Control and Population Policy in the Weimar Republic]. Münster: Westfälisches
Dampfboot.
Van der Burgt, J.M.M. 1913. 'Zur Entvölkerungsfrage Unjamwesis und Ussumb-
was' [On the Depopulation Question of Unyamwezi and Ussumbwa]. *Koloniale
Rundschau – Monatsschrift für die Interessen unserer Schutzgebiete und ihrer
Bewohner* 12: 705–28.
————. 1914. 'Zur Bevölkerungsfrage Unjamwesis und Ussumbwas' [On the Population Question of Unyamwezi and Ussumbwa]. *Koloniale Rundschau – Monatsschrift für die Interessen unserer Schutzgebiete und ihrer Bewohner* 1: 24–27.
van Laak, Dirk. 2004. *Imperiale Infrastruktur. Deutsche Planungen für eine
Erschließung Afrikas 1880 bis 1960* [Imperial Infrastructure. German Strategies for
the Exploitation of Africa 1880 to 1960]. Paderborn: Schöningh.
————. 2005. 'Der deutsche Kolonialismus und seine Nachwirkungen' [German
Colonialism and Its Aftermath]. *APuZ – Aus Politik und Zeitgeschichte* 4. http://
www.bpb.de/apuz/29265/deutschland-in-afrika-der-kolonialismus-und-seine-
nachwirkungen?p=all.
Vaughan, Megan. 1991. *Curing Their Ills. Colonial Power and African Illness*. Stan-
ford: Stanford University Press.
VENRO, ed. 2009. *Zivilgesellschaft und Entwicklung. VENRO-Jahresbericht 2008*
[Civil Society and Development. VENRO Annual Report 2008]. Bonn: VENRO.
————. 2010. 'Globales Lernen trifft neue Lernkultur. VENRO Arbeitspapier 19'
[Global Learning Meets New Learning Culture. VENRO Working Paper 19].
Bonn: VENRO. Accessed 12 July 2017. http://venro.org/uploads/tx_igpublika
tionen/2010_Arbeitspapier_19_GlobalesLernen.pdf.
Vilmar, Fritz, and Wolfgang Dumcke, eds. 1996. *Kolonialisierung der DDR: Kri-
tische Analysen und Alternativen des Einigungsprozesses* [The Colonialisation of
the GDR: Critical Analyses and Alternatives of the Unification Process]. Münster:
Agenda.

Vohsen, Ernst, and Dietrich Westermann. 1914. 'Zukunftssorgen' [Concerns about the Future]. *Koloniale Rundschau – Monatsschrift für die Interessen unserer Schutzgebiete und ihrer Bewohner* 2: 65–67.

Wainwright, Joel. 2008. *Decolonizing Development. Colonial Power and the Maya. Antipode Book Series.* Oxford: Blackwell.

Walgenbach, Katharina. 2005. *'Die weiße Frau als Trägerin deutscher Kultur'. Koloniale Diskurse über Geschlecht, 'Rasse' und Klasse im Kaiserreich* [The White Woman as Bearer of German Culture. Colonial Discourses on Gender, 'Race' and Class during the Empire]. Frankfurt am Main: Campus.

Walle, Nicolas van de. 2009. 'The Institutional Origins of Inequality in Sub-Saharan Africa'. *Annual Review of Political Science* 12 (1): 307–27. doi: 10.1146/annurev. polisci.11.063006.092318.

Walter, Bernita. 1992. *Von Gottes Treue getragen. Die Missions-Benediktinerinnen von Tutzing – Band II: Gottes Treue verkünden. Wegbereitung für die Kirche in Ostafrika* [Supported by God's Faithfulness. The Missionary Benedictines from Tutzing – Volume II: Announcing God's Faithfulness. Paving the Way for the Church in East Africa]. Erzabtei St. Ottilien: EOS.

Weber, Reinhold. 2003. 'Globalisierung: Aspekte einer Welt ohne Grenzen – Einleitung' [Globalization: Aspects of a World without Borders]. *Politik & Unterricht. Zeitschrift für die Praxis der politischen Bildung* 29 (4): 3–7.

Weiter, Matthias, ed. 2000. *Noch die internationale Solidarität? Ansichten und Informationen zur Vereinigung der deutsch-deutschen Entwicklungspolitik* [Is International Solidarity Still Alive? Views and Information on the Unification of German-German Development Policy]. Bonn and Berlin: BMZ; Deutsche Stiftung für Internationale Entwicklung; Stiftung Nord; and Sud Brücken.

Weltfriedensdienst. 1999. *Partnerschaft und Dominanz. Das Antirassismusprojekt des WFD* [Partnership and Dominance. The Anti-Racism Project of WFD]. Berlin: Weltfriedensdienst. Accessed 12 May 2017. http://w4p.wfd.de/fileadmin/pdf/Diverse/Partnerschaft_und_Dominanz_-_Das_Antirassismusprojekt_des_WFD.pdf.

Welthaus Bielefeld. 2014. *Koloniale Kontinuitäten II. Unterrichtsmaterial für das Fach Geschichte (Klasse 10–12)* [Colonial Continuities II. Teaching Material for the Subject of History (Class 10–12)]. Bielefeld: Welhaus Bielefeld. Accessed 12 May 2017. http://www.schulen-globales-lernen.de/fileadmin/user_upload/SGL_OWL/BM_Kolonial-II_EZ.pdf.

Welthaus Bielefeld, Stadt Bielefeld, Bildung trifft Entwicklung, Brot für die Welt, Deutsche Lepra- und Tuberkulosehilfe, Stiftung Entwicklungszusammenarbeit Baden-Württemberg, Unicef, and World Vision. 2012. *Die Welt braucht Dich. Ein Heft für Schülerinnen und Schüler (ab Klasse 8)* [The World Needs You! A Booklet for Students (from Class 8)]. Bielefeld: Welthaus Bielefeld.

Welthungerhilfe. 2015. 'Es reicht! Für alle. Mit ihrer Hilfe' [It's Enough! For Everybody. With Your Help]. Accessed 12 May 2017. http://www.welthungerhilfe.de/es-reicht-fuer-alle.html.

Werlhof, Claudia von, Maria Mies, and Veronika Bennholdt-Thomsen. 1988. *Frauen, die letzte Kolonie. Zur Hausfrauisierung der Arbeit* [Women, the Last Colony. On the Housewifization of Labour]. Reinbek bei Hamburg: Rowohlt.

White, Sarah. 2002. 'Thinking Race, Thinking Development'. *Third World Quarterly* 23 (3): 407–19. doi: 10.1080/01436590220138358.

Widmer, Alexandra. 2008. 'The Effects of Elusive Knowledge: Census, Health Laws and Inconsistently Modern Subjects in Early Colonial Vanuatu'. *Journal of Legal Anthropology* 1 (1): 92–116. doi: 10.4059/jla.2008.2606.

Williams, Patrick, and Laura Chrisman, eds. 1994. *Colonial Discourse and Post-Colonial Theory. A Reader*. New York: Columbia University Press.

Wilson, Kalpana. 2012. *Race, Racism and Development*. London: Zed Books.

———. 2017. 'Re-Centring "Race" in Development: Population Policies and Global Capital Accumulation in the Era of the SDGs'. *Globalizations* 14 (3): 432–49. doi: 10.1080/14747731.2016.1275402.

Wolfsperger, Douglas. 2005. *Der lange Weg ans Licht* [The Long Way to Light]. Documentary. Douglas Wolfsperger Filmproduktion.

Wollrad, Eske. 2005. *Weißsein im Widerspruch. Feministische Perspektiven auf Rassismus, Kultur und Religion* [Whiteness in Contradiction. Feminist Perspectives on Racism, Culture and Religion]. Königstein/Taunus: Ulrike Helmer.

Woolcock, Michael, Simon Szreter, and Vijayendra Rao. 2011. 'How and Why Does History Matter for Development Policy?' *Journal of Development Studies* 47 (1): 70–96. doi: 10.1080/00220388.2010.506913.

Worboys, Michael. 2000. 'Colonial Medicine'. In *Medicine in the Twentieth Century*, edited by Roger Cooter and John Pickstone, 67–80. Amsterdam: Harwood Academic Publishers.

———. 2001. 'The Colonial World as Mission and Mandate: Leprosy and Empire, 1900–1940'. In *Nature and Empire: Science and the Colonial Enterprise*, edited by Roy MacLeod, 207–20. Chicago: University of Chicago Press.

World Bank Group. 2016. *Migration and Remittances Factbook 2016*. 3rd ed. Washington, DC: World Bank. Accessed 12 May 2017. https://openknowledge.world bank.org/handle/10986/23743.

World Health Organization. 2005. 'The World Health Report 2005'. Geneva: WHO. Accessed 12 January 2012. http://www.who.int/whr/2005/en/.

———. 2006. 'The World Health Report 2006'. Geneva: WHO. Accessed 12 January 2012. http://www.who.int/whr/2006/en/.

World University Service. 2014. 'Ausgaben von Industriestaaten für Informations- und Bildungsarbeit im Bereich der Entwicklungszusammenarbeit' [Spending of Industrialised States for Information and Education Work in the Field of Development Cooperation]. WUS-Informations stelle Bildungsauftrag Nord-Süd. Accessed 12 January 2017. http://www.kooperation-international.de/uploads/media/OECD_ Flyer_2014_Ausgaben_2012.pdf.

Yeboah, Ian. 2006. 'Subaltern Strategies and Development Practice: Urban Water Privatization in Ghana'. *Geographical Journal* 172 (1): 50–65. doi: 10.1111/j.1475–4959.2006.00184.x.

Young, Robert. 2001. *Postcolonialism: An Historical Introduction*. Oxford: Blackwell.

Zantop, Susanne. 1997. *Colonial Fantasies. Conquest, Family and Nation in Precolonial Germany, 1770–1870*. Durham and London: Duke University Press.

Ziai, Aram. 2007. *Globale Strukturpolitik? Die Nord-Süd-Politik der BRD und das Dispositiv der Entwicklung im Zeitalter von neoliberaler Globalisierung und neuer Weltordnung* [Global Structural Policy? The GDR's North-South Policy and the

Dispositif of Development in Times of Neoliberal Globalization and New World Order]. Münster: Westfälisches Dampfboot.

———. 2011. 'The Millennium Development Goals: Back to the Future?' *Third World Quarterly* 32 (1): 27–43. doi: 10.1080/01436597.2011.543811.

———. 2013a. 'Das Imperium schlägt zurück. Georg Krämers Kritik am Antirassismus zeichnet ein verzerrtes Bild' [The Empire Strikes Back. The Critique of Anti-Racism by Georg Krämer Gives a False Picture]. Welt-Sichten 10. Accessed 12 January 2012. https://www.welt-sichten.org/brennpunkte/18347/das-imperium-schlaegt-zurueck.

———. 2013b. 'Frohe Weihnachten, Afrika! Rassismus in der Entwicklungszusammenarbeit' [Merry Christmas, Africa! Racism in Development Cooperation]. *ZEP – Zeitschrift für internationale Bildungsforschung und Entwicklungspädagogik* 36 (2): 15–19. https://www.waxmann.com/index.php?eID=download&id_artikel=ART101306&uid=frei.

Ziai, Aram, and Josephine Brämer. 2015. 'Die deutsche Entwicklungspolitik unter Niebel: Eine handlungslogische Analyse des FDP-geführten BMZ' [German Development Policy under Niebel: An Analysis of the Ministry of Economic Cooperation and Development under Liberal Leadership]. *PERIPHERIE – Politik • Ökonomie • Kultur* 140: 400–18. doi: 10.3224/peripherie.v35i140.22996.

Zimmerer, Jürgen. 2010. *Von Windhuk nach Auschwitz? Beiträge zum Verhältnis von Kolonialismus und Holocaust* [From Windhuk to Auschwitz? Contributions to the Relation of Colonialism and Holocaust]. Münster: LIT.

———. 2012. 'Expansion und Herrschaft: Geschichte des europäischen und deutschen Kolonialismus' [Expansion and Domination: The History of European and German Colonialism]. *APuZ–Aus Politik und Zeitgeschichte* 62: 10–16. http://www.bpb.de/apuz/146973/geschichte-des-europaeischen-und-deutschen-kolonialismus?p=all.

Index

About the Author

Daniel Bendix is a post-doc researcher and lecturer in Development and Postcolonial Studies at the Institute of Political Science of the University of Kassel, Germany. During the writing of this book, he was a junior fellow in the research group 'Landnahme, Acceleration, Activation. Dynamic(s) and (De-)Stabilisation of Modern Growth Societies' at the University of Jena, Germany. He is on the editorial board of the journal *PERIPHERIE – Politik • Ökonomie • Kultur*. His work has been published in *Development and Change*, *Progress in Development Studies*, *Postcolonial Studies*, *Critical Literacy: Theories and Practices*, *Darkmatter. In the Ruins of Imperial Culture*, and *JEP – Austrian Journal of Development Studies*.

Daniel grew up in Berlin, Germany, and spent a high school year in Maseru, Lesotho. Instead of compulsory military service, he worked with an NGO for marginalised youth in Cape Town, South Africa. He then studied political science at the Freie Universität Berlin, Germany, and the Université de Lausanne, Switzerland. Daniel holds a PhD in development policy and management from the University of Manchester, UK, is active with glokal e.V., a Berlin-based association for postcolonial development education and consulting, and is a member of kassel postkolonial.

Lightning Source UK Ltd.
Milton Keynes UK
UKHW01n1427150518
322645UK00001B/32/P